A Consumer's Arsenal

A Consumer's Arsenal

John Dorfman

Praeger Publishers
New York

Published in the United States of America in 1976
by Praeger Publishers, Inc.
111 Fourth Avenue, New York, N.Y. 10003

Second printing, 1976

© 1976 by Praeger Publishers, Inc.

Library of Congress Cataloging in Publication Data

Dorfman, John.
  A consumer's arsenal.

    1.   Complaints (Retail trade) 2.   Consumer protection
—United States. I.   Title.
HF5415.5.D66   381'.3   75-39956
ISBN 0-275-56390-1
ISBN 0-275-89610-2 pbk.

Printed in the United States of America

For Michael Magzis

Contents

PART I

A Tactics Manual for Consumers

1

Consumers Who Win

Let me introduce you to Harriet Ganes.*

No, I'm not a matchmaker. Anyway, Mrs. Ganes is already married. I want you to meet her because she's a consumer who wins.

Mrs. Ganes wins her consumer disputes even though she is not outstandingly well educated, remarkably well spoken, or breathtakingly attractive. She wins because she has the one quality that all winning consumers share: the willingness to fight back.

The silent majority of consumers are losers. One time or another, they'll be short-weighted at the supermarket, gypped at the auto repair shop, overcharged by the moving company, pinched at the shoe store, or ripped off by a roofer. Half the time they won't know what's happened to them. And the other half, they'll swallow the affront without complaining, or with only a token grumble. Then they'll sigh about how hard it is to get justice in this world.

Mrs. Ganes and other consumers who win know that to obtain justice in this world you have to fight for it. For example, there was the time Mrs. Ganes wanted a lamp for her son's room. Well before his birthday, she went to a major Chicago-area department store chain and picked out a lamp with a blue lampshade to match his room's décor. The lamp arrived right on schedule,

* Because she wants her privacy protected, I'm using an anagram of her real name.

but with a red shade. Only a few days were left before the birthday.

When she called back to the lamp department, Mrs. Ganes was informed by a young woman working there that she "must have been nuts, because there never were any blue lampshades on display." So she telephoned the store's executive offices and asked to be put through to the president. Her request was brushed aside, but she repeated it–and repeated it again. Finally she was put through. The president told her to go to the chain's main branch and pick out any shade she wanted—without charge, of course. But, when Mrs. Ganes got there, not a blue shade was to be found either on the main floor or in the merchandise-storage area in the basement. She contacted the store manager and soon was once more on the phone to the president. The upshot: The store sent out a rush order for more blue lampshades, and one was delivered by special messenger to Mrs. Ganes's door. That was three days after the wrong shade had been delivered and still a couple of days before her son's birthday.

On another occasion Mrs. Ganes ordered a new television set. Right from the beginning, there was a problem with the sound. It would start out all right, then begin to fade gradually to inaudibility. When she took it to the store's repair shop, the problem seemed to disappear. The set, she recalled, was "back and forth, in and out of the shop for nine or twelve months. Finally, I told them I wanted a new set." Nothing doing, said the store. So Mrs. Ganes wrote to her state Attorney General's office. "About a week later the man called me and said he would give me a new set if I'd give him twenty-five dollars. I said no. I said you should be able to give me *two* sets for all this trouble." The upshot: Mrs. Ganes got her new television set for no extra cost. "The new set," she reported, "works beautifully."

I'm tempted to give you more success stories from Mrs. Ganes's file. As it happens, there are quite a few more. But you might think that she has some kind of magic touch that other people can't duplicate, so I'll tell you about some other people's success stories instead.

Jim Van Buskirk is only twenty-six years old, but he has rheumatic arthritis and walks with a cane. Because his health prevents him from working regularly, he lives on very little income. "I'm eating macaroni and tuna fish salad and spaghetti," is the way he puts it. "I can't afford meat." When Jim was living in San Francisco, he saw some advertisements for an art course. The ads promised that a local artist of some note would teach the course and that the classes would be small. Jim plunked his money down. When the courses began, he found the classes to be large, the teacher (not the one whose name appeared in the ads) to be inexperienced, and the chief attraction of the course for most of the students to be the suggestive poses of the models.

Jim had nothing against other people's paying their money to see girls model in suggestive poses. But that wasn't quite what he had in mind. "I just wanted to learn legitimate art," he said, "so I asked for a refund, covering all the classes but the two I had already attended." The people running the course refused to give the refund, saying they needed the full amount to cover rent on the building and other expenses. Jim called the San Francisco police, but they told him they had more important things on their minds. So "I went to Woolworth's, got me two pieces of posterboard and some paint, and made a sandwich sign. I walked up and down in front of the shop where the classes were held, carrying this sign that said these people were engaged in misrepresentation, and I wanted to warn the public. You'd be surprised how effective one person can be in front of a store, especially if he's disabled and has to carry a cane to walk. After about an hour and fifteen minutes they came out and gave me my refund —in cash."

Here's one from a woman I'll call Jackie Tucker (another disguised name). In early July 1975 she discovered that her toilet wouldn't flush. She told the landlord about it but soon realized that talking to the toilet itself would have done as much good. So she called a plumber at her own expense and had it fixed— temporarily. About two weeks later the problem returned. She insisted that the landlord this time should call his own plumber. He responded with an ultimatum. Ms. Tucker, he said, had three choices: She could use the toilet as it was; she could repair it at her own expense; or she could move.

Ms. Tucker wasn't too enthralled with the landlord's attitude.

"So I got busy talking to people to find out my rights as a renter. I called the Board of Health and the Building Commissioner. I got on their backs and didn't get off. Once I found out I had a legal right to a working toilet, I called the landlord and said if he didn't fix it right away I was going to report him. He said, 'Okay, just don't bother me.' So I filed a formal complaint. The building commissioner told the landlord the toilet had to be in working condition. And the next day the landlord came with a plumber and put in a new toilet."

Harriet Ganes, Jim Van Buskirk, Jackie Tucker—just ordinary people with a willingness to fight for their rights. Evelyn Melody is another. She bought some shoes in a well-known brand-name shoestore. At the store she told the salesman they didn't seem to fit quite right. "Oh," he said, "take them home and wear them for a while." They would feel fine once she'd broken them in. So she took them home and wore them—and got corns. When she went back to the store she was told that such a problem had never come up before, and the store wouldn't do anything to square accounts. So she wrote to the manufacturer. Same story again: They had never gotten such a complaint.

As it happened, the state consumer-protection agency was practically across the street from Ms. Melody's shoe store. Though she'd never done anything like it before, she found herself walking into the consumer-protection office. Was her complaint the kind they could deal with? Yes, it was. Did they think she had a legitimate complaint? Well, it sounded that way. The agency undertook to investigate the case by sending a letter to the store. Very shortly thereafter, the store offered Ms. Melody a different pair of shoes at no charge.

A pair of shoes . . . a toilet . . . an art course . . . a television set . . . a lampshade. These are not the stuff of epic drama. They are, however, exactly the stuff of everyday life. They're the kinds of transactions on which consumers get rooked every day. Many of us smolder under such affronts. Some of us flare up briefly. But how many of us really fight back?

Many of us are especially reluctant to fight if the ill-fated transaction occurs in a place some distance from home. There's a tendency to return home, lick your wounds, and shrug it off. If you follow that resigned route, however, you're not only letting a little bit more of your hard-earned money trickle down the drain. You're also encouraging the people who victimized you to continue to prey on strangers. It was heartening, therefore, to read about Janice and Dennis Trick, whose actions were written up in the *Dayton* (Ohio) *Daily News*. On a trip to Chicago, their taxi driver asked them if it was their first trip to the Windy City. Assured that it was, the driver took a route that appeared to make the Minoan labyrinth look straightforward. The Tricks paid his $10.50 charge, but later learned that the trip in question should have cost only $7.00. When they got home, they took the trouble to write the Illinois Public Utilities Commission. Within a few days they got a letter from the commission. The driver's taxi license had been suspended for one week, and the company would send the Tricks a refund. A few days later the check for $3.50 was in the mailbox.

Automobiles—particularly automobile repairs—account for more consumer aggravation than any other single category. That's why I'd like you to meet another Ohioan, whose name is Ralph Perrotto. His case was described in *Everybody's Money,* the quarterly publication of the Credit Union National Association. Perrotto owned a 1968 Pontiac, which started giving him trouble in May of 1973. Luckily, his car was still under warranty. (Yes, Virginia, five-year warranties still existed as recently as 1968.) So he took it to the dealer in Cleveland, where he had bought it. The dealer fixed the camshaft, and—as per the warranty—charged nothing for the work. The only trouble was that the car still didn't run right.

When Perrotto talked with the mechanic who had worked on the car, he learned that the engine had been carbonized by the defective camshaft and needed to be decarbonized. This would take one more day in the shop, and then the car would be in tip-top shape. Perrotto left the car for the further repairs, figuring the work would be covered by the warranty since, after all, it was the defective camshaft that had caused the carbonizing problem. The dealer, however, didn't see it that way. When Perrotto went in to pick up his car, he also received an unexpected present: a bill for $146.44. Perrotto took his car and refused to pay the bill.

Later, though, another problem came up (involving the pistons), and he had to take the car in again. This time the dealer refused to release the car until Perrotto paid that $146.44 for the decarbonizing job. The case ended up in small claims court—a forum originally designed as a bastion of justice for ordinary consumers. In practice, such courts often function today as collection agencies for merchants. (You *can* make them work for you, however, as we'll see in Chapter 3.) This time, the court fulfilled its original mission: The judge ruled in favor of Perrotto.

The cases cited here all involve consumers without any special influence or fame. Each one uses the weapons that come most readily to hand. And you'll notice there are quite a few of them: complaints to top management, complaints to government agencies, suits in small claims courts, and unconventional tactics such as picketing, to name only a few. The chapters that follow will attempt to fill you in on all of the weapons in a consumer's arsenal. But the most fundamental necessity is your own willingness to use these weapons—to fight back. That determination is the critical factor in helping you join the ranks of consumers who win.

2

Basic Weaponry

As a consumer, you have access to some extremely powerful dispute-settling weapons. But there's absolutely no point in rolling out the heavy artillery until you've tried your sidearms. This chapter will familiarize you with those sidearms—light weapons that can often bring you a quick and favorable settlement of a dispute.

First is the telephone. Use it right, and it can help you cut through all kinds of red tape. Use it wrongly, however, and you may find your problem is getting *more* annoying instead of less. The first key to successful telephonemanship can be stated like this: Put the phone back on the hook. That's right. Don't use the phone *until* you've done a couple of other things. Gather up your sales slip and any other documents you have related to the transaction. Get something to write on and something to write with. And, most important, decide what it is you want. Most likely it will be a refund (full or partial), repairs, or a replacement. But give careful thought to which one you want. Should you demand a full or only a partial refund? Will you accept repairs on that air conditioner, or is it such a lemon that you should demand a replacement? Decide what's fair and what will meet your needs. Do *not* decide based on what would be most convenient for the store or what you think the store would be most likely to grant. Once you know what you want—and only then—you should pick up the phone and dial.

Eventually (and I grant it sometimes takes quite a while with some establishments), someone will answer. Here you face a second turning point that will determine whether you cut through red tape or merely entangle yourself in it. You have to decide whom to ask for. If the store has a complaint department ("customer service" is now the standard, rather agreeable, euphemism), it's reasonable to try it first. But if the complaint department can't handle your complaint, quickly insist on speaking to the person who has the authority to handle it.

Some stores have given their complaint (or customer service) departments broad powers to make customers happy. (Whenever I find such a store, I usually continue to give it my patronage; I'd guess many other people respond the same way. So you'd think more stores would do it.) But even with the good ones you sometimes have to press a little. For example, I bought a lawn sweeper recently from a major nationwide department store chain. It swept the lawn magnificently—when it was feeling all right. Unfortunately, it was prone to a disturbing ailment: Its nuts and bolts had a tendency to fly off in use like popping popcorn. After a few searches through the grass for lost parts and a trip or two to the hardware store for replacement nuts and bolts, I decided I had been unduly forbearing with the seller. So I called the store's customer service department. I explained that I was growing tired of playing nursemaid to this machine and that I would accept—in lieu of a new machine—two complete sets of replacement nuts and bolts. The young woman at customer service sympathized and said she could order the parts. They would arrive, she said, in eight weeks.

I thanked her for her concern but explained that, by the time eight weeks had elapsed, both the lawn sweeper and I would probably be in smithereens. I asked her to connect me with someone who could arrange a faster delivery. The young woman put me on hold, then returned to say she now had the number of the warehouse I could call. Fine, I said. But why didn't she call the number and let me know the outcome? She promised to do so within the next two hours. The two hours passed without a call, however.

The next morning I learned from my answering service that the store had called back while I was out. I was to call a different woman, also in the customer service department. I did so, and she told me the parts would be forthcoming in ten days, rather than eight weeks. They would be mailed directly to me at no charge.

Unfortunately, many calls to the complaint department have a less happy outcome. And many stores don't have any department specifically for handling complaints. In these cases the general rule is: Aim for the top. Insist on speaking to the manager of the department that sold you the item in question, or to the store manager, or to the president (depending on the type of business you're dealing with and the way your previous calls have been handled). The key thing is to speak with someone with the authority to make the decision you want made. Otherwise you're wasting your time.

Two things can happen now: You actually reach the person you want to speak with, or this person's assistant earnestly assures you that your problem can be handled by Mr. Smith, vice president in charge of miscellaneous malfunctions. At this point you should start keeping records. Get the name of the assistant or secretary who's making the referral. Get Mr. Smith's exact name and title. Never speak with anyone who won't give you his or her name. Write down the names of the people you talk to, the dates and times of the conversations, and what was said or promised. Whenever you speak to a new person, ask immediately whether he or she has the authority to do whatever it is you want done. If not, ask who *does* have that authority. Don't waste your time dealing with people who really don't have the power to help you.

If you finally get the answer you want, take the time to confirm it. ("So you'll send me two complete sets without charge then? Fine. And I can expect them by August 3, is that right? Okay, very good.") And make sure your understanding includes a specific time by which the goods are to be delivered, the repairs made, the check sent out, or whatever. A promise without a date attached may be valid between lovers, but in business dealings it's of dubious value.

I suppose I should say something about what tone to take on the telephone. If pressed, I would say polite, but very firm. That works for me, and it seems to be what most other consumer-writer types recommend. But, frankly, the tone you should probably take is the one that brings *you* the best results. Some people could charm the scales off a snake—especially if the snake is of the opposite sex. Some people just naturally inspire fear and trembling. You know how people react to you. And you know what your strong points are, so take advantage of them. Sympathy, sex appeal, fear, a request for simple justice—they all have their place.

Your second effective sidearm is the practice of keeping records. I've already alluded to the desirability of keeping a log of all your telephone conversations concerning a troublesome transaction. It's getting to be common knowledge now that you should keep sales slips, contracts, invoices, receipts, canceled checks, and the like. If you didn't know that, you do now. If you did know it but haven't been doing it, just think about how much more effectively you can solve a problem when you have these records than when you don't.

One of my favorite examples of record-keeping involves a friend of mine named Harry, who is a radio buff. A local station was running a contest in which you could send in a postcard in answer to some quiz questions. If you were successful, you were supposed to get a prize of cash and merchandise. Harry didn't win (he missed Nikita Khrushchev's official title) but his cousin did. The radio announcer told his cousin that she would receive $65 and a watch. He also said that the tape of his telling her the good news would be on the air that night between 11 and midnight. She called Harry, and he taped the segment just for fun. Weeks went by, and she received no cash and no watch. When she called the station, she was told there must be some mistake, but they had no record of her winning any prize. So Harry's cousin went to the state consumer-protection agency. The agency brought some pressure to bear on the station, and Harry's cousin got her money and her watch. The primary instrument used by the agency was a transcript prepared from—that's right—Harry's tape.

Not all record-keeping will have such serendipitous results. But in a large number of cases, careful record-keeping *can* be the key to victory.

One type of record you should always keep is copies of your complaint letters. Carbon copies are better than nothing. But photocopies are by far the best, because—as we'll see in Chapter 3—you may need to reproduce a complaint letter many times in the course of your quest for action.

That brings us to your third sidearm, which is the well-written complaint letter. Whole articles can be, and have been, written on how to write a good complaint letter. One company even offers a commercialized kit of fill-in-the-blanks complaint letters. (I suppose these canned complaint forms are good for those who lack confidence in their writing ability. They have an impressive appearance, with an urgent-looking red border surrounding the message.) I've also seen a number of people advise consumers to complain on the most expensive stationery they can afford or to use an official letterhead, perhaps the stationery of the place where they work.

Well, all of these suggestions make interesting reading, and I see no way you could hurt your case by following any of them. But neither do I see such externals as having a marked effect on your success or failure. What *does* make a difference is what you say and, to some extent, how you say it.

What you say matters a great deal. Not only will it condition the response of the party to whom you're sending the letter, but it will also condition the response of any third party to whom you send a copy later. Therefore, suppress your strong emotions and stifle your vitriol. Project an image as cool and self-possessed, as if you were a lawyer filing a court brief. Because, in effect, that's what you're doing.

A couple of distinctions should be pointed out, though. Legal "briefs" often run on for dozens, or hundreds, of pages. Your complaint letter, if at all possible, should be kept to one page. Why? Well, first of all, you may have to photocopy it a lot, if the problem should blow up into a major battle. Second, anyone who reads your letter and has the ability to help solve your problem is, almost by definition, a busy person. Busy people appreciate brevity.

By the same token, while legal briefs often bristle with complex jargon, your letter should be stated in straightforward language.

You're trying to get speedy action on a complaint. You are not trying to impress anyone with your erudition.

That doesn't mean you shouldn't write the letter as well as you can. This world being as it is, it's hard to deny that a letter from a person who appears well educated, forceful, and well organized will get action more quickly than a letter from a person who seems unsure of his use of the language, and therefore possibly unsure of his own rights and how to get them. But writing a complaint letter is not like entering an essay contest. You can get a fast refund with a letter that would never be printed in the *Harvard Law Review* or the *New York Review of Books*. All you have to do is convey, briefly and simply, some important facts.

Right at the outset, convey what it is you want the recipient of the letter to do for you. Do you want a full refund? A partial refund? Repairs or service? A replacement for a defective article? Shipment of late goods? Whatever it is, say it immediately and directly.

Then give the historical background of the transaction. What did you purchase? Describe the item (or service), and give any applicable model numbers or serial numbers. State the date of the transaction and the price you paid. Say whom you dealt with, if you know. If you don't know his name, and his promises are relevant to your complaint, give a brief description. (For example, "The salesman, a tall, redheaded man who works in the major appliances division, assured me that the air conditioner would run on normal house wiring.") Say when the item was delivered or installed, if that's relevant. Say how you paid for it (installments, credit card, cash, check), if that's relevant. If it's not relevant, skip it. Keep this section as brief as possible, but attach photocopies of any sales slips, contracts, or other documents you have to the letter. (Never send the originals of these documents to anyone, not even to a state consumer-protection agency. Keep them yourself.)

Then say what went wrong, and when. Here's where you'll be tempted to go on for page after page. Don't. It's pointless. Just sketch the problem in a few choice sentences. "Two weeks after I bought the television set, it suddenly became incapable of receiving any colors except green and orange. At my request, your service department sent repairmen out on three occasions, but their efforts resulted in partial and temporary improvements, at best." Or, "On July 4, I noticed the dishwasher leaked almost a quart of water. The next day, when I attempted to use it, it began to smoke. I turned it off and did not use it again until July 17, following a visit from your repairman on July 16. This time there was no leakage and no smoke, but, when the cycle was done, the dishes were still dirty." And so on. It takes only a few sentences to convey the basic problem. Let the small details slide.

You should then renew the request you made at the start of the letter, and in most cases set a deadline for action. I think it's in order to set a deadline unless the letter is your first complaint to the company on this matter. Since a letter usually has been preceded by telephone complaints, you should briefly summarize any complaints you've made and the reaction to them.

Should you make a threat in connection with your deadline? Should you, for example, say, "Unless positive action is taken within two weeks, I intend to complain about your firm's practices to the Better Business Bureau, the Federal Trade Commission, and the state Attorney General's office"? The answer is purely a matter of tactics. I think it's rude and therefore counterproductive to include such a threat in a first letter. In a second or third letter, such threats are very much in order. The choice of agencies you mention will vary, of course. Threats should never be made idly, so you should mention those agencies to which you actually intend to complain if the company doesn't give you satisfaction. The rest of this book will help you determine which are the appropriate agencies for you to use in a variety of complaint situations.

So there you have the basics of a well-written complaint letter. Its hallmarks are brevity, firmness, and precision. Its elements include (1) a request, (2) details of the original transaction, (3) what went wrong, (4) an account of preceding complaints and responses, (5) a deadline, in most cases, and (6) a threat, in some cases.

There is also another element that should be worked into some complaint letters (probably slipping in somewhere between the description of what went wrong and the setting of a deadline). That is a reference to any warranty that came with the purchase. For the warranty—prosaic, boring, and little-understood as it is—is in fact the consumer's fourth and final sidearm.

If people understood warranties, they would love them, demand them, and read them before they made a purchase. As things stand now, most consumers don't even read the warranty *after* they make a purchase. But a warranty is nothing less than the manufacturer's (or merchant's) statement of what he will do for you if something goes wrong.

If you've been in the habit of paying scant attention to warranties, you couldn't pick a better time to change your practice. A new federal law, the Magnuson-Moss Warranty and Federal Trade Commission Improvement Act, will take a lot of the ambiguity and doubletalk out of warranties, making them a stronger weapon in your hands. The basic points of the law are clear and unmistakable.

- The law applies to all products manufactured after July 4, 1975, and sold for $15 or more.
- Warranties must be written in language that it's reasonable to expect people to understand.
- No one is forced to offer a warranty. But if one is offered, it will have to be labeled either a "full warranty" or a "limited warranty."
- If a full warranty is offered, the manufacturer must repair or replace any defective product without charge within a reasonable time. If this is not done, the consumer must be given a full refund.
- If a limited warranty is offered, the limitations will have to be clearly spelled out. No manufacturer may use the warranty to disclaim the "implied warranty of merchantibility" (the common-law doctrine that any product must be reasonably fit for its intended use). Such disclaimers have been common in the past.
- A manufacturer may specify a limited time period during which the warranty applies and still call it a full warranty.

In such a case the time period will have to be indicated right in the title of the warranty. It could be called, for example, a "full one-year warranty" or a "full ninety-day warranty."

Under rules passed by the Federal Trade Commission (FTC) to implement the Magnuson-Moss Act, retailers are required (as of January 1, 1977) to have warranties on hand for your inspection. You will be able to read every word of the warranty *before* you buy a product. And that will be a pleasant change.

The Magnuson-Moss Act won't be fully effective until 1977, but it's already having some strong effects in the market place. One of the chief effects so far has been to cause many manufacturers to take warranties off their products altogether. Many other manufacturers have reduced the term of their warranties or are opting for "limited" warranties rather than "full" ones. Some observers, seeing this trend, have concluded that the new law is turning into a defeat for the consumer. One newsletter, for example, headlined, "New Warranty Law and Regulations Leave Consumer Worse Off." To my way of thinking, that is poppycock. What's happening, to use the vernacular, is that manufacturers are being told to put up or shut up. Those who are really willing to stand behind their products are now becoming easier to distinguish from those who aren't. That's good news for the consumer, not bad news.

You now have a working acquaintance with your sidearms: the well-used telephone, the well-kept record, the well-written complaint letter, and the well-read warranty. These four weapons, used singly or together, will win you an early victory in most consumer disputes. They also lay the necessary groundwork for cases in which you have to roll out your more powerful weapons. In the next chapter we'll see how your sidearms fit into the continuum of weaponry that constitutes a consumer's arsenal.

3

The Strategy of Escalation

At the height of the cold war, this country's official military posture was called brinkmanship. Our adversaries around the world were put on notice that any provocation or military action on their part could result in our unleashing nuclear weapons.

At the time, pretty much the same "all-or-nothing" approach was applicable to consumer disputes. If you felt you had been victimized or provoked beyond endurance, you could get a lawyer and sue. And that was just about it.

Today our nation's military posture is "flexible response"—the ability to meet any contingency with the (supposedly) correct amount of force. As a consumer, you too have a wide range of weaponry at your disposal, allowing you to respond flexibly to any threat or actual harm done to you in the market place. How you deploy your available weapons will be a test of your skill as a consumer—and, in a sense, your survival in the market place. Too little force, and you'll surely be trampled upon. Too much force, and you'll find yourself bogged down in a costly conflict demanding more of your time, resources, and energy than the goal is worth.

To help you in choosing the appropriate weapons and gaining the most results for the least effort, I've constructed a ladder of consumer complaint escalation. In general, start on the lowest rung and go up a step if the step you've already taken doesn't produce results.

CONSUMER COMPLAINT ESCALATION LADDER

Step   1. Telephone complaints
Step   2. Written complaints to the retailer
Step   3. Complaints to the manufacturer
Step   4. Complaints to trade association, Better Business Bureau, or Chamber of Commerce
Step   5. Complaints to local or state agencies
Step   6. Complaints to federal agencies
Step   7. Legal action (small claims court, lawyer, or conventional courts)
Step   8. Enlisting the help of voluntary consumer organizations
Step   9. Enlisting the help of the media
Step 10. Unconventional tactics

You should never consider yourself defeated in a consumer dispute unless and until you've tried all ten steps on this ladder. Even then, you need not necessarily admit defeat, because the variety of unconventional tactics you can try is limited only by your imagination (and the law).

The consumer complaint escalation ladder shown here is purposely general. Essentially, it's a simplified model consumer complaint procedure. You can deviate from it—indeed, you *should* deviate from it—according to the type of problem you have, the effectiveness of particular agencies in your area, and your own judgment and sense of tactics.

How to ascend steps 1 and 2 of the complaint escalation ladder is the subject of the previous chapter. Most of the remaining steps are discussed in this chapter. However, step 5, complaints to local and/or state agencies, is such a pivotal one for most consumer problems that an entire section of this book is devoted to it. In Part II ("Consumer Protection, State by State"), I tell you about every broad-gauge consumer-protection agency available to you on the state and local levels. A few specialized state and local agencies are described as well. To the best of my ability, I comment on their effectiveness, so you can judge which agencies to approach first and which to use as second or last resorts.

In Part III, you'll find advice on how to cope with fifty of the most common consumer problems. (A considerable number of additional problems are covered through a cross-referencing system.) The emphasis is on providing you with specific ideas, tactics, and agency addresses to help you give impetus to steps 2 through 7 of the escalation ladder. It's usually assumed that you've started with telephone complaints and that it's not necessary to mention that you can seek redress through voluntary consumer organizations, the media, and your own unconventional approaches. Steps 1 and 8 through 10 are omitted to avoid repetition, but they're still available to you as part of your tactical arsenal.

Another word about the methodology of this book. You'll notice that addresses are often given, while phone numbers rarely are. (The exception: All toll-free numbers that I'm aware of are mentioned for your convenience.) The reason is simply that telephone numbers of government and private organizations change more often than their addresses do. Armed with the address, you'll usually have no difficulty finding the current phone number.

You'll notice, too, that state laws are often described in Part II even if there's a similar federal law (which may be described in Part III). There's a definite method in this madness. Consumer-protection and law-enforcement agencies are often overburdened. If you have a choice of enforcement agencies, you stand a better chance of finding one that can get to your problem quickly. Also, either the state or the federal law may have some special twist to it that makes it especially applicable (or plainly inapplicable) to your particular complaint.

Let's take a guided tour now through the ten steps of the consumer complaint escalation ladder.

Step 1—Telephone complaints. The art of complaining by phone is discussed in detail in Chapter 2. Among the key points to remember are these: Always talk to someone in authority. Know exactly what you want. Get the name and title of anyone you talk to. Keep a written log, detailing exactly what was said or promised and when.

Step 2—Written complaints to the retailer. The fine art of the complaint letter is also discussed in Chapter 2. Among the points to remember: State clearly what you want from the company, whether it be repairs, a replacement item, or a refund. Give a brief but explicit history of the transaction and your complaint. Include a summary of your telephone complaints and the store's response to them so far. State a deadline for action, after which you will feel compelled to seek outside help in resolving the dispute.

Under no circumstances should you omit the step of writing the retailer! It doesn't matter if the store is in your own city, on your own block, or right across the street from you. Write anyway! There are two reasons for this. Number one, the retailer will probably take your complaint more seriously when he sees you took the trouble to put it in writing. Number two, you need copies of your complaint letters to the retailer in case you wind up in a situation where you need a record of what's happened. Your complaint letters to the retailer may prove to be excellent evidence in a small claims court or in an arbitration proceeding. If you seek the help of a local, state, or federal agency, or of a voluntary group, the media, or anyone else, attaching copies of these letters can be invaluable to your case. And having the letters available will save you a lot of time, since you needn't describe the dispute all over again if you're seeking someone's help. A short covering note, with your previous letter or letters attached, will do the trick.

Since you never know how many times you're going to have to reproduce your original complaint letter, I recommend making a photocopy of the original for your own records (rather than a carbon copy). The photocopy will probably be much more suitable for further reproduction than a carbon copy would be.

Step 3—Complaints to the manufacturer. Usually, by the time you write the manufacturer, your complaint already has a history. This isn't always the case, though. You might, for example, have bought a bicycle in New Jersey and then moved to Illinois (or a toaster in Texas and then moved to California). You might have bought furniture from a retailer who's since gone out of business. In short, the retailer as a remedy isn't always available.

The manufacturer should be told why you're writing to him. If it's because the retailer isn't available to you, say so. If it's because the retailer *told* you to write the manufacturer, say that. And if (probably the most common situation) it's because the retailer has proved unable or unwilling to resolve your complaint, say that too. A responsible manufacturer wants to know why he's getting complaints. If it's because he's chosen retailers who don't stand behind their merchandise, he may want to consider changing his distribution outlets.

In your letter to the manufacturer, include a succinct but explicit account of your original purchase, the problem that arose, and any efforts to solve it thus far. Include specific dates where possible and copies (never originals) of any relevant documents, including your previous letters to the retailer. Courteously but directly say exactly what it is you want. Usually this will be a refund, repairs, or a replacement.

In a first letter to the manufacturer, I would avoid making threats or setting deadlines. You can do those things, if necessary, in a later letter. The tone of your initial approach, I think, should be cordial and positive. You *expect* the manufacturer to respond in a timely and ameliorative way to your problem. You are confident that he wants to do the right thing, to maintain good customer relations. Such a tone of positive expectations will often produce favorable results. If not, you can always adopt a harsher tone in future correspondence.

Of course, if time is really of the essence, you should press for a prompt response even in a first letter. This might be the case, for example, with an air conditioner purchased early in the summer or with gardening equipment purchased at the same time. Any substantial delay in resolving your complaint here would substantially impair the value of the product to you, and you should point this out in your letter.

How much can you hope for in writing the manufacturer? More than many people would think. To be sure, you may get a runaround or a brushoff. But you may be pleasantly surprised. When this route works, it's often quicker, more effective, and less costly than the remedies on the higher rungs of the complaint escalation ladder.

Here's a case in point, condensed from the Complaint Ledger

of the publication *Everybody's Money.** Margaret Helwig of Lewiston, New York, bought two half-gallon containers of Purex bleach and left them overnight on her carpeted kitchen floor. The next morning she discovered that one of the containers had a pinpoint-size leak and that bleach had leaked out, leaving a circle of white on her carpet. She was especially upset because the carpet had been bought on sale, and would cost $40 to $50 more to replace than it had cost initially. She called her insurance company, which told her the homeowner's policy didn't cover the damage. She went to the supermarket, which told her to write the manufacturer. So (despite the pessimistic predictions of her husband) she wrote the manufacturer. "They'll probably send you a coupon for a free bottle of bleach," her son joked.

Instead, Purex's Consumer Complaint Department sent Mrs. Helwig a "bleach damage report" to complete and asked her to supply the company with two estimates for replacing the carpet. Mrs. Helwig filled out the report and got the two estimates. She then received in the mail a check for $112.45, covering the cost of new carpeting, installation of the new carpeting, and the postage for sending in the bleach container.

Of course, you might not fare that well with your complaint to a manufacturer. But then again, you might. In any case, all you have to do is find the manufacturer's address and take a few minutes to write. Many people seem to be at a loss when it comes to finding the manufacturer's address, but there's no need to be. Your local library probably carries several reference books with manufacturer's addresses listed. Often you can also find the name of the president or the chief complaint officer listed. Among the reference books you can use are *Poor's Register of Corporations,* the *Thomas Register of American Manufacturers,* and the financial manuals published by Moody's and Dun and Bradstreet.

For your convenience, this book also provides a small sampling of corporate addresses. Those for the big four American automakers are listed in the Part III entry for "Automobile repairs."

* Publication by the Credit Union National Association, Box 431, Madison, Wisconsin 53701.

Those of some major appliance manufacturers are listed under "Appliances and Appliance Repairs." And those of some major television, radio, and stereo manufacturers are listed in the entry "Stereo, Audio, and Audio-visual Equipment and Repairs."

Here's a selective list of some key manufacturers in other consumer-goods industries:

BICYCLES

- AMF, Inc., 777 Westchester Ave., White Plains, N.Y. 10604 (R. C. Gott, chairman of the board)
- Raleigh Industries of America, Inc., 1168 Commonwealth Ave., Boston, Mass. 02134
- Schwinn Bicycle Co., 1856 N. Kostner Ave., Chicago, Ill. 60639

BOATS

- Bangor-Punta Corp., 1 Greenwich Plaza, Greenwich, Conn. 06830 (David W. Wallace, chairman of the board)
- AMF, Inc., 777 Westchester Ave., White Plains, N.Y. 10604 (R. C. Gott, chairman of the board)

If your complaint concerns the motor, the following names and addresses may be useful:

- Evinrude Motors, 4147 N. Twenty-seventh St., Milwaukee, Wisconsin 53216 (James Reigor, sales manager)
- Johnson Motors, 3145 Central Ave., Waukegan, Ill. 60085 (Thomas Kalbfus, sales manager)
- Chrysler Corp., Marine and Industrial Operations, P.O. Box 2641, Detroit, Mich. 48231 (William Pearson, sales manager)
- Mercury Marine, Pioneer Road, Fond Du Lac, Wisconsin 54935 (William Hamberger, sales manager)

CAMERAS AND FILM

- Eastman Kodak Co., 343 State St., Rochester, N.Y. 14650 (W. A. Fallon, president)
- Polaroid Corp., 549 Technology Square, Cambridge, Mass. 02139 (Edward H. Land, president)
- Ehrenreich Photo Optical Industries, Inc. (Nikon), 623

Stewart Ave., Garden City, N.Y. 11530 (Joseph Ehrenreich, president)
- Berkey Photo, Inc., 842 Broadway, New York, N.Y. 10003 (H. Berkey, president)

FISHING EQUIPMENT

- Shakespeare Co., 241 E. Kalamazoo Ave., Kalamazoo, Mich. 49001
- Garcia Corp., 329 Alfred Ave., Teaneck, N.J. 07666
- Berkley & Co., 1617 Hill Ave., Spirit Lake, Iowa 51360
- Zebco Division, Brunswick Corp., P.O. Box 270, Tulsa, Okla. 74120
- Johnson Reels Co., 1231 Rhine, Mankato, Minn. 56001

LINENS

- Burlington Industries, Inc., 1345 Avenue of the Americas, New York, N.Y. 10019
- Cannon Mills, Inc., 1271 Avenue of the Americas, New York, N.Y. 10019
- Fieldcrest Mills, Inc., 60 W. Fortieth St., New York, N.Y. 10018
- Dan River, Inc., 111 W. Fortieth St., New York, N.Y. 10018
- Wamsutta Mills Division, Lowenstein & Sons, Inc., 1430 Broadway, New York, N.Y. 10036
- West Point-Pepperell, Inc., 111 W. Fortieth St., New York, N.Y. 10018

LUGGAGE

- American Luggage Works, Inc. (American Tourister), 91 Main St., Warren, R.I. 02885
- Samsonite Corp., 1050 S. Broadway, Denver, Colo. 80217
- Airway Industries, Inc. (Boyle), West Pittsburgh, Pa. 16160

MOTORCYCLES

- American Honda Motor Co., 100 W. Alondra Blvd., Gardena, Calif. 92705
- Yamaha International Corp., 7733 Telegraph Road, Montebello, Calif. 90640

- Harley-Davidson Motor Co., Inc., 3700 W. Juneau Ave., Milwaukee, Wis. 53201
- U.S. Suzuki Motor Corp., P.O. Box 2967, Santa Fe Springs, Calif. 90670

For the many companies not listed here, a quick trip to the library should give you the address. Then put your pen or typewriter to work. If satisfactory results don't follow, move another rung up the ladder.

Step 4—Complaints to a trade association, Better Business Bureau, or Chamber of Commerce. Many people shun these resources, figuring that members of business organizations are always probusiness, and therefore anticonsumer. Probusiness they are. But anticonsumer they often aren't. At the very least, business associations usually want to combat unfair competition on the part of fly-by-night operations. At their best some business groups really want to improve the efficiency and morality of the market place. Such groups are, in short, worth a try.

The names of a number of trade associations that can help you with consumer complaints in specific areas are given in Part III of this book. Among them are the AUTOCAPS (for car complaints), MACAP (for appliance complaints), FICAP (for furniture complaints), the National Home Improvement Council and its affiliates (for home improvement and repair complaints), the National Association of Home Builders (for complaints about new homes), and the Direct Mail Marketing Association (for mail order complaints).

Fairly often the merchant with whom you have a dispute belongs to some trade association or other. You can call the association, if it's a local one, and find out whether it will mediate complaints involving its members. If it's not a local group, you can write (check the address at a library if you don't want to ask the merchant) and make the same inquiry.

You may also be able to learn which trade associations to consult by asking your local Better Business Bureau (BBB) or Chamber of Commerce. These also may have their own complaint-handling procedures. The BBB, of course, will take consumer complaints at any of its offices. But what's done from there on varies tremendously from one BBB to another. Some merely put the complaints on file and use them for reference when consumers call to inquire about a firm's reputation. Others forward complaints to the offending business for reconsideration, with varying degrees of follow-up to see whether a resolution was reached. An increasing number of BBBs, however, are now going beyond these mild measures. Many of them are making available panels for the arbitration of consumer-business disputes. And there's often a genuine effort to include consumer representatives, as well as business representatives, on the arbitration panels.

The Council of Better Business Bureaus has been urging its member bureaus (about 150 of them around the country) to get going with consumer dispute arbitration. The mechanics, including the method of selection of arbitrators, vary. According to *Changing Times* magazine,

> The Long Island, N.Y., BBB's arbitrator pool includes attorneys, educators, housewives, and a 17-year-old high school student. The volunteer pool in Asheville, N.C., utilizes many retirees. In Wichita, Kan., the arbitrators are all volunteer lawyers selected by the local bar association. In Seattle, Wash., the regional office of the Federal Trade Commission helps recruit arbitrators.

Some factors are fairly constant, though. The BBB always tries first to resolve disputes through mediation. If that fails, both sides are asked to submit written statements on the dispute. Normally, the panel of arbitrators will already have read these statements when they sit to hear a case. Proceedings are informal, with no lawyers needed. Both sides get to state their cases, and each can cross-examine the other. The decision normally won't be made in your presence. The panel of arbitrators (or, at times, a single arbitrator) will mail the ruling to you and your adversary, typically in a month or less. There's no cost to you for using the service.

The BBB won't arbitrate a case unless both sides state in writing that they're willing to be bound by the decision. Once both parties agree, the BBB's decision is as legally binding as any other contract and can be enforced by the courts. The finality (for all practical purposes) of the arbitration panel's judgment raises two potential problems for you. First, you have to get the merchant to agree to enter this type of binding arbitration. Second, you have to be reasonably satisfied yourself, before entering such a proceeding, of the impartiality of the panel members. If you call your local BBB office, you may be able to arrange to attend some arbitration sessions. At the least, you should be able to obtain a list of the arbitrators and their backgrounds.

In some localities, the consumer-protection functions of the BBB are performed instead by a Chamber of Commerce. Few Chambers, however, have gone so far as to offer a consumer dispute arbitration service.

Many Better Business Bureaus are designed to serve a fairly sizable region, rather than just one city. Some are even statewide. So if there's no BBB in your hometown, you can try one in a city nearby. Here's a list (organized state by state) of cities with BBBs. Check the phone book of the city in question for addresses and telephone numbers.

Alabama: Birmingham, Huntsville, Mobile (eastern Alabama is served by the BBB in Columbus, Ga.)
Alaska: None
Arizona: Phoenix, Tucson
Arkansas: Fort Smith, Little Rock
California: Bakersfield, Fresno, Long Beach, Los Angeles, Oakland, Orange, Palm Desert, Sacramento, San Bernardino, San Diego, San Francisco (3), San Jose, San Mateo, San Rafael, Santa Barbara, Stockton, Vallejo, Van Nuys
Colorado: Denver
Connecticut: Bridgeport, Hartford, New Haven
Delaware: Wilmington
District of Columbia: Washington
Florida: Miami, West Palm Beach (northwest Florida is served by the BBB in Mobile, Ala.)
Georgia: Atlanta, Augusta, Columbus, Savannah
Hawaii: Honolulu, Maui
Idaho: Boise
Illinois: Chicago, Peoria
Indiana: Elkhart, Fort Wayne, Gary, Indianapolis, South Bend

Iowa: Des Moines, Sioux City

Kansas: Topeka, Wichita

Kentucky: Lexington, Louisville

Louisiana: Baton Rouge, Lake Charles, Monroe, New Orleans, Shreveport

Maine: None

Maryland: Baltimore, Bethesda

Massachusetts: Boston, Springfield, Worcester

Michigan: Detroit, Grand Rapids

Minnesota: Minneapolis, St. Paul

Mississippi: Jackson

Missouri: Kansas City, St. Louis, Springfield

Montana: None

Nebraska: Lincoln, Omaha

Nevada: Las Vegas, Reno

New Hampshire: Concord

New Jersey: Collingswood, New Brunswick, Newark, Paramus, Trenton

New Mexico: Albuquerque

New York: Buffalo, New York City, Rochester, Syracuse, Utica, Westbury, White Plains

North Carolina: Asheville, Charlotte, Greensboro, Winston-Salem

North Dakota: None

Ohio: Akron, Canton, Cincinnati, Cleveland, Columbus, Dayton, Toledo

Oklahoma: Oklahoma City, Tulsa

Oregon: Portland

Pennsylvania: Philadelphia, Pittsburgh, Scranton

Rhode Island: Providence

South Carolina: None

South Dakota: None

Tennessee: Chattanooga, Knoxville, Memphis, Nashville

Texas: Abilene, Amarillo, Austin, Beaumont, Bryan, Corpus Christi, Dallas, El Paso, Fort Worth, Houston, Lubbock, Midland, San Antonio, Waco

Utah: Salt Lake City

Vermont: None

Virginia: Norfolk, Richmond, Roanoke
Washington: Seattle, Spokane, Tacoma, Yakima
West Virginia: None
Wisconsin: Milwaukee
Wyoming: None

Where you find no BBB available, check to see if the Chamber of Commerce performs similar functions. If not, it's time to move up the complaint escalation ladder to the next rung.

Step 5—Complaints to local or state agencies. The state consumer-protection agencies are the real spine of government efforts at consumer protection. A strong state agency can accelerate and coordinate the efforts of citizens' groups, trade groups, and local agencies. By promptly and vigorously tending to complaints it can discourage market place transgressions in the first place. Without a strong state agency, consumer-protection activities in a state will always be diffuse and haphazard. Individual consumer groups and local agencies may do a spectacular job. And if you live in a state where they are the best available resource, you may very well be able to gain satisfaction on your complaints through them. But without strong state laws and statewide enforcement, your struggle for redress will almost always be more difficult. And others less resourceful than you will inevitably give up the struggle and forfeit their rights.

For these reasons, I've devoted an entire section of this book to consumer protection state by state. In Part II you'll find names and addresses of your statewide and local consumer-protection agencies, plus a few specialized agencies. Rather than merely giving you a directory, I've attempted to give my opinion (in some cases, my guess) of the effectiveness of the state agencies in handling complaints. To this end I sent questionnaires to key agencies in all fifty states. After some gentle prodding, forty-four states responded. Some responses were extremely detailed and helpful; others were cursory. All have been summarized in the state-by-state entries.

At first you'll probably read only the information applicable to your own state, and your own city or county. That's fine, for a start. But this book will have failed as a tactical manual if it doesn't help you in as many troublesome situations as possible. Some of those situations—and some of your resultant complaints —will inevitably concern merchants or manufacturers far away from your own territory. Even if you rarely travel, the goods you buy may have traveled hundreds or thousands of miles. It's surprising how few people think to write the consumer-protection agency in the state where a product was manufactured or shipped (or, as the case may be, not shipped). So, if your letter to a manufacturer runs into a stone wall of silence or draws only a token, placating response, put some pressure on the manufacturer by writing the consumer-protection agency in *his* home state.

When you write to any government agency, you can let copies of your previous complaint letters to the retailer or manufacturer do much of your talking for you. Attach them to a short covering letter, which might go something like this:

> I'm having a severe problem with the Such-and-So Manufacturing and Distributing Co., whose address is 543 Unfair Practices Road, Fraudsville [name of state and zip code]. In essence the problem is that Such-and-So sold me a widget that has consistently failed to widge and has refused to make restitution or offer me a replacement. The attached copies of letters and documents will provide you with details on the course of the dispute to this point. I have had no answer to my letter dated [date of your most recent letter]. Because it is difficult for me to compel the firm to act responsibly or to make an effort to settle our dispute equitably, I would greatly appreciate your agency's intervention on my behalf.

Then sit back and wait for the agency to intervene. For state agencies, an effort is made in Part II to estimate how long you'll probably have to wait. Your complaint should at least be acknowledged within a month. If you haven't heard from an agency within that time, write again. With local agencies you can supplement your letter with phone calls.

Step 6—Complaints to federal agencies. If a state agency can't spark a solution to your problem, perhaps a federal agency can. On some complaints (airlines, drugs, national banks, and product safety, to name only a few) a federal agency should probably be your *first* resort. You'll find some guidance as to when to contact federal agencies—and which ones to contact—in the "Complaint Encyclopedia" that constitutes Part III of this book.

One extremely useful resource is the **U.S. Office of Consumer Affairs (OCA)**, which receives several thousand complaints every month. The OCA, 330 Independence Ave., S.W., Washington, D.C. 20201, doesn't handle very many of these complaints itself. But, by all accounts I've heard, it does a very good job of referring them to other organizations that have the capability to handle them. In short, when you're stumped at where else to turn, write the OCA. (By the way, the OCA is often known in popular parlance as "Virginia Knauer's office" after its longtime and present director.)

Six other federal agencies are important enough, in terms of their role in handling consumer complaints, to merit discussion here. They are the Federal Trade Commission, the Food and Drug Administration, the Consumer Product Safety Commission, the Securities and Exchange Commission, the Interstate Commerce Commission, and the Civil Aeronautics Board. Let's have a brief look at each.

The **Federal Trade Commission (FTC)** is really our basic national consumer-protection agency. It promulgates trade-regulation rules designed to curb unfair practices by businesses and to protect consumers. It has a major role in the enforcement of the nation's antitrust laws. It administers the Truth in Lending Act (along with the banking agencies). It polices the market place for false or misleading advertising. And it has a variety of miscellaneous responsibilities that have been tossed its way over the years, including textile and wool and fur labeling, and the prevention of misleading packaging.

How well does the FTC discharge its multiple responsibilities? And how much help can you, as an individual consumer with a problem, expect from the FTC? The answer to the first question, in my opinion, is fairly well, considering the immensity of the task. But I wouldn't be too sanguine about the FTC as a recourse agency for your personal complaints. The agency just doesn't have a big enough staff to investigate all the abuses reported to it. What it will do, many times, is just take your complaint and file it. If it gets a lot of complaints about a particular business practice, it may eventually issue a trade-regulation rule barring that practice. If it gets a lot of complaints about a particular company, it may take action against that company (possibly after conducting its own investigation). So your complaints to the FTC are far from wasted, but they may or may not bring you a solution to your immediate problem. Your chances of getting direct action are far higher when you're bringing to the FTC's attention a violation of its own regulations.

Some further insight into the FTC's complaint-handling methods can be gained from a study commissioned by the U.S. Office of Consumer Affairs. The study, conducted by Technical Assistance Research Programs, Inc., was titled, "Feasibility Study to Improve Handling of Consumer Complaints." It will be referred to, from here on, as the TARP study. During the first phase of the TARP study (later phases are still in progress at this writing), some fifteen federal agencies were scrutinized to see how quickly, how appropriately,* and how clearly they responded to consumer complaints. The FTC responded to the average consumer complaint in thirteen days. TARP researchers judged the FTC to be satisfactory (though just barely) in the appropriateness of its responses, and also satisfactory in the clarity of its responses. (About 93 per cent of FTC responses were considered clear, in light of the estimated sophistication and education level of the consumer making the complaint.)

It should be noted that the effectiveness of the FTC in handling individual complaints varies considerably from one regional office to another. For example, a spokesperson for the Chicago regional office said that, although it was "not a Commission policy" to help individual consumers get their money back, "informally, we do try to help people if we can." The Chicago office has set up an informal hot-line system with about two hundred major companies in the area to expedite the handling of complaints. "We don't pressure anyone into belonging," the

---

* An agency's answer was considered "appropriate" if it was directly responsive to a consumer's complaint or inquiry, regardless of whether it was positive or negative.

spokesperson noted. Membership in the hot-line arrangement is informal, and the FTC won't tell callers how many complaints are filed against each member. It's just an arrangement to try to get the most action on complaints, using limited staff.

Since passage of the Magnuson-Moss Act reforming the FTC's structure and functioning, the agency has some broad new powers. One thing it can now do is negotiate out-of-court settlements with companies allegedly involved in wrongdoing in such a way that the company agrees to set up a restitution fund. The FTC then collects the money and disperses it to consumers who inform the FTC that they've been bilked by the company in question. One of the first such cases (settled in the summer of 1975) involved a string of vocational schools franchised by Career Enterprises, Inc. Consumers who responded to the FTC's public announcements were entitled (if they'd attended the school's classes since 1969 but had failed to land a job as a result) to share in a $1.25 million restitution pool. Individual consumers stood to get back up to 75 per cent of the money they had spent for the courses. Many similar restitution-pool proceedings can be expected in the future.

The FTC's national headquarters address is simply Federal Trade Commission, Washington, D.C. 20580. For most complaints, though, you'll do best to contact the FTC regional office nearest you. Here's a list of the offices (arranged alphabetically by city) and the territory served by each of them:

- Atlanta Regional Office, 730 Peachtree Street, N.E., Room 800, Atlanta, Ga. 30308 (serves North Carolina, South Carolina, Georgia, Florida, Alabama, Tennessee, Kentucky, and Mississippi)
- Boston Regional Office, 150 Causeway St., Room 1301, Boston, Mass. 02114 (serves Maine, Vermont, New Hampshire, Massachusetts, Connecticut, and Rhode Island)
- Chicago Regional Office, 55 East Monroe St., Suite 1437, Chicago, Ill. 60603 (serves Indiana, Illinois, Wisconsin, Minnesota, Iowa, and Missouri)
- Cleveland Regional Office, 1339 Federal Office Building, 1240 East Ninth St., Cleveland, Ohio 44199 (serves Ohio,

Michigan, New York State west of Rochester, and Pennsylvania west of Pittsburgh)

- Dallas Regional Office, 500 South Ervay St., Room 452-B, Dallas, Texas 75201 (serves Louisiana, Arkansas, Oklahoma, Texas, and New Mexico)
- Denver Regional Office, 1006 Federal Office Building, 1961 Stout St., Denver, Colo. 80202 (serves Kansas, Nebraska, North Dakota, South Dakota, Wyoming, Colorado, Montana, and Utah)
- Honolulu Field Station, 605 Melim Building, 333 Queen St., Honolulu, Hawaii 98613 (reports to San Francisco Regional Office)
- Kansas City Field Station, 2806 Federal Office Building, 911 Walnut St., Kansas City, Mo. 64106 (reports to Chicago Regional Office)
- Los Angeles Regional Office, 13209 Federal Building, 11000 Wilshire Blvd., Los Angeles, Calif. 90024 (serves Southern California and Arizona)
- New York Regional Office, 2243-EB Federal Building, 26 Federal Plaza, New York, N.Y. 10007 (serves New York east of Rochester, and New Jersey)
- San Francisco Regional Office, 450 Golden Gate Avenue, Box 36005, San Francisco, Calif. 94102 (serves Northern California, Nevada, and Hawaii)
- Seattle Regional Office, 28th Floor, Federal Building, 915 Second Ave., Seattle, Wash. 98174 (serves Washington, Oregon, Indiana, and Alaska)
- Washington, D.C. Regional Office, 600-C Gelman Building, 2120 L St., N.W., Washington, D.C. 20037 (serves Virginia, West Virginia, Maryland, District of Columbia, Delaware, and Pennsylvania east of Pittsburgh)

The **Food and Drug Administration** (**FDA**) is another agency whose importance to consumers is almost impossible to overestimate. It's responsible for keeping off the market any drugs, food products, or cosmetics that may be hazardous to people's health. To do this, it necessarily relies on citizen complaints.

If you complain to the FDA, you may not be helping yourself

directly. "We don't get involved in getting consumers' money back," said a spokesperson. "But their complaints help us do our job properly." In the long run an FDA investigation or recall *might* help you get your money back. (It could be used as evidence in court, for example.) But in any event a successful complaint gives you the satisfaction of knowing that you may be saving someone else from possible injury. And you're helping to see that companies putting out defective products are held accountable for their actions.

According to the TARP study, the FDA answers the average consumer complaint in twenty-two days. The responses were found to be appropriate (that is, fitted to the complaint) in 100 per cent of the cases investigated—a record shared by no other agency among the fifteen checked. About 97 per cent of the time, the response to a complaint was judged to be clear, in light of the apparent level of sophistication and education on the part of the complainant.

When you make a complaint, the FDA asks you to use the following procedure:

> Give your name, address, telephone number, and directions on how to get to your home or place of business. State clearly what appears to be wrong. Describe in as much detail as possible the label of the product. Give any code marks that appear on the container. . . . Give the name and address of the store where the article was bought, and the date of purchase. Save whatever remains of the suspect product or the empty container for your doctor's guidance or possible examination by FDA. Retain any unopened containers of the product you bought at the same time. If any injury is involved, see your physician at once. Report the suspect product to the manufacturer, packer, or distributor shown on the label, and to the store where you bought it [as well as to FDA].

You can send your complaint to FDA national headquarters at 5600 Fishers Lane, Rockville, Md. 20852. But your complaint might get faster action if you use one of the ten regional offices, nineteen district offices, or ninety-seven inspection stations around the country. (Ten of the district offices are also regional offices.) Check the U.S. Government listings in the white pages of your phone book to see if there's an inspection station near you. The regional and district offices are listed below:

- Atlanta Regional Office, 880 W. Peachtree St., N.W., Atlanta, Ga. 30309
- Baltimore District Office, 900 Madison Ave., Baltimore, Md. 21201
- Boston Regional Office, 585 Commercial St., Boston, Mass. 02109
- Buffalo District Office, 599 Delaware Ave., Buffalo, N.Y. 14202
- Chicago Regional Office, Room 1222, Main Post Office Building, 433 W. Van Buren St., Chicago, Ill. 60607
- Cincinnati District Office, 1141 Central Parkway, Cincinnati, Ohio 45202
- Dallas Regional Office, Suite 470-B, 500 S. Ervay, Dallas, Texas 75201
- Denver Regional Office, New Customhouse Building, Room 500, Twentieth and California Sts., Denver, Colo. 80202
- Detroit District Office, 1560 E. Jefferson Ave., Detroit, Mich. 48207
- Kansas City Regional Office, 1009 Cherry St., Kansas City, Mo. 64106
- Los Angeles District Office, 1521 W. Pico Blvd., Los Angeles, Calif. 90015
- Minneapolis District Office, 240 Hennepin Ave., Minneapolis, Minn. 55401
- New Orleans District Office, U.S. Customhouse, Room 222, 423 Canal St., New Orleans, La. 70130
- New York Regional Office, 850 Third Ave., Brooklyn, N.Y. 11232
- Newark District Office, Room 831, 970 Broad St., Newark, N.J. 07102
- Philadelphia Regional Office, Room 1204, U.S. Customhouse, Second and Chestnut Sts., Philadelphia, Pa. 19106
- San Francisco Regional Office, Room 544, Federal Office Building, 50 Fulton St., San Francisco, Calif. 94102

- San Juan District Office, P.O. Box 4427, Old San Juan Station, San Juan, P.R. 00905
- Seattle Regional Office, Room 5003, Federal Office Building, 909 First Ave., Seattle, Wash. 98104

The U.S. **Consumer Product Safety Commission (CPSC)** is the agency to contact when you spot any safety-related defect in any product (except for food, drugs, and cosmetics). This is another agency that can give you a great deal of satisfaction—but not monetary satisfaction. "We're of no help in terms of getting a refund or replacement on an individual product," said a spokesperson, "but our investigative staff follows up every safety-related complaint. Let's say you buy a mixmaster. If you get an orange one when you ordered green, that's no concern of ours. But if you find it's easy to get your finger caught in the mechanism, we'd be interested.

"When we have an indication of a defect," the spokesperson continued, "we go to the company involved. The company can propose voluntary corrective action, such as making a design change, and repurchasing the units that are already on the market. We monitor the corrective action. If we're not satisfied with it, we can conduct hearings and then order a recall and a correction. If other products of the same type are affected by the same hazard, then we put out a public request inviting interested parties to develop safety standards for that type of product. Of course, we have the last word on what standards are adopted."

The TARP study found the CPSC responded to the average consumer complaint within nineteen days. The agency's replies were almost always found to be directly responsive to the complaint. And 98 per cent of the time they were found to be clear in terms of the probable level of sophistication and education on the part of the complainant.

One extremely valuable feature of the CPSC's operations is its nationwide toll-free telephone number. Unless you live in Hawaii, Alaska, or Maryland, you can just pick up the phone and dial 800-638-2666. It won't cost you a dime. But it might save somebody from injury—or help keep some company from perpetrating market place mayhem.

In Maryland, the number to call is 800-492-2937. In Hawaii and Alaska there's no toll-free phone connection, but you can write the CPSC at 1750 K St., N.W., Washington, D.C. 20006.

If you prefer, you can contact one of the CPSC's fourteen area offices around the country. They're in Atlanta, Boston, Chicago, Cleveland, Dallas, Denver, Kansas City, Los Angeles, Minneapolis, New Orleans, New York, Philadelphia, San Francisco, and Seattle. Check your phone book for addresses and telephone numbers.

The **Securities and Exchange Commission** (**SEC**) is the agency to call when you have problems involving stocks, bonds, options, or misconduct on the part of a brokerage firm or other securities dealer. While the SEC has proved unable to stop financial swindles, it has certainly slowed them down. In a large number of cases it has caught and punished the culprits.

SEC headquarters are at 500 North Capitol Street, Washington, D.C. 20549. It also has nine regional offices and eight branch offices. The branch offices, serving only a relatively small area, are in Cleveland, Detroit, Houston, Miami, Philadelphia, Salt Lake City, San Francisco, and St. Louis. If you don't live near one of those cities, you can contact the regional office serving your area. The addresses and jurisdictions of the nine SEC regional offices are listed below.

- Region 1 Office, 26 Federal Plaza, New York, N.Y. 10007 (serves New York and New Jersey)
- Region 2 Office, 150 Causeway St., Boston, Mass. 02114 (serves Maine, New Hampshire, Vermont, Rhode Island, Connecticut, and Massachusetts)
- Region 3 Office, 1371 Peachtree St. N.W., Suite 138, Atlanta, Ga. 30309 (serves Florida, Alabama, Georgia, North Carolina, South Carolina, Mississippi, Tennessee, Puerto Rico, the Virgin Islands, and eastern Louisiana)
- Region 4 Office, Room 1708 Everett M. Dirksen Office Building, 219 S. Dearborn St., Chicago, Ill. 60604 (serves Illinois, Iowa, Indiana, Kentucky, Ohio, Wisconsin, Michigan, Missouri, Minnesota, and the city of Kansas City in Kansas)

- Region 5 Office, 503 U.S. Court House, Tenth and Lamar Streets, Fort Worth, Texas 76102 (serves Texas, Oklahoma, Arkansas, western Louisiana, and Kansas except for Kansas City)
- Region 6 Office, 7224 Federal Building, 1961 Stout St., Denver, Colo. 80202 (serves Colorado, North Dakota, South Dakota, Utah, Wyoming, Nebraska, and New Mexico)
- Region 7 Office, Room 1043 U.S. Courthouse, 312 N. Spring St., Los Angeles, Calif. 90012 (serves California, Arizona, Nevada, Hawaii, and Guam)
- Region 8 Office, 900 Hoge Building, Seattle, Wash. 98104 (serves Washington, Oregon, Idaho, Montana, and Alaska)
- Region 9 Office, Ballston Centre Tower #3, 4015 Wilson Blvd., Arlington, Va. 22203 (serves District of Columbia, Virginia, Maryland, West Virginia, Delaware, and Pennsylvania)

The **Interstate Commerce Commission (ICC)** regulates truck lines, bus lines, and (to an extent) railroad lines. When you have a complaint concerning a moving company, a freight shipment, or a bus or train company, this agency is often the place to turn. You should also be on the lookout for other avenues of recourse, however. The ICC is sometimes slow in responding to consumer complaints. (It takes thirty-one days to answer the average one, according to the TARP study.) And the agency has been much criticized in the past for being a captive of the very interests it was supposed to regulate. It does seem to have been improving recently in this regard, however. And the TARP study gave it high grades for the directness and clarity of its responses to consumer complaints—when it finally gets around to answering them.

The ICC has seventy-eight offices scattered around the country. If you can't find the one nearest your home by checking a phone book or a library—or if you don't get satisfactory treatment at a local ICC office—you can write to the agency's national headquarters or to one of its six regional offices. The national headquarters address is simply Interstate Commerce Commission,

Washington, D.C. 20423. The six regional offices and the territories they serve are as follows:

- Region 1 Office, 150 Causeway St., 5th floor, Boston, Mass. 02114 (serves Massachusetts, New York, New Jersey, Connecticut, Rhode Island, Vermont, New Hampshire, and Maine)
- Region 2 Office, 1518 Walnut St., Room 1600, Philadelphia, Pa. 19102 (serves Pennsylvania, Virginia, West Virginia, the District of Columbia, Maryland, Delaware, and Ohio)
- Region 3 Office, 1252 W. Peachtree St., N.W., Room 300, Atlanta, Ga. 30309 (serves Georgia, Florida, Alabama, Mississippi, Tennessee, Kentucky, North Carolina, and South Carolina)
- Region 4 Office, Room 1086 Everett M. Dirksen Building, 219 S. Dearborn St., Chicago, Ill. 60604 (serves Illinois, Indiana, Minnesota, Nichigan, Wisconsin, North Dakota, and South Dakota)
- Region 5 Office, 9A27 Fritz Garland Lanham Federal Building, 819 Taylor St., Fort Worth, Texas 76102 (serves Texas, Louisiana, Oklahoma, Missouri, Nebraska, Arkansas, Kansas, and Iowa)
- Region 6 Office, 13001 Federal Building, 450 Golden Gate Ave., San Francisco, Calif. 94102 (serves California, Hawaii, Oregon, Washington, Idaho, Colorado, Alaska, Arizona, Montana, Nevada, New Mexico, Utah, and Wyoming)

Last, and in some people's opinion least, of the six specialized federal agencies with broad consumer-protection functions, is the **Civil Aeronautics Board** (**CAB**). The CAB has been something of a public whipping boy for politicians and the press in the last year or two. The charges are that the agency is inefficient as a regulator, tends to drive up the price of airline travel rather than lowering it, and is subservient to the airline interests it is supposed to regulate. In my opinion, all these charges have some truth in them, but not enough truth to merit singling out the CAB as the agency to criticize while ignoring similar faults in many other federal agencies.

Besides, whatever criticisms one may wish to level at the CAB's regulation of airline fares, its handling of consumer complaints has been, in many respects, quite good. For example, the TARP study found the average consumer complaint was answered by the CAB in ten days. The agency was also given extremely high marks for the directness and clarity of its responses. In short, if you have a problem involving an airline, and you can't straighten it out using steps 1 through 4 on the complaint escalation ladder (step 5 is inapplicable to airline complaints), by all means send your complaint to the CAB. Write the Office of Consumer Affairs, Civil Aeronautics Board, 1825 Connecticut Ave., N.W., Washington, D.C. 20428.

If the federal agencies mentioned here (and those mentioned in Part III of this book in the discussion of particular problems) can't help you, it's time to move another step up the consumer complaint escalation ladder. This would be a reasonable time to consider court action, or the threat of court action.

Step 7—Legal action.   This step really involves three possible strategies or substeps. If your dispute could be settled by the return of a specific sum of money, and if that sum is less than the ceiling of small claims court jurisdiction in your state, then small claims court might provide the perfect solution for your problem. If that's not the case, you can hire a lawyer. Many times your lawyer's advice or a letter from your lawyer to your adversary will produce a quick breakthrough in the case. If that doesn't happen, you can go all the way and file a conventional lawsuit. (That, you'll remember, is what most consumers had to do ten or twenty years ago if they wanted to assert their rights.) Let's look at each of these three in turn.

First, small claims court. One of the beauties of this forum is that you don't need a lawyer. Indeed, some jurisdictions actively discourage the use of lawyers, or even ban them. Another beauty of the system is that its costs are small. Usually you'll pay $15 or less to have your day in court. And if you win this money will often be refunded. Perhaps the best point of all is that you stand an excellent chance of winning. A survey by Consumers Union in 1970 found that consumers won in about two-thirds of the actions they brought. Other surveys have noted similar results.

Well, with all these good points, why isn't small claims court the universal answer to consumer problems? There are several answers to this. Some consumers don't know about small claims courts. Some are embarrassed or frightened to appear before a judge. Some are put off by the investment of time necessary to see that summonses are served and to make the court appearance itself (possibly preceded by one or two continuances). Finally, and perhaps most important, some people are discouraged by the fact that the consumer must still exert an effort to get paid even after he wins a small claims court judgment. As Douglas Matthews beautifully put it in his book *Sue the B*st*rds*, a court judgment is not cash in hand but a "hunting license" to go out and try to collect the amount the court has awarded you.

Matthews, an unabashed proponent of the use of small claims courts, underestimates the importance of this collection problem, in my opinion. (He does, however recommend that courts should start paying victorious plaintiffs themselves and then collect from the guilty party. This certainly makes sense, since the court is in a far better position to make the guilty party pay up than the consumer is. So far, however, no small claims court of which I'm aware uses this system.) If you can't collect a judgment after winning in small claims court, Matthews recommends the use of the local sheriff to help you rather than the marshall. (No, we're not back in the Wild West; these offices still exist in most counties and states.) The reason is that the marshall operates by charging the debtor a fee, which is a percentage of the money collected. With a small claims court judgment, that fee will be so small that the marshall is likely to give low priority to collection of your claim. I personally got involved in a case where a couple had purchased a defective refrigerator. They went to small claims court and won, but a year later the guilty company still hadn't paid, and the marshall had been "too busy" to collect the debt! Such difficulties arise all too frequently. They occurred about 20 per cent of the time in the Consumers Union survey. In some states they occur in about one-third of all cases.

Let's not overemphasize these difficulties, however. In most cases you will win if you have a valid case. And in most cases where you win, you will collect. Hence, small claims courts are a very logical resource for you to use. You can learn the location of the small claims court nearest you by calling or writing your county office or, in large cities, city hall. Once you locate the court—which may be called Small Claims Court, Justice of the Peace Court, or some other name—speak to the clerk's office. Be sure to find out:

- The current dollar ceiling on cases the court will hear (this averages about $500)
- The procedures you have to go through to serve your adversary with a summons
- Whether your adversary's exact legal name and address must appear on the summons, and, if so, where you can most easily find it
- Whether you can sue your adversary in the small claims court nearest your home, or whether you must use the one closest to his place of business

People at the court clerk's office are usually glad to help you with these technicalities and any others that may arise as you go along. When you get to court, the proceeding will be informal, much like the BBB arbitration panel proceedings described earlier. (One key difference, of course, is that your adversary has to answer to you in court, willingly or not. BBB arbitration proceedings are strictly voluntary.) You'll get to tell your story briefly, then be cross-examined. Then the other side will present its defense, and you can ask questions if you wish. The judge may ask some questions of his own. Then he'll retire to make his decision (of which you'll probably be notified by postcard). Bring with you to court all copies of letters and other documents that you have relating to the complaint. Let the judge know you have them, but don't trot them out or quote from them extensively. Judges usually have heavy caseloads, and the qualities they'll appreciate most from you are brevity, forthrightness, and directness. If the judge or your opponent asks you a question that you can answer yes or no, do so. I, for one, always find this kind of straightforward answer extremely impressive. My lawyer friends tell me that judges do, too.

Of course, small claims courts aren't for every situation. Your complaint may not be translatable into a dollar sum. Or, conversely, it may translate into a dollar sum too great for the jurisdictional limit of the court. What then? In terms of legal action, your next step is to get a lawyer. Some people dismiss this step out of hand, either because of a general aversion to lawyers or (more often) because of their perception of lawyers' fees. Many people assume that lawyers' fees are (1) always large, (2) always calculated on a payment-per-hour-of-the-lawyer's-time basis, and (3) always paid out of your own pocket. These assumptions aren't universally true. It is true that lawyers, especially good lawyers, rarely come cheap. But they don't all charge penthouse-high rates, either. Fees can be discussed frankly when you first sit down with an attorney. If you're particularly concerned about the subject, you can open the discussion by saying you feel you need legal help but aren't sure you can afford it.

On some types of cases, fees are often calculated not on an hourly basis but as a flat percentage (perhaps 20 per cent) of any award or settlement the lawyer may win for you. If you prevail, he gets a healthy cut. But if you lose, his services have cost you nothing.

And, while you will probably have to pay your lawyer his fee out of your own pocket, at least at first, some courts will order your adversary to pay your (reasonable) attorney's fees, if the court believes the interests of justice are best served that way. According to the U.S. Office of Consumer Affairs, at least sixteen states had legislation permitting courts to do this as of 1974. Your lawyer or your state consumer-protection agency can advise you on the situation in your state.

Some further notes on low-cost sources of legal advice will be found in the entry on lawyers in Part III. But let's look now at the other side of the cost-benefit coin: What will a lawyer do for you? It sounds like gamesmanship to say it, but one thing he can often do is impress or intimidate your adversary—perhaps to the point of producing, for the first time, a genuine effort on that adversary's part to settle the dispute. I've heard of, read about, and personally seen several examples of the impact the entrance of an attorney can have on a dispute. One of the best examples, because of its elegant simplicity, concerns a young man, soon to be married, who had a bathroom with a leaky roof and falling tiles. Requests to the landlord for service were met with the standard "we'll-look-into-it" response. The requests were escalated to complaints with no more results. Finally the young man turned to his uncle, a lawyer, for help. The uncle sent the landlord a letter on his firm's stationery. The letter was quite simple. It contained no assertions about the facts of the case, the condition of the bathroom, or the alleged irresponsibility of the landlord. All it said, in essence was, "I represent Mr. Kenneth Green, the occupant of apartment 2B in your building at 439 Riverside Boulevard.* I understand you are having a dispute with him over certain conditions in the apartment. I would appreciate your informing me, in writing, of your version of this dispute at your earliest convenience." That's all, just a simple request for the landlord's side of the dispute. The result: The landlord fixed up the bathroom immediately, several weeks, as it turned out, before the new bride moved in.

Your adversary, of course, might not be intimidated by the appearance of a lawyer on your behalf. He might be one of those people whom the devil himself couldn't intimidate. (I know what you're thinking. But, really, there is only a slight statistical possibility that your adversary *is* the devil himself.) Your next step is to consider a lawsuit. If by now you feel you have a good relationship with your attorney, and you trust his judgment, ask *his* advice on whether a lawsuit is worthwhile. Among the factors you want to consider are the probable delays, the probable costs to you in time and money, your chances of winning, and the amount you can realistically hope to win. Weigh these factors and decide if a suit is the route you want to go. If so, take all the relevant documents, organize them well, and store them in a convenient place. Then settle in to wait for your day in court—a wait that may range from a couple of

---

* The name and address given here are fictitious.

months to a few years depending on the court backlogs in your jurisdiction. Do not go on with any further actions, such as picketing, that might prejudice your case. You can, of course, continue to bargain with your adversary. Once your suit has actually been filed, he may finally begin to think seriously about a settlement. And then the horse-trading begins. The general rules in such bargaining are (1) don't be rushed, and (2) if the other side makes you an offer worth considering, get it in writing. Needless to say, you'd huddle with your attorney before deciding whether to accept any out-of-court settlement. The vast majority of lawsuits *are* settled out of court. And there's probably no reason why yours shouldn't be. But neither need you jump at the first offer that comes along.

When considering lawsuits, give thought to filing yours as a class action, together with other plaintiffs. If several people were victimized by the same merchant or manufacturer, you may be able to share valuable information and pool funds for top-rank legal representation. In some cases filing your suit as a class action may speed up its path through the courts; in other cases it may slow it down. You and your lawyer will have to investigate the status of class action suits in your state to find out. As of 1974, according to the U.S. Office of Consumer Affairs, class action suits were legal in nineteen states, plus the Virgin Islands and Puerto Rico. (The nineteen were Alaska, California, Connecticut, Hawaii, Illinois, Indiana, Iowa, Kansas, Maine, Massachusetts, Missouri, Nebraska, Ohio, Oregon, Rhode Island, Texas, Utah, Vermont, and Wyoming.) In many of those states, however, restrictive rules regarding these suits make their use difficult and cumbersome. In Alaska, for example, according to *Consumer Reports* magazine, "the Attorney General must approve any class action suit before it's brought, and the plaintiff must post a $5,000 bond to cover the defendant's legal fees and court costs should the plaintiff lose."

Even tighter restrictions have been clamped on class action suits in the federal courts. Currently, each party to the suit must have suffered at least $10,000 worth of harm. And the party initiating the suit must bear the costs of notification to all other members of the class of aggrieved consumers. These restrictions may topple, however, if one of the reform bills before Congress achieves passage. So watch your newspapers. The federal court class action suit may someday again become (as it briefly was, before the Burger Supreme Court) a spearhead in the drive for consumer rights.

If you decide a suit—no matter what type—is not your style, or if you prefer to settle your problems without getting into the realm of lawyers and courts, then move on to the next step on the consumer complaint escalation ladder. If you do go to court and lose, but you're convinced your loss turned on a technicality rather than the merits of the case, you may also want to forge ahead with further action. So, up another rung we go.

Step 8—Enlisting the help of voluntary consumer organizations. It's one thing for a merchant or manufacturer to incur your lasting ill will, to forfeit your future business (and that of your close friends, perhaps), and even to risk litigation. But it's quite another for him to continue an intransigent stand when faced with the active interest or opposition of a well-organized consumer group. A medium-size group may include a fair number of potential customers. Through picketing and access to other means of publicity, it may scare off many more. So a group has to be taken seriously.

Some groups demand, if you want them to help you, that you help them in turn. You may have to pay dues or do a certain amount of work or join in picketing on behalf of some other consumer's complaint. (This is not to imply that picketing is the favored strategy of all consumer groups, by any means. But it is used by some, and quite effectively. The best-known group that uses picketing is CEPA—the Consumers Education and Protective Association. Founded in Philadelphia, it has spread to more than a dozen other cities. You can inquire of CEPA if it has a branch in your area by writing Consumers Education and Protective Association, 6048 Ogontz Ave., Philadelphia, Pa. 19141.)

Many of the best and most active groups are local. I can't list them all here. Your local newspaper and your local library may be able to furnish you with some names and addresses, if you don't know the consumer organizations in your area. You can also ask for leads from your state consumer organization, if there is one. And, of course, the state association may be worth joining itself. Here's a list of some statewide consumer groups:

- Arizona Consumers Council, 6840 Camino de Michael St., Tucson, Ariz. 85718
- Consumer Federation of California, 2200 L St., Sacramento, Calif. 90005
- Connecticut Consumer Association, Inc., 8 Ellsworth Road, W. Hartford, Conn. 06107
- Florida Consumers Federation, P.O. Box 1466, Tallahassee, Fla. 32301
- Georgia Consumer Council, Box 311 Morris Brown College, Atlanta, Ga. 30314
- Consumer Federation of Illinois, 53 W. Jackson Blvd., Room 1625, Chicago, Ill. 60604
- Consumers Association of Indiana, Inc., 1330 W. Michigan, Indianapolis, Indiana 46202
- Iowa Consumers League, 200 Walker, Suite A, Des Moines, Iowa 50317
- Consumers Association of Kentucky, Inc., P.O. Box 154, Grayson, Ky. 41143
- Louisiana Consumers League, P.O. Box 1332, Baton Rouge, La. 70821
- Maryland Consumers Association, Inc., Box 254, Courthouse Station, Rockville, Md. 20850
- Association of Massachusetts Consumers, Box M-378, Chestnut Hills, Mass. 02167
- Consumer Alliance of Michigan, P.O. Box 1051-A, Detroit, Mich. 48232
- Minnesota Consumers League, P.O. Box 3063, St. Paul, Minn. 55101
- Mississippi Consumer Association, 1601 Terrace Road, Cleveland, Miss. 38732
- Missouri Association of Consumers, 805 Edgewood, Columbia, Mo. 65201
- Montana Consumers Affairs Council, Inc., P.O. Box 417, Helena, Mont. 59601

- Consumers Alliance of Nebraska, 1301 North Forty-first St., Lincoln, Neb. 68503
- Consumers League of Nevada, 1663 La Jolla Ave., Las Vegas, Nevada 89109
- Consumers League of New Jersey, 20 Church St., Montclair, N.J. 07042
- Consumer Association of New York, 109 Heather Drive, Rochester, N.Y. 14625
- North Carolina Consumers Council, Inc., 1200 Hunting Ridge Rd., Raleigh, N.C. 27609
- Consumers League of Ohio, 940 Engineers Building, Cleveland, Ohio 44114
- Oregon Consumers League, 3131 N.W. Luray Terrace, Portland, Ore. 97210
- Pennsylvania League for Consumer Protection, P.O. Box 948, Harrisburg, Pa. 17108
- South Dakota Consumers League, P.O. Box 72, Brookings, S.D. 57006
- Tennessee Consumer Alliance, P.O. Box 12352, Acklen Station, Nashville, Tenn. 37312
- Texas Consumer Association, P.O. Box 13191, Austin, Texas 78711
- League of Utah Consumers, 180 E. First St., Salt Lake City, Utah 84111
- Virginia Citizens Consumer Council, Box 777, Springfield, Va. 22150
- Washington Committee on Consumer Interests, 2700 First Ave., Room 206, Seattle, Wash. 98121
- Consumer Association of West Virginia, 707 Forestry Tower, Morgantown, W.Va. 26505
- Wisconsin Consumers League, 7017 Dorchester Lane, Greendale, Wis. 53129

In addition to local and state groups, you may want to contact one or more national consumer organizations. They can feed you valuable information; they can sometimes put you in touch with local or state groups you didn't know about; and occasionally they can even help you with an individual problem.

The three national consumer organizations of the greatest interest (and possessing the greatest clout) are Ralph Nader's conglomerate, Consumers Union, and the Consumer Federation of America.

Nader, a man of remarkable intelligence, energy, and persistence, has founded or helped to found more than a dozen consumer groups. His base of operations is the Center for the Study of Responsive Law, 1910 K St., N.W., Washington, D.C. 20006. Among the other groups that Nader helped found, and that he still keeps in close contact with, are the Corporate Accountability Research Group, the Tax Reform Research Group, the Aviation Consumer Action Project, the Health Research Group, the Capitol Hill News Service, and the Public Citizen Visitors Center. There's also Public Citizen, Inc., which is in essence a fund-raising arm for most of the other groups. And—perhaps most important from your point of view—there are the Citizen Action Group (133 C St., S.E., Washington, D.C. 20003), and the National Public Interest Research Group (1832 M St., N.W., Washington, D.C. 20036). The first group helps citizens to form local and state consumer-action organizations; the second oversees the activities of the existing network of more than twenty Nader-oriented state and local consumer-action groups. Most of these groups are called Public Interest Research Groups, or PIRGs, for short. The one in Connecticut is called the Connecticut Citizen Action Group. There are currently PIRGs in California, the District of Columbia, Florida, Illinois, Indiana, Iowa, Maine, Maryland, Massachusetts, Michigan, Minnesota, Missouri, Montana, New Jersey, North Carolina, Oregon, South Carolina, Texas, Vermont, West Virginia, and Wyoming. If you want to join your state's PIRG but can't find it, write to the National Public Interest Research Group. If you'd like to help in forming a PIRG or other consumer action group under Nader's auspices, write to Citizen Action Group. If you just want to get in touch with Nader, write him care of the Center for the Study of Responsive Law. He gets such a titanic volume of mail that you can't expect a personal reply. But you'll probably get a reply of some kind.

The same is true when you write Consumers Union, the non-profit testing organization and publisher of *Consumer Reports,* whose circulation was recently more than 2 million. Though rocked by monetary troubles recently, this long-term mainstay of the consumer movement, founded in 1936, continues to offer the movement some of its most intelligent, thorough, and responsible leadership. Its chief activities are the publication of its monthly magazine, product testing, and the filing of public-interest lawsuits by its Washington, D.C., office. The main office is at 256 Washington St., Mount Vernon, N.Y. 10550. If you write to Consumers Union, your letter may be answered by a form letter or postcard. A fair percentage of the time, however, you'll later receive a more detailed personal response from a member of the staff.

The Consumer Federation of America (CFA) is an umbrella group including hundreds of state and local consumer groups. It may be particularly useful in helping you find a group near you, if you're having trouble. It also conducts lobbying efforts in favor of proconsumer legislation and against what it considers anticonsumer legislation. You can reach the CFA at Suite 406, 1012 Fourteenth St., N.W., Washington, D.C. 20005.

One more organization that may be worth writing to is *Everybody's Money*, the quarterly publication of the Credit Union National Association, Box 431, Madison, Wisconsin, 53701. It forwards all complaints it receives to the top executives of the company in question. You, of course, can do that for yourself. But when a national publication has expressed interest in your complaint, it may get faster—or fairer—treatment.

Getting involved with local, state, and national consumer groups has certain rewards, entirely aside from the help you get in resolving your own complaint. Those rewards have to do with helping other people, exposing unfair or illegal practices on the part of some business, and generally bringing a little bit more justice into the world.

But let's return now to your personal quest for justice. If working with consumer groups fails to get you action on your complaint, you can move up one more rung on the ladder.

Step 9—Enlisting the help of the media. You can seek to put the power of the media to work for you in one of two ways. Number one, you can try to get a news story about your plight into the local newspaper or on radio or television. This can be extremely effective, but it's also an extremely long shot. Number two, you can seek help from a paper's or station's "action line," "complaint line," "hot line," or whatever it may call the problem-solving service it may run. Not all newspapers and radio stations have action lines, of course.

I am personally acquainted with the writers of two action line-type newspaper columns. I can tell you that one is an old fuddy-duddy who couldn't scare a flea and rarely gets people much of their money back. The other is a young tiger who's dedicated, fast, and reasonably effective in getting results. If someone were to spend a few thousand dollars to do a survey, I'm sure they would discover that newspaper and broadcast action lines run the whole spectrum between these two extremes, probably falling into some kind of bell curve.

You, however, don't really need the results of such a survey. You're interested primarily in the effectiveness of the action lines near your hometown—those you can evaluate by reading them or listening to them.

There's one more wrinkle that few people think of—writing an action line in the home area of a distant merchant or manufacturer with whom you're having a dispute. This technique isn't half so hard as you'd think, and it's potentially effective. The mere fact that you took the trouble to write from so far away may impress the action line personnel and tend to make your complaint rise to the top of their in-box or file drawer. Your technique goes like this: Go to the library. Look up the address* of one or two major newspapers and one or two major television stations in the area where the merchant or manufacturer is located. Write them, explaining *very briefly* your problem and asking if they have some type of action line service. When you get a positive reply, you're in business. Just ask for their help in a persuasive covering note, include the usual photocopies of complaint letters and documents, and sit back to wait—preferably with your fingers crossed for good luck.

Having given you the urge to use action lines, let me also

---

*Some useful reference sources are the *Ayer Directory of Publications, Spot Radio Rates and Data,* and *Spot Television Rates and Data.*

sketch briefly the dark side of the picture. Many of these help services are able to respond to only a small percentage of the requests for help they get. Some newspaper and broadcast journalists are at least as callous as any corporate official you'd care (or not care) to meet. They may toss your complaint into the wastebasket and never so much as notify you. "I'd say that some of these lines probably print such a minuscule portion of the letters they get as to make them totally useless to the average consumer," said Dr. Salvatore Davita, a professor in the school of business and government at George Washington University. That may be true to varying degrees in various places. But it's also true that action lines sometimes break through to solve a problem when no one else could.

If an action line doesn't seem to have the sword to slash through your particular Gordian Knot, you can still go one step higher on the consumer complaint escalation ladder.

Step 10—Unconventional tactics.   There's really no limit to the number of imaginative approaches you may be able to think of when you really try. One consumer who's put his intelligence and imagination to work is Professor David Klein. The *New York Times* on Dec. 8, 1974, described what Professor Klein did one day when he arrived in Montreal after a long trip, and discovered that the hotel reservation he had made long before wasn't going to be honored.

> "I will give you three minutes to find me a room," he told the clerk, quietly, but firmly. "After three minutes, I am going to undress in the lobby, put on my pajamas and go to sleep on one of the sofas."
>
> He got a room. He also got a lot of cheers and pats on the back from scores of other men waiting for overbooked rooms.
>
> "But," Professor Klein recalled, a little sadly, "none of them would go ahead and do the same thing."

Remember our friend Jim Van Buskirk from Chapter 1? He's a successful user of unconventional tactics. You've already read about the incident with the art course. Here's another one that occurred recently: Jim rented a car from one of the major rental companies. The rate was to be $14 a day, and no mileage charge. He entered the rental office at 5:45 P.M., left with the car at 6:15 P.M., and returned it at 7:00 P.M. the next day at a gas station that was licensed by the rental agency to accept returned vehicles. The charge came to an inexplicable $36, which Jim paid. Infuriated, he then went back to the rental office (taking a train and a bus to get there). "I can't afford to have you ripping me off," he told the manager. "I'm going to be out here picketing this weekend, and I'm going to bring my friends. What's more, I'm going to charge you three dollars an hour for my time, and the time of each person picketing your place, until you give me twenty dollars back on this bill."

The manager became extremely animated and began to raise his arms and his voice. "What do you want?" he asked, in seeming exasperation. (This, by the way, is a question every complaining consumer should always be glad to hear.)

"I want twenty-five dollars," Jim said.

"Wait a minute," said the manager, suddenly rational again. "A minute ago, you said twenty dollars."

"I decided I should add on the cost of my transportation here and back," Jim replied. The upshot: Jim got a $20 refund, and the manager personally drove him home. "It was," Jim recalls, "one of the quietest trips I've ever taken."

By the way, it should be noted that, even though Jim used unconventional methods to solve his problem, he used very conventional ones to lay the groundwork. He had saved a copy of the rental agreement, spelling out clearly what the charges were supposed to be. "The manager knew that I had proof that would stand up in court," he said.

Another of my favorite unconventional tactics was used by a group of tenants on the East Side of New York. This was not what you would call an underprivileged group. I'd say all of the tenants were paying at least $500 a month in rent, and some more than $1,000. Nonetheless, they had formed a fairly militant tenants' organization because of their concerns about two issues. Number one, they felt the landlord was destroying the aesthetic charm of their vintage building. Number two, the landlord had cut expenses by reducing the security in force at the building.

(Several of the tenants held diplomatic posts at the United Nations, and some of them were from controversial countries.) The landlord claimed the security was still perfectly adequate, but the tenants felt otherwise. I once strolled into the building unannounced and unchecked, so I was inclined to side with the tenants.

Well, push came to shove. The landlord wouldn't comply with their requests; the tenants went on rent strike; the landlord prepared eviction notices. So the tenants did some intensive research on the landlord. They discovered that a major avocation of his was racing horses. He took it so seriously, in fact, that he even had a horse entered in the Belmont Stakes, which was coming up in just a few days. The tenants, many of whom were no strangers to the craft of public relations, called up major newspapers and television stations to tell them about a very interesting demonstration that would take place outside the gates of Belmont Park the day of the race. When reporters and cameramen arrived, they found the tenants picketing for their cause. Some of them had rented a horse costume for the occasion. The result: a big splash of media publicity, which provided some needed leverage in their battle with the landlord.

And here's one more example of unconventional tactics. This one's dear to my heart, because of its simplicity and humbleness. The editorial-page editor at a paper I used to work for once bought a beef roast for dinner. (That was in the days when reasonably well-paid people could afford roasts.) When he got it home and unwrapped it, there was a lot of uncut fat—for which, of course, he'd paid a premium price. He and his wife decided to save the fat and cook the roast. When they did, a huge amount of additional fat drained off. The editor fished the package label, with weight and price indicated, out of the garbage can. He took the label and the remains of the cooked roast, plus the trimmed fat, to the store on a plate. Eyes turned. A crowd gathered. The editor patiently waited for service at the butcher's counter. When the butcher finally got to him, the editor gave a loud and lengthy explanation of why he felt the butcher had not given him his money's worth. He left the store with a full refund, plus a new roast, compliments of the house.

Well, there you have them: the ten rungs on the consumer complaint escalation ladder. They are, in essence, ten ways for you to fight back, ten strategies for you to pursue. The remainder of this book is intended to help you adapt these strategies for use in your own situation. Part II will give you an idea of the governmental resources available to you in your state. Part III will suggest which are the best weapons to choose from your basic arsenal as you grapple with a particular consumer problem.

Consumer Protection, State by State

Alabama

Getting action on a consumer complaint in Alabama isn't easy, but it can be done. There are two consumer-protection agencies in the state, one in the Office of the Governor and one in the Office of the Attorney General. Unfortunately, they operate in a legislative climate that is basically anticonsumer or indifferent to the consumer.

To sense this climate, you need only scan a few of the clouds on the horizon. Cloud number one: Alabama is one of only two states without an Unfair and Deceptive Trade Practices law. Cloud number two: Alabama is one of only six states where a pharmacy isn't allowed to post prices, even *within* the store. (This issue is being fought out in the courts.) Cloud number three: The consumer-protection agencies in Alabama operate on shoestring budgets. The Governor's consumer-protection office, for example, had a 1974 budget of $15,000.

Yet, despite the clouds, you still have a fighting chance. The **Governor's Office of Consumer Protection** does resolve about 40 per cent of the consumer complaints it receives. The average waiting time for a consumer seeking help from that office is about four weeks. The office is located at **138 Adams Avenue, Montgomery, Ala. 36104.** And here's some good news: There's a toll-free statewide hotline on which you can call in a complaint. The number is **1-800-392-5658.**

If you want to have two state agencies working for you instead of one, you can also try the **Consumer Services Coordinator, Office of the Attorney General, 669 South Lawrence St., Montgomery, Ala. 36107.** This agency has a smaller staff than the Governor's agency, but it has somewhat more funding and broader legal powers to deal with certain types of abuses.

The ten most common consumer-complaint areas in Alabama are (1) automobile sales and repairs; (2) mobile homes; (3) mail orders; (4) home improvements and repairs; (5) insurance; (6) housing and real estate; (7) appliances; (8) credit problems; (9) furniture; and (10) unfair business practices. You'll find specific guidance on dealing with all ten of these problems in Part III of this book.

Alaska

The oil-pipeline fever sweeping Alaska is probably only the beginning of a period of explosive growth for the state. History tells us that with wild growth usually come wild schemes and con men seeking to take away other people's newfound money. So Alaskans will be needing a lot of consumer protection in the next few years.

The state seems reasonably well prepared to provide it. In 1974 it greatly strengthened its basic consumer protection law. The law now includes broad language against unfair and deceptive trade practices in general, plus a list of twenty-one acts or practices that are specifically held to be illegal. (Among these are pyramid schemes, chain referral selling, rolling back an odometer, misrepresenting used parts as new when making repairs, and gaining business through deceptive advertising.) For violators, civil penalties now go as high as $5,000; criminal (misdemeanor) penalties range up to $10,000 and a year in jail.

While it was revamping its basic consumer law, the Alaska legislature also strengthened the powers of the Attorney General's office to enforce it. That office now has powers to help consumers comparable to those of just about any other office in the county—

at least on paper. The actual amount of consumer-protection activity, of course, depends in part on budget and staff. Right now the levels of both in Alaska are reasonable but hardly awe-inspiring. The Consumer Protection Section of the Attorney General's office runs on a budget of a little more than $100,000. Its staff consists of two lawyers, two investigators, and four secretaries.

To file a complaint with this office, write **Consumer Protection Section, Office of Attorney General, 3600 K Street, Anchorage, Alaska 99501.** Or you may increase your chances of personal or telephone contact with the person handling your complaint by using one of the two branch offices. They're at Pouch K., State Capitol, Juneau, Alaska 99801; and 604 Barnette, Box 1309, Fairbanks, Alaska 99701.

I'd like to tell you how long your complaint will take to process or what your chances of success are. These questions were in my questionnaire to the state agency. But Alaska's was one of the handful of agencies that didn't respond. After my first two letters went unanswered, I telephoned and was told by a senior agency official that the information would be sent right out. It never came.

We can hope though, that your complaint will be handled better than my inquiry was. Indeed, since the Consumer Protection Section is the only full-time consumer-protection office in all of Alaska, we had better hope so. If the time that might have gone into answering my questionnaire went into helping consumers with complaints, so much the better.

If the agency does fail you, though, you're still not entirely without governmental recourse. Like most states, Alaska has a small claims court system. And, unlike most, it permits class action suits. These are a valuable consumer weapon in which you can band together with other aggrieved consumers to press a case. The pooling of information here is advantageous. So is the pooling of funds for legal expenses. The amount at stake for any one individual might not be worth hiring a lawyer at all. But with a class action, the group might be able to afford an excellent lawyer. And here's some more good news. When you use the courts in Alaska, whether in a class action or as an individual, you may be able to recover some or all of your attorney's fees as part of your award if you win.

In recent years, the Alaska legislature has taken several pro-consumer steps, besides those already mentioned. Collection agencies, vocational schools, and mobile-home dealers have been licensed. A three-day "cooling-off period" is provided, during which you can change your mind about something you bought from a door-to-door salesman. To cancel the sale, you need only notify the seller in writing. (It's smart, of course, to keep a carbon of the letter and to send the original by certified mail). Alaska's law here has good and bad points. The bad point is that you have to know about it; the salesman doesn't have to tell you or notify you. The good point is that the Alaska cooling-off period law applies to most sales of $10 or more—a relatively low limit.

That's only a sampling of the laws that have been passed to help you. You can get a more complete summary, plus a list of what specialized agencies to turn to for help, by writing the Consumer Protection Section, Office of Attorney General. Ask for the "Consumer Protection Kit."

Arizona

It used to be that if you wanted to settle a complaint in Arizona you pulled out your six-shooter. Today's procedures are less dangerous, but they are slower—and sometimes less effective.

The basic state consumer-protection agency is the **Consumer Protection and Antitrust Division, Office of the Attorney General, 159 State Capitol Building, Phoenix, Ariz. 85007.** The division was unable to tell me what percentage of cases it resolves successfully. But it did say, "The average waiting time for complaint processing is six to eight weeks." And "We require that complaints be in writing."

Before you go running for that six-shooter, however, there's a sunny side to the consumer-protection picture in Arizona. To begin with, if you live in the right place, you may be able to take advantage of county or city agencies that appear to be staffed and funded as well as their big-sister state agency. If you live in Tucson, try the **Consumer Affairs Division, City Attorney's Office.** It's at **180 North Meyer, Tucson, Ariz. 85703.** In Pima County, there's a large **Consumer Protection Division** in the **Pima County Attorney's Office, 199 North Stone Ave., Tucson, Ariz. 85701.** The **Cochise County Attorney's Office** in **Bisbee, Ariz. 85603,** also performs consumer-protection functions.

Then there are the courts. Though surely slower than a speeding bullet, they have become more open to consumer-protection cases since a 1974 Arizona Supreme Court decision. In essence, that decision said that private individuals may bring suit to collect damages under the Arizona Consumer Fraud Act. You may collect not only actual damages but also punitive damages, if the conduct of the business that wronged you was sufficiently outrageous.

With vast stretches of open land available, land sales have provided a booming business in Arizona—and a source of major problems for some unwary buyers. If you run into a land-sales problem, it's worth knowing that Arizona has a **Real Estate Commissioner.** You'll find him at **3777 East Broadway, Tucson, Ariz. 85716.** He has the power to take quick action to suspend a developer's license or to halt sales of subdivision lots. Penalties for illegal land-sale shenanigans have recently been strengthened to include jail terms up to a stiff five years and fines up to a lukewarm $5,000.

On the price-fixing front, there's also been some recent movement. Arizona belatedly passed an antitrust statute in 1974. Though late, it is a good one in that it provides for a portion of damages collected to go into a fund to pay for future investigations and prosecutions.

The top eight consumer complaints in Arizona in 1974 were (1) automobile sales and repairs, (2) mobile homes, (3) credit problems, (4) home improvement and repairs, (5) housing and real estate, (6) furniture, (7) appliances, (8) TV and radio. You'll find advice for dealing with each of these areas in Part III.

Arkansas

Folks in Arkansas have been shown an increasing amount of consumer-protection activity lately. And, apparently, they like what they see. In the year that ended July 1, 1975, Arkansans filed 2,356 written complaints with the Consumer Protection Division of the Attorney General's office. This outpouring was double the complaint total of the previous year and about ten times the total of four years ago. In addition to the written complaints, there were about 13,000 telephone complaints and inquiries.

This increase in complaint handling by the state agency coincides with a flurry of activity on the part of the state legislature. In 1974–75 the General Assembly

- Repealed so-called Fair Trade laws that permitted manufacturers to set minimum prices for their products at retail outlets (these have since been repealed nationwide)
- Passed Act 436, permitting druggists to substitute a low-cost generic drug for a high-priced brand-name prescription drug, at the customer's request
- Prohibited credit discrimination according to marital status
- Gave the state Mobile Home Commission power to set standards for the manufacture and sale of mobile homes
- Required a written disclosure of a car's mileage at the time a car is sold (rolling back the odometer to falsify the mileage figure can bring penalties up to $1,000 and a year in jail.)

Just how this activity will translate into action on your particular complaint is difficult to say. The Consumer Protection Division has annual funding of about $70,000 and a staff of nine. At that level of staffing, it's possible that complaints may become backlogged. My questionnaire, asking (among other things) for the percentage of complaints resolved and the average waiting time for action on a complaint, was returned with the notation, "Unfortunately, we do not have sufficient staff to research the answers to all your questions." Will you have better luck with the agency? You may—and one tool you can use is a statewide toll-free telephone number: **1-800-482-8982.** The address is **Consumer Protec-**

tion Division, Office of the Attorney General, Justice Building, Little Rock, Ark. 72201.

Another avenue for getting your complaints resolved may be opening up soon. The Consumer Protection Division recently sponsored legislation to set up a series of small claims courts throughout the state. The status of that legislation was unknown when this book was written, but you can check for yourself by calling the toll-free line in Little Rock.

The list of the most commonly heard consumer complaints in Arkansas largely runs parallel to national trends. An exception is that Arkansas seems to have a lot of trouble with magazines, which rank unusually high in the tallies. Despite the state's controversial limit of 10 per cent on loan interest charges, credit problems in Arkansas seem neither more nor less frequent than they are nationwide.

The most common complaints are about (1) automobile sales and repairs, (2) magazines, (3) home improvements and repairs, (4) mobile homes, (5) real estate, (6) home furnishings, (7) mail orders, and (8) credit problems. You'll find advice for coping with each of these problems in Part III.

California

It's a maxim of pop sociology that social trends in America begin in California. Sexual liberation, the counterculture, strict pollution controls on cars—you saw them all first, as the saying goes, on the West Coast.

To the extent that there's some truth in this cliché, it applies also to the consumer-protection movement. The state has an abundance of laws on the books designed to protect you, and an abundance of people on the public payroll to see that those laws are enforced. If you have a legitimate complaint in California, there's every reason for you to expect to get satisfaction.

Of course, you may find that consumer protection has burgeoned to the point where it has created its own bureaucratic red tape. But slicing through it shouldn't be too hard. The complaint game in California is played in two steps. First you contact the **Department of Consumer Affairs.** Its main office is at **1020 N Street, Sacramento, Calif. 95814.** There are branch offices at **107 South Broadway, Los Angeles, Calif. 90012,** and at **30 Van Ness Ave., San Francisco, Calif. 94102.**

Your complaint—like 90 per cent of the more than 100,000 complaints the Department receives each year, will probably be referred to one of the thirty-six boards and bureaus that regulate various professions and businesses in California. If your case doesn't happen to fit into one of those thirty-six categories, it will be turned over to the department's own Consumer Services Division.

The historical genesis of this system is a bit suspect. The Department of Consumer Affairs was, in effect, superimposed on an existing structure (or hodge-podge) of licensing boards, some of which have been accused of being captives of the very industries they were supposed to regulate. As a result, the effectiveness of the action you'll get depends to a good degree on which board or bureau your complaint is referred to. Most of the boards and bureaus have the power to discipline firms that break their regulations. The discipline can take the form of a fine, a suspension of a firm's license, or an outright revocation of a license.

Perhaps the best of the thirty-six boards and bureaus is the state's Bureau of Automotive Repair. In California, as in the vast majority of states, cars and automotive repairs are the number one consumer problem. Unlike most states, California has taken decisive action to deal with the problem. After its creation in 1972, the Bureau of Automotive Repairs set up a statewide toll-free hot line to take complaints from consumers. Heavy demand quickly pushed the number of complaint-takers up from ten to fifteen. The number, **1-800-952-5210,** is still in operation, and busier than ever, as the bureau handles more than 25,000 complaints a year.

After listening to your complaint, the bureau will attempt to mediate it, getting you and the repair shop to resolve your differences. If that fails—and if you have a serious, legitimate beef—the bureau can suspend or revoke the shop's license through administrative proceedings. Or it can go to court and seek penalties up to six months in jail and $1,000 in fines against the people who ripped you off.

To further discourage auto repairmen from taking advantage of consumers, the bureau has sent inspectors into the field to pose as customers in order to detect fraud. In case you're wondering how all this activity is financed, the answer is that the repair shops pay for it. Each of some 35,000 repair shops around the state pays a licensing fee. Ultimately, of course, the consumer pays, since the repair shops raise their charges to cover the cost of the fees. But a lot of consumers find the protection is worth the price.

We won't name all the other boards and bureaus here. They run the gamut (and the alphabet) from the Board of Accountancy to the Board of Vocational Nurse Examiners. The total staff of the Department of Consumer Affairs is about 850; the annual budget is around $22 million.

This huge staff enforces a battery of consumer-protection statutes passed by a consumer-conscious legislature. In May 1975 the Department of Consumer Affairs published a thirty-nine-page digest of recent state consumer-protection legislation (worth sending away for, by the way, if you're an active consumer). It contained no fewer than 180 laws passed in 1973 and 1974. Besides such standard subjects as advertising and warranties, it touched on such arcane realms as astrology (cities may prohibit its practice for money) and pay toilets (which were banned in state-run or city-run public facilities).

Here are a few highlights of recent California consumer legislation:

- California courts now have inherent powers to order refunds to customers who have purchased goods or services as a result of misrepresentation or unfair business practices.
- Mail-order firms must deliver their goods within six weeks of your order, or else do one of three things: (a) send you your money back, (b) send you a letter explaining the delay and giving you the opportunity to request a refund, or (c) send you substitute goods, which you may keep or exchange for a full refund.

- Drug stores must post the prices of their 100 most frequently prescribed drugs.
- Mobile home dealers must offer a one-year warranty and must have the warranty available for your inspection.
- If a merchant sells goods or services by speaking Spanish to a customer, and if the customer requests that the contract be written in Spanish, the merchant must comply with that request.

Large as it is, the Department of Consumer Affairs isn't the only agency available to go to bat for the consumer in California. The Consumer Protection Unit, Office of the Attorney General, has offices in Los Angeles and San Francisco. Several counties have consumer-protection bodies; those in Fresno County and Sacramento County are particularly well staffed and well funded.* On the whole, you may as well start with the Department of Consumer Affairs, using the other agencies as your second resort.

The top seven consumer complaints in California (all discussed in the final section of this book) are about (1) automobile sales and repairs, (2) mobile homes, (3) landlord-tenant problems, (4) appliances, (5) TV, radio, and stereo sets, (6) credit problems, and (7) unfair or deceptive business practices.

Colorado

Outsiders think of Colorado as a place of rustic beauty, a step back in time. There's truth to the image, of course. But, as Denver's smog attests, Colorado faces the normal array of problems encountered by all of an increasingly urban America.

The profile of the complaints most commonly filed with the state's Office of Consumer Affairs present anything but a rustic picture. Here are the top ten, with the number of complaints for

*Other California counties with consumer-protection offices are Del Norte, Los Angeles, Marin, Monterey, Orange, San Bernardino, San Diego, Santa Barbara, Santa Cruz, Stanislaus Ventura, and Yolo. There are city offices in Long Beach, Los Angeles, Merced, and San Diego.

each in 1974: automobile sales and repair, 730; home improvement and repair, 500; mail-order and publication-subscription problems, 400; home furnishings and appliances, 380; mobile homes, 300; credit problems and collection practices, 180; landlord-tenant problems, 180; advertising, 100; TV, stereo, and radio repair, 100; and health spas, 100.

All ten of these areas are discussed in detail in this book. If one of them—or some other problem—has you beating your head against what feels like a Rocky Mountain, there are two types of government agencies you can turn to for help. First, there's the **Office of Consumer Affairs, 112 East Fourteenth Avenue, Denver, Colo. 80203.** It reports that it resolves the average consumer complaint in about four weeks. However, "We solve approximately thirty-five to forty per cent of our cases to the consumer's satisfaction. The remaining cases are either not valid claims or do not fall within our jurisdiction."

If you live in one of the five counties in or around Denver (Adams, Arapahoe, Boulder, Denver, and Jefferson), you may want to use a five-county regional agency instead of (or in addition to) the state agency. The Metropolitan District Attorney's Consumer Office was created in 1974 to serve the five counties. It describes itself as "the first multicounty office of its type engaged in the prosecution of economic crime in the nation." Sponsored by the district attorneys of the five counties, it is funded partly by a federal Law Enforcement Assistance Administration grant and partly with local funds. In its first six months of operation it processed more than 2,400 consumer complaints (plus more than 8,000 securities fraud cases). That pace of operations is about equal to the state's; what's more, the five-county agency has staff and funding about equal to the state's (at least as long as the federal funds last). The Metro Office says it is resolving some complaints that formerly went unattended because they involved consumers in one county and merchants in another. If you want to give this new agency a try, here's the address: **Metropolitan District Attorney's Consumer Office, 655 South Broadway, Denver, Colo. 80209.**

El Paso County, Teller County, and Pueblo County also have consumer specialists within their district attorneys' offices, but I was unable to evaluate their effectiveness. You'll have to check them for yourself.

Connecticut

On July 19, 1974, a new regulation took on the force of law in Connecticut. It's one that you, as a consumer, should know about, if you don't already. Basically, it's designed to guarantee you a full refund if you return something within seven days after you bought it.

That rule, promulgated by the state Department of Consumer Protection, has all kinds of qualifications and caveats. Knowing them will help you use the rule wisely. So sit down for a moment, take a deep breath, and let's go. First, you must save the sales slip or have some other proof that you did indeed buy the item in question from the store in question within the last seven days. Second, the rule doesn't apply if the merchant has conspicuously placed a sign in the store saying that it doesn't. Such a sign may be posted in one of three places: at the store entrance, at the place the item is displayed, or at the cash register.

If there's no sign saying otherwise, then the merchant is obliged to give you a full refund for goods you return within a week. It can be a cash refund or credited to your account. Not a bad regulation, is it? Of course, it would be even better if it weren't for the exceptions. Items that are wholly or even partly custom-made are exempt from the regulation. So are food and other perishables, used merchandise, things that can't be resold legally, and items that were marked "as is" or "final sale" at the time you bought them.

In addition to this handy refund regulation, Connecticut has—like most states—a broad statute prohibiting unfair and deceptive trade practices. The agency charged with seeing that you don't get ripped off and helping you if you do is the **Department of Consumer Protection.** It's in the **State Office Building, Hartford, Conn. 06115.** The department has a staff of about 150 people and a budget of about $1.7 million. Those figures can be misleading, though, in that not all that money and manpower go into handling of citizens' complaints. The department has extensive responsibilities in the areas of meat and poultry inspection, drug control, weights and measures, consumer education, the regulation of pharmacies, and even the regulation of boxing and wrestling. (Because a woman is usually named Commissioner of the Department of Consumer Protection, Connecticut was the first state with a woman boxing commissioner.)

So far as complaint-handling goes, Connecticut does have the always welcome touch of a toll-free number for you to call. It's 800-842-2649. Exactly how well you'll fare is difficult to predict. In response to my questionnaire, Commissioner Mary M. Heslin wrote, "We cannot rate our success in terms of cases successfully resolved, other than to state that each and every complaint is reviewed, analyzed, evaluated, and proceeded on based on our statutory authority. At the present time we are investigating complaints that were submitted three to five weeks previous, although a preliminary contact has been made with the complainants." A curious phenomenon is the relatively low number of complaints received by the department; it appears to be processing fewer complaints than comparable agencies in smaller, more rural states. Barring a statistical quirk, this must mean that (1) the department isn't publicizing its services well enough; (2) it isn't performing its services well enough, causing people to stay away; (3) Connecticut consumers are so well educated they are less likely than others to need help; or (4) some combination of the above. Let's hope the answer is (3), because the Department of Consumer Protection is essentially the only game in town. According to a federal compilation, the only other government consumer office in the state is the one operated by the city of Middletown, which has a staff of two people.

However, other state agencies not formally designated as consumer-protection agencies can help you with many problems. You can get a list of these, plus advice on a variety of consumer topics (food buying, car buying, warranties, contracts, insurance, and credit, for example), by sending for the publication *$HELP$*. Single copies are free from the Department of Consumer Protection.

Delaware

Most consumer complaints in Delaware seem to fall close to home. "Dwellings" is the number one complaint category in the records kept by the state Division of Consumer Affairs. Those complaints seem to consist mainly of gripes against unsatisfactory home repairs. The number-two consumer problem in the state is "home furnishings." Landlord-tenant problems and difficulties with mobile homes also rank near the top of the complaint ladder.

Outside their homes, Delaware residents are most troubled by cars that don't work, clothing that proves unsatisfactory, mail-order sales, recreational vehicles, publications, and credit problems (in that order). For help with these and other problems, residents of the First State needn't go too far from their homes. To begin with, nobody in Delaware is more than 100 miles from Wilmington, where the **Division of Consumer Affairs** is located (**200 W. Ninth Street, 6th Floor, Wilmington, Del. 19801**). To make things even more convenient, the division maintains local telephone numbers in New Castle County, Kent County, and Sussex County. When you dial the local number, your call is put through to Wilmington. The numbers, at last notice, were 302-571-3250 for the Wilmington office, 658-9251 in New Castle County, 678-4000 in Kent County, and 856-2571 in Sussex County.

The division claims a good batting average: "75 per cent plus" of its cases successfully resolved. Unlike some states, which require that all complaints be in writing, the Delaware Division of Consumer Affairs handles a lot of complaints informally, by phone. "We receive between eight hundred and nine hundred telephone inquiries monthly," a staff investigator says. "Many of these are handled by making a telephone call or writing a letter and may not become formal complaints. An initial consumer's call will result in either advice, some immediate action, or our sending out a formal complaint form calling for additional documentation."

A second consumer-recourse agency in the state is the **Consumer Protection Division** of the **Department of Justice**. This office, located in the **Public Building, Wilmington, Del. 19801,** has been active in enforcing Delaware's forward-looking statutes on mobile-home parks and landlord-tenant relations. On those types of problems, plus others involving clear violations of law, contact with this agency is recommended. In addition, you can use it as a backup on other types of problems.

District of Columbia

Since its very birth, Washington, D.C., has lived in a kind of legal limbo. In some ways it resembles a state, in other ways a no man's land. Thinking of it for the moment as a jurisdiction comparable to a state, it would join California and Connecticut as the only ones that license and regulate both auto repair shops and electronic repair dealers (such as radio, TV, and stereo repairmen). The Board of Consumer Goods Repair Services is in charge of watching over these two areas and is studying the question of adding to the list. The regulated facilities are required to give you a written estimate before doing any repair work, to tell you about all service charges in advance, and to give you all the parts that were replaced. (This is to prevent phony replacements.) In this city where "cost overrun" has become a household word, repair shops are allowed to exceed their estimates by 20 per cent on repairs costing $300 or less, and by 10 per cent on repairs costing more than that. Any further overruns require your consent. If you don't give it, the shop must put your car (or television, or whatever) back into as good shape as it was in when they got it. They may charge you a reasonable fee for the job of reassembly—providing that the fee was disclosed to you in advance.

If you want to get in touch with the Board of Consumer Goods Repair Services, you can reach it through the District of Columbia **Office of Consumer Affairs, 1407 L Street, N.W., Washington, D.C. 20005.** The District Office of Consumer Affairs is also your primary complaint-handling agency. Established in 1973 as part of the office of the mayor, the office claims to resolve successfully 75 per cent of the complaints it receives. The average waiting time for a consumer needing help is highly variable, but a rough average, the Office says, would be one week.

The categories of complaints received most often by the Office are (1) auto repairs and sales, (2) home improvements and repairs, (3) television, electronic, and appliance repair, (4) credit problems, including billing and debt collection practices, (5) furniture, (6) retail stores, and (7) mail-order houses. You'll find advice on grappling with these problem areas in Part III.

Florida

This vast peninsula, dipping its lacquered toes into the Atlantic, is like no other state in the union. With its bright birds, alligator swamps, and miles of beaches, it has long been a magnet for tourists. Unfortunately, it's also been a magnet for some fast-buck operators. Victimized Florida consumers, however, have a plethora of agencies designed to help them.

The pattern of consumer complaints in Florida is quite different from the standard pattern. Auto complaints, normally first, are only third here. Home improvements, normally second, are eighth.

At the top of the list in Florida are condominiums. Fully 55 per cent of the new housing being built in Florida takes the form of condominiums, and the state Department of Legal Affairs (Attorney General's Office) believes that many of the developers have been in a position to gain "unconscionably large" profits at the consumer's expense. In 1974 the department filed charges against one of the state's largest developers in an attempt to get rid of the notorious ninety-nine-year leases that developers have held on important parts of condominium developments (the recreation facilities, for example). About the same time the state legislature passed a reform law (Chapter 711) affecting condominium developments. Among other reforms, it will require that prospective condominium-unit owners be notified if they are going to be required to belong to a recreation facilities club.

The state Glenn Turner made his base of operations has also

had an unusually high number of complaints regarding franchises and distributorships. Such problems rank seventh here. Ranking ninth (high compared to their incidence in the average state) are complaints about contracts for delivery of future consumer services—such as health spas, singles clubs, and country clubs.

Complaints involving landlord-tenant relations rank fourth here, but Florida tenants have a number of powerful weapons at their disposal under a recent state law. Tenants who are denied the basic services that make an apartment habitable can legally withhold their rent under the statute. This is best done, though, in consultation with a lawyer.

Other complaints in Florida's top ten are land sales (second), mobile homes (fifth), deceptive advertising (sixth), and mail-order problems (tenth). If you run into a problem in these or other areas, there are a whole battery of state agencies that may be of use in clearing things up.

For most problems, your first recourse (after the seller or manufacturer) should probably be the **Fair Trade Practice Office** in the **Department of Legal Affairs, The Capitol, Tallahassee, Fla. 32304.** The Fair Trade Practice Office has branches at **1350 Northwest Twelfth Ave., Miami, Fla. 33136,** and at **305 Morgan Street, Tampa, Fla. 33602.** This office has the strongest legal powers for dealing with abuses.

However, it's strongly recommended that you also seek help from the **Division of Consumer Services, Department of Agriculture and Consumer Services, 106 W. Pensacola Street, Tallahassee, Fla. 32301.** The Division of Consumer Services lacks some of the legal powers of the Department of Legal Affairs. But it has more staff (and more money) to devote to coping with your complaint. It also has that great convenience, a toll-free telephone number, **1-800-342-2176.**

On problems involving banking, securities, or finance, the **Office of the Comptroller** (same address as the Department of Legal Affairs) stands ready to help. The comptroller's office has six branches around the state; it also has a toll-free number, **1-800-342-3557.**

If you find that you have a problem with some branch of the state government, you can call the state **Ombudsman.** The Ombudsman can also help you if you don't know which state agency you should go to with a particular problem. The number—again toll-free—is **1-800-342-3556.**

Besides these state agencies, you may be able to get help from one of the nine county and two city consumer-protection agencies that exist in Florida. Jacksonville has a well-staffed Division of Consumer Affairs in its Department of Human Resources (220 East Bay Street, Jacksonville, Fla. 32202). Saint Petersburg has a City Division of Consumer Affairs at 175 Fifth Street, North, Saint Petersburg, Fla. 33701.

Among the county agencies, the Consumer Protection Division of Metropolitan Dade County appears to be particularly active. It's located at 1399 N.W. Seventeenth Ave., Miami, Fla. 33125. Brevard County has a Consumer Fraud Division within its State Attorney's Office in Titusville. Broward County maintains a County Department of Consumer Affairs in Fort Lauderdale. There's a joint State Attorney's Office that handles consumer complaints in DeSoto, Manatee, and Sarasota counties. In Hillsboro County the place to turn is the county Office of Consumer Services in Tampa. In Palm Beach County it's the county Office of State Attorney in West Palm Beach. And in Pinella County it's the county Office of Consumer Affairs in St. Petersburg.

Georgia

The switchboard in the Atlanta office of the Georgia Consumer Services Program is lit up like the proverbial Christmas tree. It's a typical day: About two hundred people are calling in with problems, and many of them are being put on "hold" for long periods of time.

Just another instance of red tape and bureaucracy, you say? Well, it might look that way at first. But many of the consumers put on "hold" are actually experiencing an unusually intelligent complaint-handling system at work. For, while they're holding the phone, a complaint-handler at the other end may be calling the business with whom they have a dispute, bringing a fast wrap-up to the whole tangle.

Here's how the procedure works, as described by Steve Johnson, a legal intern with the Consumer Services Program. A consumer calls in on the Tie Line, a toll-free number set up to "aid citizens in threading their way through state bureaucracies and finding the person they need to talk with." (The number is 1-800-282-4900.) If the call should be handled by someone in another agency, the call will be immediately "bridged" to an appropriate person in that agency. Otherwise, information will be taken by one of sixteen trained telephone counselors. If the counselor can put the consumer on "hold" and solve the problem with a quick phone call, that's how it will be done. If not, the counselor will take down information about the problem. The counselor then has twenty-four hours to resolve the complaint. Of some two hundred-odd calls per day, about one hundred eighty-five are handled within twenty-four hours by the telephone counselors. The remaining fifteen, along with some ten complaints per day arriving by mail, are turned over to the case closure unit. This unit "screens the complaints to see which ones need legal action or appear to reveal a pattern of deception by a particular company. . . . The vast majority of consumer complaints are handled within a week, while a small minority, usually involving hardcore fraud or complex issues, may require months of work, if a trial is required," Steve Johnson explains. "We are fortunate in having the telephone counselors, since we therefore do not have the extensive delays experienced by other agencies which use form letters and require all complaints to be in writing before taking action. . . . I would guess overall that we resolve 80 per cent of our cases, with another 10 per cent being unsolvable and another 10 per cent involving problems that we are too late in finding out about, but which could have been solved, had we been notified earlier."

The successful-solution rate, however, is much lower on those cases that actually reach the case closure unit. On these more knotty cases, the solution rate is only about 20 per cent. Many consumers with these special problems will be referred to small claims court, or will be advised to retain a lawyer on their own. "We do have the authority to sue for actual damages lost by a consumer," Johnson said, "but not as a class action, so if the deception is egregious we can provide some legal assistance.

Limitations on staff and time make this rather unlikely, however, unless a major operation is involved."

In light of the way the Consumer Services Program works, you'll probably want to phone, rather than write, at least at first. Should you need it, the mailing address is **Georgia Consumer Services Program, 618 Ponce De Leon Ave. N.E., Atlanta, Ga. 30303.**

When it comes to consumer-complaint handling in Georgia, the Consumer Services Program is pretty much the only game in town. You can try the **Assistant Attorney General for Deceptive Practices, Office of the Attorney General, 132 State Judicial Building, Atlanta, Ga. 30334.** But its staff allocation for handling consumer complaints is rather limited. If you live in Atlanta, you can try the Atlanta Office of Consumer Affairs, City Hall–Memorial Drive Annex, 121 Memorial Drive S.W., Atlanta, Ga. 30303. But its staff consists of one person. On the county level, there are no consumer-protection agencies as such.

The most common complaints in Georgia are about (1) automobile repairs, (2) appliance repairs, (3) landlord-tenant problems, and (4) door-to-door sales. Others often heard involve utilities, credit, mobile homes, mail-order problems, furniture, and insurance. In Part III of this book you'll find discussions of these topics, arranged alphabetically.

Hawaii

There's good news and bad news about consumer protection in Hawaii. The good news: Hawaii has an active, vigorous Office of Consumer Protection, which in certain ways has been innovative in protecting the consumer. The bad news: The agency does have some flaws, and if it can't (or doesn't) help you, there's not likely to be a second chance—at least on the governmental level. The Office of Consumer Protection (which is part of the Governor's office) is the only broad-gauge state consumer-protection agency; and there are no county or city agencies.

The OCP's director, Walter T. Yamashiro, claims that 85 per

cent of the cases that come to the agency are successfully resolved. However, this statement is accompanied by a warning that "in no case may OCP act as an individual's private counsel." It may be that your definition of success and Mr. Yamashiro's would not agree.

The director's estimate of the average waiting time for a consumer needing aid is far less impressive than the reported success rate: six to eight weeks. So if you file a complaint with OCP, be prepared to sit back for quite a while to await results. Knowing this wait lies in store for you may make you more prone to try a small claims court, a voluntary organization, or some unconventional tactic in your quest for redress.

To its credit, though, the state has tried some unconventional tactics of its own. Take car sales and repairs, for example. In Hawaii, as in the vast majority of states, auto sales and repairs constitute the number one source of consumer complaints. In 1974 OCP had accumulated a large number of complaints against a major auto dealer, and had charged the dealer with eleven counts of unfair or deceptive practices. After negotiations with the dealer, it was agreed to bring together some auto industry leaders in a so-called board of experts to resolve complaints against the dealer that weren't resolved by OCP mediation. OCP was reportedly considering the use of similar panels in the future in disputes involving other dealers.

Next to car problems, the OCP gets the most calls about landlord-tenant disputes. The largest number of these calls concern security deposits. OCP staffers usually listen to a description of the circumstances surrounding a landlord's keeping a tenant's security deposit. They inform the tenant about the law, and if they think the tenant has a case, they usually urge him to go to small claims court. No lawyers are allowed in security-deposit cases heard there, so the tenant needn't fear costly legal expenses. On security deposits and other matters, tenants' rights are fairly well protected by Hawaii's version of the Uniform Residential Landlord-Tenant Act (URLTA). The state adopted URLTA in 1973, and in 1974 cut the time a landlord may take to make needed repairs (requested in writing by a tenant) from thirty days to twenty days. Even this is too long, of course. But if you're a tenant in Hawaii, you're probably better off than tenants in most places.

One footnote for tenants, especially those recently arrived from the mainland. According to the *Honolulu Star-Bulletin*, newcomers are prone to complain to OCP about roaches or gekko lizards in apartments. Calls about roaches are referred to the Department of Health. And, according to OCP chief investigator Mitsuo Takayama, the gekko lizards are "ugly as hell but perfectly harmless."

Complaints about contractors, which rank second in most states, rank only seventh in Hawaii. One reason may be that home improvement and other contractors are licensed here. Licensing can, of course, be an industry-controlled sham whose chief effect is simply to cut down competition. But there's some evidence that it's working to the consumer's benefit in Hawaii. Powers of the Contractors Licensing Board, and of similar boards that license some other professions, were recently expanded, enabling the boards to hold hearings on complaints that can't be resolved informally. Following a hearing, a board can order a firm to give a customer a refund or to redo the job in question to the customer's satisfaction. If a firm refuses to do these things after being told to, its license can be suspended or revoked.

In 1974 OCP reported receiving "a great number" of complaints about poor workmanship in jobs (especially home additions or repairs) by unlicensed firms. Result: a toughening up of the laws against the unlicensed practice of certain occupations. Penalties now go as high as $2,500 per offense, and a contractor's license is now a prerequisite for getting a building permit.

OCP's own powers to mediate consumer disputes have also been increased recently. It can negotiate an "assurance of voluntary compliance" with companies accused of wrongdoing. And as part of the deal it can get written agreement from such companies that they will reimburse some or all of the consumers who have been harmed. This could be a real boon to ripped-off Hawaiians—but it's not an unmitigated blessing. The amount OCP recovers for you might be less than you could have gained for yourself in the courts, if the economic harm you suffered was substantial. So, in really serious cases, think twice and consult a lawyer before signing any papers that, in effect, designate OCP as your bargaining agent.

We've already alluded to three of the problems that are most troubling to Hawaiian consumers: (1) cars, (2) landlords, and (7) contractors. For the curious, the remainder of the top ten trouble list are (3) mail-order firms, (4) appliance sales and repairs, (5) home furnishings, (6) travel, (8) food, (9) unlicensed activities, and (10) real estate. Except for unlicensed activities, discussed above, you'll find treatments of each of these problems in Part III.

If you need OCP's services, you can write **Office of Consumer Protection, P.O. Box 3767, Honolulu, Hawaii 96813.** If you're one of those who (like me) get nervous writing to P.O. boxes, you can substitute the street address: **602 Kamamalu Blg., 250 South King St., Honolulu, Hawaii 96811.** There are also three branch offices around the islands, one at 75 Aupuni St., Hilo, Hawaii 96720; one at 179 Kaahumanu Ave., Kahului, Maui, Hawaii 96732; and one at P.O. Box 191, Lihue, Kauai, Hawaii 96766.

Idaho

If you're like most Idaho consumers, your complaints are likely to fall into one of these ten areas: (1) auto repairs and sales, (2) food and drugs, (3) mobile homes, (4) home repairs and improvements, (5) appliances, (6) furniture, (7) mail-order houses, (8) credit, (9) medical treatment, (10) housing and real estate.

You'll find advice for coping with all ten of those problem areas in Part III. But, to be frank, it looks like a bit of an uphill battle for Idaho consumers. State laws here do not protect the consumer particularly well, compared to the situation in other states. As a rough gauge, let's consider a tabulation of *State Laws on Major Consumer Issues* published by the federal Office of Consumer Affairs. The tabulation lists thirty types of consumer-protection laws or regulations that are assumed useful in helping consumers defend their rights. Of these thirty, California and Oregon have twenty-two in force. Montana has fifteen. Idaho has fourteen. (If it will make you feel better, Mississippi has eleven, Alabama ten, and Arkansas five.)

Much, of course, depends on the energy and skill of the agency charged with administering these laws. In Idaho that agency is the **Consumer Protection Division, Office of Attorney General, State Capitol, Room 225, Boise, Idaho 83720.** This is also the agency to which you should submit your complaints, after first trying to hammer fair treatment out of the merchant or manufacturer.

I wish I had more information to pass on concerning this agency. What I have is not too encouraging. Its only office is in Boise, and it has no toll-free telephone number, so you'll probably be transacting your business in writing. I wrote the agency to ask (among other things) what its success rate is in handling complaints and what the average waiting time is for a consumer needing help. After two letters went unanswered, I telephoned. On my second call a senior agency official told me the information I had requested would be sent right out. It never arrived.

Don't let this discourage you from contacting the agency. Your luck may be better than mine; indeed, the agency *should* devote a higher priority to complaints than to answering authors' questionnaires. (Still, forty-four states did find time to answer.) If you find the agency is unable to help you, be prepared to use the courts, the media, voluntary groups, or unconventional methods to achieve your goal of simple justice in the market place.

To help you make the most of the protections you do have at your disposal, write the Consumer Protection Division right now to ask for a copy of its publication, *Consumer-Business Relations in Idaho,* which describes state and federal laws you may need or want to use. You might also want to subscribe to the Division's monthly newsletter, *Idaho Consumer News,* which gives you local and national consumer news as well as buying tips. Single copies (or single subscriptions) of both of these publications were free to state residents at last report.

Illinois

Illinois has a history of political rivalry between the Governor's office and the Attorney General's office. (As a convenient, if coincidental, illustration, the Attorney General declared his candidacy for Governor and his intention of opposing the current Governor while this book was being written.) One result of this traditional rivalry is the development of two separately functioning consumer-protection agencies within the state government. Both, of course, want to take credit for helping as many consumers as possible.

If you live in Illinois, you may view this arrangement unfavorably, at least in your role as a taxpayer. As a consumer, however, there's no reason not to let it work for you. Just consider that you have two recourse agencies instead of one.

As luck would have it, both state agencies replied to my questionnaire, giving me two separate lists of Illinois's top ten consumer complaints. Both the similarities and differences between the two lists are interesting. Automobile problems were at the top of both lists, with somewhat more consumers disgruntled about repairs than about sales. Home improvements, in one form or another, came next. The Governor's office received a particularly large number of complaints (414) about waterproofing firms. (Apparently it's hard to keep the drips out of your basement in Illinois—one way or another.)

Mail-order houses ranked just about neck-and-neck with home improvements on both lists. Many of the mail-order complaints are received from out-of-state consumers against mail-order houses headquartered in Illinois.

After cars, home improvements, and mail-order houses, the complaint patterns diverged. In upstate Illinois, the Attorney General's office gets a considerable number of complaints concerning real estate, furniture and draperies, credit, appliances, publications, and heating and air-conditioning. Among downstate consumers, the same office finds mobile homes a significant problem, along with publications, advertising, health centers, real estate, and leases. The Governor's office, on the other hand, is approached most often about collection agencies, landlord-tenant problems, mobile homes, credit, retail sales, and home furnishings, in about that order. If you're suffering from one of these common Illinois consumer problems, you'll probably find some advice on your specific problem in the final section of this book.

If you need government help, try both state agencies. The Attorney General's Office, with thirty-two investigators (twenty full-time), has both the staff and the legal clout to help you. Some observers, though, fault it for taking an overly legalistic approach—failing to act except in cases of apparent fraud, unless it receives a thick file of complaints on an individual company. If you live upstate, write **Consumer Fraud and Protection Division, Office of the Attorney General, Room 204, 134 North LaSalle St., Chicago, Ill. 60602.** You can expect action, according to officials in the Chicago office, within two to three weeks on the average. Your chances of success were put at 65 per cent.

Downstate, write **Consumer Protection Division, Office of the Attorney General, 500 South Second St., Springfield, Ill. 62706.** An official in the downstate office claims 90 per cent of cases handled are resolved successfully. However, he said the average waiting time is four to five weeks.

If your problem is one you think might be cleared up over the phone, you can call a special assistant to the Attorney General at one of the twenty branch offices around the state. Fourteen branch offices report to the Chicago AG office. Four of them are in Chicago; the others are in Aurora, Buffalo Grove, Des Plaines, Elk Grove Village, Joliet, Maywood, Morton Grove, Schaumburg, Skokie, and Waukegan. Six branch offices report to Springfield. They are in Carbondale, East Saint Louis, Peoria, Rantoul, Rockford, and Rock Island.

After you contact the AG office, whether by phone or by letter, you'll probably want to do the same with the Governor's office. That's the **Consumer Advocate's Office, Office of the Governor, Room 2000, State of Illinois Building, 160 North LaSalle St., Chicago, Ill. 60601.** This agency lacks the legal powers and large staff of the AG office, but it can sometimes accomplish a lot through informal mediation. It was founded in 1973 and only began to keep figures on what percentage of its cases it resolves in late 1975, so no meaningful success ratio can be given. As for waiting time, it's "two weeks at the most" for most cases, says an official.

There are a couple of areas where you should probably bypass both of the broad-gauge state agencies. One is real estate, since real estate brokers are licensed by the Department of Registration and Education, 628 E. Adams, Springfield, Ill. 62706. In 1974 the state legislature required all brokers to pay annual fees, which are pooled to form a Real Estate Recovery Fund. If you've been ripped off in a real estate transaction, you can recover up to $10,000 from the fund—plus at least some of your court costs. But to do that you'll need an order from a state circuit or district court, which means you'll need a lawyer.

The courts, rather than the consumer-protection agencies, are also likely to be your best allies in landlord-tenant disputes. That's because tenant protection in Illinois has come largely through protenant judicial decisions, not through legislation. The best way to exercise your rights as a tenant (anywhere, but especially in Illinois) is to join or form an active tenants' group. The group as a whole should have access to up-to-date legal advice. If none of your group's members is a lawyer, it's worth pooling some of your funds to pay for counsel. A good group to consult is the Metropolitan Tenants Union, at 3543 W. Jackson Street, Chicago, Ill. 60624.

If your complaint concerns a merchant in your own area—and if you live in the right area—you can seek help from a local agency. In Cook County, there's the **Consumer Complaint Division, Cook County Office of State's Attorney, Civic Center, Suite 303, Randolph at Clark, Chicago, Ill. 60602.** And in Madison County, there's the **Madison County Office of State's Attorney, 3d floor, 103 Purcell St., Edwardsville, Ill. 62025.**

In the village of Park Forest, there's the **Consumer Protection Commission, Village Hall, 200 Forest Boulevard, Park Forest, Ill. 60466.** And in the city of Chicago, there's the **Chicago Department of Consumer Sales, Weights & Measures, City Hall, 121 N. LaSalle St., Chicago, Ill. 60602.**

Oh, one more thing. If you live in Chicago, it doesn't hurt to be a friend of the mayor's.

Indiana

In thirty seconds, if you live in Indiana, you are going to put down this book. You will walk to the phone. You will dial **1-800-382-5516.** That's the toll-free number of the state Consumer Protection Division. You will ask the person who answers for a copy of a small brochure called *Consumer Assistance Agencies in Indiana.* She or he will take down your name and address, and a few days later you will get a copy of the brochure. It won't solve all your problems. But it is sure to give you a good idea of where to go with them.

If you have a problem and, even after reading the brochure, are not sure where to turn for help, you can dial that toll-free number again. Or write **Consumer Protection Division, Office of the Attorney General, 219 State House, Indianapolis, Ind. 46204.**

In 1974 Indiana consumers with gripes made more than ten thousand telephone calls to the CPD and wrote 3,627 complaint letters. As far as broad-gauge consumer complaint handling goes, the CPD is practically the only governmental agency to use. The city of Gary does have an Office of Consumer Affairs, but at last report its staff was small and its funding uncertain. If you live in Gary there's no harm trying it on local disputes. The address is **City Office of Consumer Affairs, City of Gary—Annex East, 1100 Massachusetts, Gary, Ind. 46402.** The same advice applies to using the Prosecuting Attorney's offices if you live in Lake County or Porter County. (The addresses are: **Lake County Office of Prosecuting Attorney, 232 Russell St., Hammond, Ind. 46320;** and **Porter County Office of Prosecuting Attorney, P.O. Box 390, Crown Point, Ind. 46307.**) But by all means make your first approach to the state Consumer Protection Division.

When you complain, there's a large chance it will be about either a mail-order house or a door-to-door salesman. Those two areas ranked number one and number two in the state in 1974, far above other types of complaints. This is a striking deviation from the pattern in most states, where autos and home improvements top the list (those gripes rank third and fourth in Indiana).

Partly in an effort to stem the tide of mail-order complaints, the CPD has recommended (but at last report the state legislature had not enacted) a law making it a "deceptive practice" to fail to deliver ordered goods within thirty days. If a seller couldn't meet the deadline, it could offer a refund instead. The requirement would apply in all cases except when a longer delivery time was clearly disclosed at the time of the sale. Until such a measure passes in Indiana—and even afterward—Indiana consumers would be well advised to read the discussion of mail-order problems in Part III.

Problems with door-to-door salesmen can be to some extent alleviated by making use of Indiana's home solicitation law, which was passed in 1969 and amended in 1971. It requires that a buyer be given a three-day cooling-off period to change his mind* about the sale. There's no penalty for this cancellation, so long as it occurs within three business days. And the salesman, by law, is supposed to tell the customer about the existence of the three-day rule. However, there's a hitch. The law applies only to goods that are bought on credit. If you paid cash or by a check, you're out of luck. One obvious lesson: If your sales resistance is a little weak, never pay cash to a door-to-door merchandiser.

After mail-order houses, door-to-door sales, cars, and home improvements, the most common complaints in Indiana deal with appliances, furniture, recreational vehicles, real estate, and collection agencies. Most of these problems are discussed individually in the final section of this book.

Iowa

Think about Iowa and you think about land. Mile upon mile of rich, fertile farmland is the state's chief resource. And land, ironically, is also the state's number one consumer complaint.

Most of the land Iowans have occasion to complain about

---

* Or hers—but studies have shown that men, rather than women, are most prone to fall for a door-to-door sales pitch.

isn't in Iowa. It's somewhere else. But Iowans have bought it, often without seeing it. This—it need hardly be pointed out to those who have already fallen prey to glowing sales pitches—is a mistake. Whether Iowans are particularly prone to this type of error, or whether land hucksters just like to congregate here, we won't try to resolve. But it's worth noting that Iowa is the only state where land sales rank number one on the complaint list.

As it happens, some Iowa consumers have apparently been victimized twice over when it comes to land sales. The one-two punch works this way: First some firm comes along and sells you a choice lot in Arizona (or wherever) with boundless investment potential. When you later learn that the lot is 100 miles from the nearest water supply in an area where the temperature averages 115 degrees, you feel a great deal of remorse, accompanied by an empty sensation in the wallet. You set to work trying to forget your mistake when another firm appears, and offers—for a slight fee—to resell the land at close to the price you paid for it. Glad at the chance to be bailed out, you pay the slight fee to the second firm—which then vanishes, never to be heard from again.

Of course, an ounce of prevention is invaluable here. There's a valuable real estate adage that goes, "Any piece of property worth buying is worth a plane trip to look at it." If you are victimized, though, get in touch with the Consumer Protection Division of the Iowa Department of Justice, which by now has had plenty of experience in dealing with shady and marginal land sellers.

Their address is the only address you need to know when it comes to governmental consumer protection agencies in Iowa. There are no county agencies, no city agencies, and no other broad-gauge state agencies. There's just the **Consumer Protection Division, Iowa Department of Justice, 220 East Thirteenth Court, Des Moines, Iowa 50319.**

There are other spices in life besides variety, and no one would mind the absence of other governmental agencies if the Consumer Protection Division were capable of meeting consumers' needs fully. The agency does claim a 70 per cent success rate in resolving consumer complaints—which is decent, if not superlative. However, the average waiting time for resolution of a complaint is estimated at four to six weeks. That long a wait is bound to seem excessive to many consumers—and remember, that's only the *average* wait, not the time it takes to resolve the knottiest cases.

The agency expresses a preference for written complaints. And you'll probably feel the same way, unless you live near Des Moines, since there are no branch offices and there's no toll-free telephone number. With its smallish budget and modest staff, the agency might be hard-pressed to cope with the complaint volume a toll-free line tends to fish up from the recesses of the market place. The current complaint volume is low—perhaps 4,000 to 5,000 complaints a year. And the staff numbers only thirteen, including five secretaries, four lawyers, and three investigators.

Iowa does have small claims courts and voluntary consumer organizations. On many complaints, it would be worthwhile to try these avenues in addition to the Consumer Protection Division.

After land sales, the most common consumer complaints in Iowa are about (2) buying clubs, (3) health spas, (4) trade and correspondence schools, (5) auto sales and repairs, (6) mail-order houses, (7) credit and debt collection, (8) home improvements, (9) magazines, and (10) real estate problems other than land sales. This complaint profile is unusual in that the complaints that usually rank number 1 and 2 rank 5 and 8 here. It's also unusual for discount buying clubs and health spas to have such prominence. But you'll find advice concerning each of the problem areas mentioned in Part III.

Kansas

When you first saw *The Wizard of Oz*, you probably regarded it as pure fantasy for a Kansas tornado to pick up Dorothy's house and whisk it off to a strange land. But some Kansans—particularly those living in mobile homes—have found that scenario more realistic than they would have wished. Mobile homes are susceptible to being displaced, toppled, and otherwise damaged by high winds. And of course high winds and mobile homes are two things Kansas has in abundance.

Anchoring, or "tying down," a mobile home can go a long way toward minimizing that kind of damage. Under a new state law, all mobile homes bought after July 1, 1975, must be tied down, using equipment approved by the state Division of Architectural Services. That's a step forward for Kansas mobile-home dwellers. But they still have plenty of problems.

In fact, mobile homes rank as the number two consumer problem in Kansas, following only that universal nemesis, automobiles. A large part of the problem is the close to absolute power wielded by mobile-home park owners, who can still evict almost anyone they please. In 1973 Lance Burr, then in charge of the state Consumer Protection Division, told me, "You can be kicked out if you don't mow your lawn, or if you don't have the lid straightened just right on your garbage can. These kinds of rules make ideal pretexts for eviction." Holding that ace, park owners could—and still can—make unreasonable demands for rent increases, inflated fees for services, and the purchase of goods or services from particular suppliers (with whom the owner may have kickback arrangements). Kansas, at least at the time this book was being written, had not yet joined the increasing group of states that have passed laws to regulate such goings on in mobile-home parks.

Many mobile-home problems, of course, relate not to the parks at all but to the homes themselves. Their construction has sometimes been shoddy; their warranties have traditionally been inadequate. Kansas has, however, adopted the American National Standards Institute (ANSI) code for the construction of mobile homes, with toughening amendments added in 1974. That should help some, and the Federal Trade Commission is after mobile-home makers to offer better warranties. Meanwhile, if you have a problem regarding your mobile home, consult the state Consumer Protection Division, which takes an active interest in such problems and has accumulated a lot of experience in handling them by now.

The address to write is **Consumer Protection Division, Office of Attorney General, State Capitol, Topeka, Kans. 66612.** On all types of consumer complaints, the CPD estimates its batting average of successful resolutions at 85 per cent—quite a good ratio. The average waiting time for action on a complaint is said to be only two weeks—again quite good, compared to the situation in most states.

In addition to the state agency, there are three county agencies and two city agencies you may possibly be able to use. In each of the three counties, there's a **Consumer Protection Division** in the **County Office of District Attorney.** The address in Johnson County is **County Courthouse, Box 728, Olathe, Kans. 66061.** In Sedgwick County, it's **County Courthouse, 5th floor, Wichita, Kans. 67203.** In Wyandotte County, it's **710 North Seventh St., Kansas City, Kans. 66102.**

The two city agencies are in Kansas City and Topeka. Here are their addresses: **City Department of Consumer Affairs, Municipal Office Building, One Civic Plaza, 701 N. Seventh Street, Room 350, Kansas City, Kans. 66101,** and **Consumer Protection Division, City Attorney's Office, 215 East Seventh St., Topeka, Kans. 66603.**

The Topeka office issues a little brochure called "Some facts you've always wanted to know about door-to-door peddlers, canvassers and solicitors in Topeka but didn't know who to ask." With such a catchy title it may soon be a bestseller, but at the moment single copies are free on request. It might be worth requesting one, in view of the fact that door-to-door sales are the number three consumer complaint in Kansas. You should also know that Kansas has a three-day cooling-off period law. That means you can legally change your mind about the gold-plated widget you bought from the door-to-door salesman and get your money back any time within three business days of the time the sale occurred. There's no penalty to you for canceling out, and the salesman is supposed to notify you of the law at the time the sale occurs. The Kansas law is superior to those in some other states in that it covers cash as well as credit transactions. However, it only applies to sales of $25 or more.

After cars, mobile homes, and door-to-door sales, the leading consumer complaints in Kansas are (4) lakeside lot sites, (5) home repairs, (6) receipt of unsolicited merchandise, (7) distributorships, (8) nursing homes, (9) termite inspection, and (10) missing-heir schemes. You'll find most of these problems discussed in Part III.

Kentucky

Consumers in Kentucky are growing increasingly aware of their rights. As they do, they're complaining more. Back in 1971 the state Consumer Protection Division was getting fewer than fifty complaints a month—and often only half that figure. Each year since then the total has swelled. In 1974 the average was more than 250 complaints a month—up 35 per cent from the year before, and still rising.

One reason for the rising awareness, and the rising complaint total, is that the Consumer Protection Division has been putting up posters around the state advising people of the existence of the CPD's toll-free number. (That number, by the way, is **1-800-372-2960.**)

The chief consumer-protection agency in the state is the CPD. The address is **Consumer Protection Division, Office of the Attorney General, The Capitol, Room 34, Frankfort, Ky. 40601.** Your chances of getting successful resolution of your complaint are put at around 70 per cent by the agency. And the time you'll have to wait for resolution, if your complaint is typical, will be about a month.

If you live in Jefferson County, you may also want to seek help from the **Jefferson County Department of Consumer Protection, Fifth and Market, Room 401, Louisville, Ky. 40202.** And if you live in Louisville, you should definitely keep in mind the new **City Department of Consumer Affairs,** which is located in the **MSD Building, 400 S. Sixth St., Louisville, Ky. 40203.** The city agency has a budget of $132,000 and a full-time staff of eleven, giving it money and manpower closely comparable to the CPD, which serves the entire state.

The top ten areas of consumer complaints in Kentucky are (1) auto repairs and sales, (2) mail-order houses, (3) home improvements and repairs, (4) mobile homes, (5) radio, TV, and stereo equipment, (6) appliances, (7) credit problems, (8) furniture, (9) publications, and (10) utilities. Advice on coping with each of these problem areas is found in Part III.

On some of the problems there are specific Kentucky statutes that consumers should be aware of and ready to use. To make things a little bit less thorny in the home-improvement area, the Kentucky legislature has made it much harder for workmen to hit home owners with so-called mechanic's liens. This is to deal with a situation in which a homeowner pays a contractor, who fails to pay some of his subcontractors. In the past (and still, in some states), the unpaid subcontractors could come after the homeowner for payment. Under the new Kentucky law, an unpaid subcontractor can still seek payment through a mechanic's lien if he notifies the homeowner within ten days of the time he supplies his materials or labor. Otherwise, his quarrel is with the contractor, and the homeowner is mercifully out of the picture.

In the mobile-home area, the state has established construction standards that the homes have to meet and has set up a Mobile Home Certification and Licensure Board to regulate dealers. Recently the board's powers were enlarged to allow them to set standards affecting the sale of used mobile homes as well as new ones.

To help combat abuses in the sale of publications, there's a "statute relating to salesmen of printed material." Anyone selling magazines, periodicals, encyclopedias, books, Bibles, or other printed materials on a subscription basis, "where the delivery of the materials depends on some type of future payment," has to register with the county clerk in any county where they do business. The law requires any salesperson to tell you his or her registration number before making a sale.

Information about some other consumer-protection laws in Kentucky can be obtained from a brochure entitled *10 Danger Signals in Buying,* and from a pamphlet called *Kentucky's Consumer Protection Laws.* Both can be obtained from the CPD.

Louisiana

In case anyone is harboring any mint julep images, the profile of complaints most commonly heard from Louisiana consumers reads as follows: (1) motor vehicle repair and sales, (2) household goods and services, (3) retail stores and services, (4) mobile homes, (5) home construction and repair, (6) mail-order houses, (7) residential rentals, i.e., landlord-tenant problems, (8) utilities, (9) credit, and (10) real estate. There's nothing particularly genteel about the list—but then the people who go around bilking consumers have probably never heard of Southern courtesy.

Eight of the ten problems mentioned above are discussed individually in Part III. Numbers 2 and 3 are sufficiently broad so that it's difficult to pinpoint remedies. Just reread the early chapters for advice on dealing with retailers and manufacturers.

If you need a state agency to help you, the first place to turn in Louisiana is the **Governor's Office of Consumer Protection, (GOCP), P.O. Box 44091, Capitol Station, Baton Rouge, Louisiana 70804.** If you (like me) have an innate distrust of post office boxes, it may comfort you to know that the mail ends up at 1885 Wooddale Boulevard, in Room 1218.

But wait! Before you put pen to paper, here's some good news. The GOCP also has a toll-free number. It's the same as the toll-free Public Assistance Line you can use to call any state agency: **800-272-9868.** About 40 percent of the calls on that line are for GOCP. Unlike some state agencies, GOCP will be glad to offer you advice on the phone. You need not start out by filing a formal complaint unless you want to.

The GOCP claims that it successfully resolves some 70 to 80 per cent of the complaints it receives. On the question of how long you'll probably have to wait for resolution of your problem, I couldn't pin state officials down. On formal complaints, I was told, the consumer has to request, fill out, and send in a written complaint form. "Complaint mediators initiate a contact with the business within seven working days of the return of the written complaint form," my informant said. "However, the handling of complaints of an emergency nature begins on the day of initial contact. It is not unusual for such complaints to be resolved within a matter of hours."

As this book was being written, the Louisiana legislature had set up committees to study two areas where consumers consistently have a lot of complaints: auto repairs and home improvements or repairs. On another troubled front—mobile homes—that state has already taken several actions. All mobile homes sold in the state must now meet ANSI construction standards; dealers are licensed by the state; and mobile-home park owners are subject to the provisions of a recent law affecting the relations between park landlords and their tenants. Under the new law, a tenant must be given a written rental agreement, specifying the rent and all other charges the tenant will pay. The tenant must also be given a copy of the park rules. But no matter what it says in those rules, a landlord may not require the tenant to purchase goods or services from particular vendors or charge entrance or exit fees (other than the rent), nor can he unreasonably refuse to let a tenant sell his mobile home while leaving it in the park.

Those reforms are a major help to mobile-home park tenants. But tenants in general in Louisiana have very few rights, compared to tenants in many other states. If you have a problem with your landlord, your best bet is probably to try to gain leverage by joining with other tenants in an association. See the discussion of "Landlord-Tenant Problems" in the final section of this book for advice on how to do that.

In the credit area, the state has recently passed Act 466, which contains several useful reforms. With its passage, Louisiana joined most other states in providing a three-day "cooling-off period," during which you may change your mind and cancel a sale made by a door-to-door salesman. (There is still some penalty for you in canceling, though, so don't jettison your sales resistance.) Interest on revolving charge account credit cards was limited to 1.5 per cent a month (an 18 per cent annual percentage rate), again bringing Louisiana into line with most other states. In a nice proconsumer touch, the act provides that credit card issuers must use the average daily balance method in figuring out how much you owe them, unless they substitute a method that will result in smaller interest charges.

At this writing, Louisiana has two county and two city consumer-protection agencies in addition to the GOCP. You may want to use them, if you live within their jurisdictions or have problems with merchants who do. The county agencies are the **East Baton Rouge Parish Consumer Protection Center, 1779 Government St., Baton Rouge, La. 70802;** and the **Consumer Protection and Commercial Frauds Department, Jefferson Parish Office of District Attorney, 1820 Franklin Ave., Suite 23, Gretna, La. 70053.** The city agencies are the **Monroe Office of Consumer Affairs, City Plaza, Monroe City Hall, Monroe, La. 71201;** and the **City Office of Consumer Affairs, City-1W12, New Orleans, La. 70112.**

Maine

A small psychological test: What personality characteristic would you most associate with the typical resident of Maine? Did you perhaps say, "rugged individualism"? Many people would. And that trait is one that would come in handy to you as a complaining consumer in this state.

Oh, there is a state agency to help you, all right. But it's not one of the most impressive around, and it doesn't have a particularly large battery of consumer-protection legislation to enforce. There are no consumer agencies at the county level or the city level. So brush up on your unorthodox tactics, sharpen your psychological warfare skills, and prepare to use the courts, the media, voluntary groups, or even politicians.

It's certainly worth while to *try* the Division of Consumer Fraud and Protection (DCFP). Just don't count on it. Unless you live near Augusta, you'll probably want to write, since there are no branch offices and there's no toll-free number. Write **Division of Consumer Fraud and Protection, Office of Attorney General, State House, Augusta, Me. 04330.** Despite a small staff and small budget, the DCFP claims to resolve successfully "approximately 65 to 75 per cent of the consumer complaints" received. It's difficult to say how long you'll have to wait for resolution of your complaint. The head of the agency would offer only the truism that "the time a consumer who requests aid must wait depends upon the nature of his or her complaint."

The DCFP couldn't furnish the number of complaints received in its most common complaint categories. But it said the subjects most frequently producing complaints from Maine consumers are (1) auto repairs and sales, (2) nonperformance of warranties, (3) unauthorized charges for service or repairs, (4) unsatisfactory service or repair work, (5) mail-order houses' failure to deliver merchandise after accepting a deposit, and (6) mobile homes and mobile-home parks. Federal records based on figures obtained from Maine authorities also indicate a significant number of complaints about appliances and utilities. You'll find advice on handling most of these types of complaints in Part III.

Of all these areas, the one on which Maine authorities have moved most aggressively is probably mobile homes and mobile-home parks. It was one of the first states to require that all new mobile homes sold in the state come with a warranty. While the warranty is issued by the manufacturer, it must also be signed by the dealer, who must certify that to the best of his knowledge the unit doesn't have any substantial defects in materials or workmanship. In an effort to end the runaround between manufacturer and dealer so frequently encountered by mobile-home buyers, Maine's recent law states that the consumer may hold either one of them fully liable for fulfillment of the terms of the warranty. This law is a major step forward for mobile-home dwellers. Unfortunately, Maine did less well in its law on mobile-home parks, passing a rather halfhearted measure containing enough loopholes to resemble a Swiss cheese. The holes allow mobile-home park owners to retain considerable powers, including the arbitrary eviction of tenants. And once arbitrary eviction is possible, it becomes difficult to control other abuses.

For Maine consumers who run into problems involving credit

in any way, there's a new state office worth knowing about. It's called the **Bureau of Consumer Protection, Credit,** and it's part of the **Department of Business Regulation, State Office Annex, Western Ave., Augusta, Me. 04330.**

Maryland

Maryland is the only state for which it makes sense to list the county consumer-protection agencies before the state agency. Some of the counties—most notably Montgomery—outdo the state when it comes to imagination, forceful defense of consumers' rights, and spending per capita on consumer protection. This is not necessarily to praise the state less, but rather the counties more. Chris Wheeler, who engaged in a detailed nationwide study of consumer complaint handling under the auspices of Ralph Nader's Center for Responsive Law, has gone so far as to call the Montgomery County Office of Consumer Affairs the most outstanding consumer-protection office in the nation.

There are four counties in Maryland that have consumer protection agencies. If you're a resident in any of the four, or transact business there, make these agencies your first recourse. In Montgomery County it's the **Montgomery County Office of Consumer Affairs, 24 Maryland Ave., Rockville, Md. 20850.** In Prince George's County, it's the **Prince George's County Consumer Protection Commission, Courthouse, Upper Marlboro, Md. 20870.** In Anne Arundel County, it's the **Board of Consumer Affairs, Arundel Center, Room 403, Annapolis, Md. 21404.** And in Baltimore County, it's the **Consumer Fraud Division, State's Attorney's Office, 316 Equitable Building, Baltimore, Md. 21202.**

Use the state agency if you don't live in one of those four counties, if your ill-fated transaction crossed county lines, or as a backup resource. It's the **Consumer Protection Division, Office of Attorney General, One South Calvert St., Baltimore, Md. 21202.** There are branch offices at **5112 Berwyn Road, 2d floor, College Park, Md. 20740,** and at **138 E. Antietam St., Room 302, Hagerstown, Md. 21740.** In addition, staff members of the Consumer

Protection Division (CPD) make regular monthly trips to nine locations to gather complaints and give advice. The nine are Cumberland, Easton, Fort Meade, Frederick, Salisbury, Woodlawn, and three locations in Baltimore. (The Baltimore meetings are for the sole purpose of helping people who receive social service funds.) For exact times and locations of these meetings, check with city hall in the towns mentioned, or check with the CPD itself.

Evaluating the CPD's effectiveness in aiding consumers is difficult. It is true, as a CPD spokesman put it, that "Maryland has enacted some of the more progressive legislation in the consumer protection area." But having that legislation on the books is one step removed from consumers' ability to make use of it in solving their problems. It's discouraging to learn that more than 120,000 telephone callers to the CPD have been getting a busy signal each year. It was discouraging to find Maryland among the few states that declined to provide the author of this book with an estimate of the percentage of its complaints successfully resolved, and the average time a consumer has to wait for resolution of a complaint. And it's discouraging to find in the CPD's annual report for 1974 the following statement: "We recognize that we can never hope to answer all of the consumer inquiries and complaints, however we do attempt to make the Division freely available to the general public, thereby keeping our 'finger on the pulse of the market place.'"

Unlike most states, the CPD doesn't seem to have an exact tally on the nature of the complaints it receives. Using "survey techniques," it finds that Maryland consumers are most concerned about automobiles and appliances. After those, the biggest gripes are landlord-tenant problems and mail-order merchandise that arrives late or not at all. Using the records kept by Montgomery County and Prince George's County, one can add to the list home improvements or repairs, credit problems, furniture, and radio and TV sets and repairs. Each of these problems is discussed in detail in Part III. And, for many of them, there are specific statutes on the books designed to help Maryland consumers.

Take automobile repairs. In Maryland all repair shops are licensed by the **Motor Vehicle Administration (MVA)**. If you have a complaint against a repair shop, send it in writing to the MVA at **6601 Ritchie Highway, N.E., Glen Burnie, Md. 21061.** The MVA has the right to sift through the repair shop's records to investigate your complaint; it also has subpoena power and other investigative powers. Under a 1974 law, you have a right to request a written estimate for any repair that's likely to cost $50 or more. If you ask for it, this estimate must include the estimated completion date for the work, as well as the estimated price for labor and materials. The repair shop may not exceed the estimate by more than 10 per cent without getting your consent. The shop can charge you for the estimate if it wants to, so long as the fee is reasonable and you're told about it in advance. After the work is done, you must be given an invoice (bill), describing exactly what was done and what parts were used. It must say if any of the parts were rebuilt or reconditioned. You must be given a copy of the invoice, and the repair shop must keep a copy. Finally, you must be given the parts that were replaced, unless they have to be returned to the manufacturer to fulfill the terms of a warranty. (This is to protect you against the practice of some shops, which have been known simply to clean some old parts, replace them, and charge you for them.)

Montgomery County has a Motor Vehicle Repair Registration Ordinance of its own. It reads much like the state law, but it applies to all jobs over $25. It's enforced by the Montgomery County Office of Consumer Affairs.

Appliances, TV sets, and radios all rank high as a source of complaints in Maryland, as we noted earlier. There's no statewide law regulating people who install or service these items. In Montgomery County, though, these installers and repairmen have to register with the County Office of Consumer Affairs. They must give consumers a written estimate if they're asked to. As with the auto repair regulation, they must return replaced parts to the consumer (unless the parts have to be sent back to the manufacturer under the warranty). And they must display their registration certificate at their place of business.

In the landlord-tenant area, again, some counties offer the consumer (in this case the tenant) more protection than do others. Because laws are changing rapidly in this field, we won't describe any of the county ordinances here. The best way to familiarize yourself with them is to consult with (or, better yet, join) a local tenants' association. Statewide, there is a law against a landlord's evicting you in retaliation for your making a complaint against him to a government agency (such as a buildings department, health department, or rent-control agency). There is also a law that landlords must return your security deposit to you within forty-five days after your lease expires (unless you've significantly damaged the apartment) and must pay you interest on it.

With regard to home repairs, it's worth knowing that contractors must be licensed by the **Maryland Home Improvement Commission.** If you have a complaint about a contractor who worked on your home, notify the commission at **1 South Calvert St., 7th floor, Baltimore, Md. 21202.**

Massachusetts

If you can't get action on a consumer complaint in Massachusetts, your complaint probably isn't valid. The state is among the most progressive in passing consumer-protection legislation. Two state agencies, one county agency, and five city agencies devoted solely to consumer protection stand ready to help you translate that legislation into reality.

For most complaints, your basic resource is the **Executive Office of Consumer Affairs (EOCA), Consumer Complaint Division, One Ashburton Place—14th floor, Boston, Mass. 02108.** This office handles a heavy volume of complaints: The number of complaints about furniture (4,000), for example, exceeds the total of all complaints received by state agencies in some states. And furniture is only the fourth-ranking complaint on the list in Massachusetts!

Despite this heavy pace of work, the EOCA claims it's able to resolve successfully about 95 per cent of the complaints it receives. And the average waiting time for a consumer needing help is said to be only about two weeks.

So, if complaining to the company doesn't work, direct your

next complaint letter to the EOCA. Then, if you want to enlist the help of another government agency, you can also write to the **Consumer Protection Division, Department of Attorney General, State House, Room 167, Boston, Mass. 02133.** The Attorney General's office is less oriented toward individual complaint handling than the EOCP is, but it wields formidable legal powers.

If you live in one of the five cities that have consumer-help agencies, or if your ill-fated transaction took place in one of them, it might be worthwhile to enlist their aid. The largest, of course, is the **Boston Consumers' Council, City Hall, Room 721, Boston, Mass. 02201.** It has a staff of about eighteen people and a budget of more than $100,000. It maintains fourteen branch offices as part of Boston's "Little City Hall" program; for their locations call (617) 722-4100. And it claims a success rate of 70 per cent, with an average waiting time of only a week.

In Fitchburg, you can write to the **Fitchburg Consumer Protection Service, 455 Main St., Fitchburg, Mass. 01420.** In Lowell, it's the **Lowell Consumer Advisory Council, City Hall, Lowell, Mass. 01852.** Quincy recently started a **City Consumer Assistance Center** in the **Adams Building, Room 306, 1354 Hancock St., Quincy, Mass. 02169.** And Weymouth recently launched its **Town Office of Consumer Affairs, Town Hall, 75 Middle Street, Weymouth, Mass. 02189.**

There is also, as we mentioned at the outset, one county agency —the **Consumer Protection Agency** within the **Franklin County Office of District Attorney, Courthouse, Northampton, Mass. 01060.** It serves not only Franklin County but also Hampshire County.

If you're like most Massachusetts consumers, your complaint is probably going to fall into one of the following ten areas: (1) auto repairs or sales, (2) appliances, (3) mail-order houses, (4) furniture, (5) home improvements or repairs, (6) TV, radio, and audio equipment, (7) unfair or deceptive business practices, (8) housing and real estate, (9) utilities, and (10) credit problems. Those are the ten areas on which the EOCA receives the most complaints. Within the city of Boston, the Boston Consumers' Council reports a somewhat different complaint profile. There, landlord-tenant disputes top the list. Bostonians also seem to have a greater proportion of problems involving clothing or insurance and fewer involving mail-order houses or credit.

If you're among the ranks of disgruntled tenants, you can take comfort in knowing that Massachusetts has some of the strongest tenant-protection laws in the country. If a landlord fails to make essential repairs (after you request them in writing), the law permits you to make them yourself and deduct the cost from your rent (up to a maximum of the equivalent of two months' rent). There are also legal procedures for conducting rent strikes in Massachusetts. These rights are best exercised in consultation with a tenants' association, a lawyer, or both.

Sometime when you don't have any complaints pressing for immediate attention, drop a line to the **Massachusetts Consumers' Council, Leverett Saltonstall Building, Government Center, 100 Cambridge St., Room 2109, Boston, Mass. 02202.** Though government affiliated, it's not a complaint-handling agency. It is involved in shaping future legislation and informing the public about existing consumer-protection laws. You may find its monthly newsletter, *The Commonwealth Letter,* to be useful. A single subscription is free to Massachusetts residents.

Michigan

Have you ever noticed that people who victimize consumers are timid, easily cowed, and prone to part with their ill-gotten gains the moment someone looks at them harshly? No? You haven't? Frankly, I haven't either. But perhaps the majority in the Michigan state legislature have that impression. They set up two state consumer-protection agencies and sent them out to police the market place armed with a feather duster.

The two agencies are the **Michigan Consumer Council, 414 Hollister Building, Lansing, Mich. 48933;** and the **Consumer Protection/Antitrust Division, Office of Attorney General, 670 Law Building, Lansing, Mich. 48913.** Considering what they have to work with, their efforts may be praised, albeit faintly. The Consumer Council claims to resolve successfully about 60 per cent of the complaints it receives. The average waiting time for the embattled consumer is about a month. The Consumer Protection/Antitrust Division claims a shorter waiting time—only a week to a week and a half, on the average. But its success rate is even lower than the Consumer Council's, about 50 per cent.

Christine Mikrut, a complaint examiner for the Consumer Protection/Antitrust Division, put it this way: "If the problem cannot be resolved through your own negotiations or with the assistance of a local or state consumer agency, consider exercising your rights through the court system. In small claims court, attorneys are not allowed, but there is a limit ($300 in Michigan) as to how much in damages you can claim. If your dispute involves a greater amount of money than is allowed in small claims court, consult an attorney about the feasibility of starting litigation. Although this avenue of recourse may be the very thing you wish to avoid (for financial and/or time reasons), bear in mind that the Attorney General or whatever other agency you contact is only as effective as the authority given it by your state legislature."

In Michigan that authority does not include the power, for either agency, to hold hearings or issue subpoenas. Both agencies can seek court restraining orders to make a business stop a particular form of conduct. But neither agency can seek a court order mandating restitution to abused consumers! What's more, neither has the power to negotiate so-called voluntary assurances of discontinuance with businesses suspected of unfair or illegal practices. An assurance of discontinuance is an agreement by the business not to engage in a certain kind of conduct in the future. It's useful for two reasons. First, it's fast, since the business doesn't formally admit wrongdoing, and lengthy court proceedings are avoided. Second, it can help where there are gray areas in the law. If a firm is engaged in a practice that seems clearly undesirable to state consumer-protection authorities but may not be illegal, it can sometimes be stopped promptly by this method. If the firm later does the same thing again, it can be punished for violating its agreement with the state agency. But this tool, part of the arsenal of most state consumer agencies, isn't available in Michigan.

Perhaps because they expect few results, Michigan consumers haven't used the two state agencies in great numbers. It appears that the Consumer Protection/Antitrust Division gets fewer than 6,000 complaints a year, and the Consumer Council fewer than 1,500. For a state the size of Michigan, this is a small outpouring indeed (perhaps outtrickling would be a better word). One could argue that Michigan consumers may be victimized less often per capita than consumers in other states. Or possibly they are smarter. That would be a nice argument, but I wonder who would believe it. Data submitted by forty-four states in response to my questionnaire convince me that there are two things that account for a high complaint total. One is the existence of a toll-free "hot line" for phoning in complaints. (Michigan has one— 1-800-292-2431—but for land sales only.) The other is an expectation that complaining will bring results.

These harsh words over, I would still recommend to Michigan residents that they try using the state agencies. There's little to lose, and their batting averages suggest that you have at least a fifty-fifty chance. Try the Consumer Council first; it is somewhat more geared to arbitrating individual complaints.

If the state agencies can't help you, you're not without resources. To begin with, as Ms. Mikrut said, there are the courts. But there are also plenty of other places to look. If you live in Detroit, Bay County, or Washtenaw County, you can take advantage of strong, well-funded local agencies whose legal powers in many ways exceed those of the state bodies. In Detroit use the **City Consumer Affairs Department, 809 City-County Building, 2 Woodward Ave., Detroit, Mich. 48226.** In Washtenaw County, try the **Consumer Action Center, Consumer Protection Division, Washtenaw County Office of Prosecuting Attorney, 200 County Building, Main and Huron Streets, Ann Arbor, Mich. 48108.** In Bay County, contact the **Consumer Protection Unit, Bay County Office of Prosecuting Attorney, 515 Center Ave., Bay City, Mich. 48706.**

The agency in Wayne County has a large budget and staff and is interested in helping mediate complaints, though it's no tiger when it comes to legal powers. That's the **Wayne County Consumer Protection Agency, 356 E. Congress, Detroit, Mich. 48226.**

Three other counties also perform some consumer-protection functions through the **County Office of Prosecuting Attorney.** In Gennessee County the address is **105 Courthouse, Flint, Mich. 48502.** In Jackson County it's **464 County Building, Jackson, Mich. 49201.** In Saginaw County it's **115 S. Michigan Ave., Saginaw County Courthouse, Saginaw, Mich. 48602.**

Some other agencies can be useful to you in handling particular sorts of problems. The problems that most gripe Michigan consumers, according to the Attorney General's office, are related to (1) auto repairs and sales, (2) refunds, (3) contractors, (4) credit, (5) mail-order houses, (6) mobile homes, (7) home furnishings, (8) landlord-tenant problems, (9) advertising, and (10) television, radio, and stereo. (By the way, you'll find advice on coping with nine of these problems in Part III. The exception—refunds—is discussed directly or indirectly throughout this book.)

The Michigan state legislature, to its credit, has set itself up for a head-on collision with the state's number one consumer problem: cars. It has passed a law intended to put auto repair shops under stringent regulation by the state. The administering agency is not to be either of the consumer agencies, but the Secretary of State's office. The regulations are to take effect in stages and are designed to be fully effective by January 1, 1978. All repair shops (except gas stations that do only very minor repairs) will have to be licensed. Individual mechanics will be licensed as specialists in various lines of repair work. The law recognizes eight such lines. Starting in 1978, a suitably certified mechanic will have to oversee any repairs a shop does. If a customer wants emergency service from an outfit that has no one specialized to do the particular repair needed, he'll have to sign a form waiving his rights under the law.

Before any repair is done, the shop will have to give the customer a written estimate, itemized as exactly as possible. If, once the car is up on the lift, the shop discovers that the job will cost more than the estimate said, the customer must be given a chance to cancel the whole job. In that case the shop may charge a reasonable fee for returning the car to its former condition. If a customer wants to tell a repair shop, "Just fix it, whatever it costs," he may do so, but again he would have to sign a form waiving his rights under the law.

When the customer gets his car back, the repair shop must also give him a written statement containing a veritable encyclopedia of information: (1) the repairs the shop found were needed, (2) the repairs the customer requested and authorized, (3) the amount of the estimate, (4) the amount it actually cost to fix the damned thing, (5) the names of all the parts replaced, with a notation as to whether they were new, used, rebuilt, or reconditioned, and (6) the name of the mechanic who did the repairs. Then the owner or his agent must sign a statement to the effect that the repairs were done satisfactorily, or else the garage must give a written explanation of why they couldn't be.

All of this, though some may fear it will require greasemonkeys to be scribes, seems on balance to be a tremendous step forward for the consumer. If the law looks as good in practice as it does on paper, it could well become a model for the rest of the country. The inspiration for this major piece of legislation, by the way, came from a survey done in 1974 by the Consumer Protection/Antitrust Division, which drove unmarked state cars with preinduced defects into scores of repair shops. After repeated instances of having a costly whoosis replaced when merely adjusting the whatsis would have done the trick, the division concluded that 70 per cent of auto repair outfits in the state were dishonest, incompetent, or both.

Contractors (chiefly home improvement and repair outfits) rank third on Michigan's complaint list, and there's a separate board already in existence to deal with them. If you have trouble with a contractor, the people to talk to are at the **State Residential Builders' and Maintenance and Alteration Contractors' Board, 1033 S. Washington Ave., Lansing, Mich. 48926.**

Michigan has recently passed laws affecting two other areas where complaints are rife: mobile homes and credit. Every new mobile home sold in the state must carry a warranty, and the law sets forth minimum standards to make sure the warranty is worth the paper it's printed on. Sex discrimination in credit has been outlawed, along with discrimination by marital status. And the Collection Practices Act limits what collection agencies can do to try to squeeze money out of debtors. To exercise your rights under this act, write to the **Department of Licensing and Regulation, 1033 South Washington Ave., Lansing, Mich. 48926.**

Minnesota

Minnesota is one of the states with two consumer-protection agencies that operate fairly independently of each other. If you have a complaint that needs attention, you can try one, then use the other as a backup if the first fails. Or you can try both at once.

The Minnesota Office of Consumer Services has a specific legislative mandate to involve itself in the solving of individual consumer complaints. It is legally empowered to act as a mediator and to seek court orders of restitution for consumers. Over all, according to Tom Tahnk, supervisor of complaint handling, it probably resolves 70 per cent of complaints successfully. "But it varies by category," Tahnk notes. "Many problems with autos and mobile homes are almost unsolvable. There we succeed maybe 40 per cent of the time in a good month. With other problems, like undelivered merchandise or false advertising, our success rate would be near 100 per cent." The time a consumer has to wait for resolution of his complaint probably averages thirty-five to forty days, according to Tahnk. The agency's address is **Minnesota Office of Consumer Services, Department of Commerce, Metro Square Building, Seventh and Robert Streets, 5th floor, Saint Paul, Minn. 55119.** There's also a branch office at **332 West Superior St., Duluth, Minn. 55802.**

The other agency is the **Consumer Protection Division (CPD)** of the **Office of Attorney General.** It's located at **102 State Capitol, Saint Paul, Minn. 55155.** The CPD's legal powers are geared more to prosecution of businesses that rip off consumers and less to mediation of individual complaints. Nevertheless, it claims to resolve successfully 85 per cent of the complaints it receives, with an average waiting time of only three weeks.

In addition to the two state agencies, there are three broad-gauge consumer-protection agencies at the city and county levels. All three have small staffs but enough legal powers to give them a good chance of being able to help you with your complaint. In Hennepin County there's the **Consumer Protection Division, Hennepin County Attorney's Office, 248 Hennepin County Courthouse, Minneapolis, Minn. 55415.** The city of Minneapolis has the **City Department of Licenses and Consumer Services, 101 City Hall, Third Ave. and Fourth St., Minneapolis, Minn. 55415.** And in St. Paul, there's the **City Office of Consumer Affairs, 179 City Hall, Saint Paul, Minn. 55415.**

The problems that most trouble Minnesota consumers, as reported by the Office of Consumer Services, are about (1) unfair business practices, (2) collection agencies, (3) credit problems, (4) auto repairs and sales, (5) home repairs and improvements, (6) mobile homes, (7) landlord-tenant disputes, (8) food and drugs, (9) miscellaneous, and (10) mail-order houses. You'll find advice on handling all of those problems (except miscellaneous) in Part III.

Considering the unusually large number of complaints about collection agencies, it's surprising that Minnesota hasn't, at least at this writing, joined the ranks of states that regulate debt collectors. (Some thirty-two states do.) However, threats and harassment are illegal, whether for debt collection or whatever other purpose. It's also against the regulations of the Federal Communications Commission to use the phone to harass anyone, including a debtor. Anyone receiving frequent calls at work or at home should complain to the telephone company. The same goes for debt-collection calls made at late hours.

People with credit problems other than bill collectors—such as incorrect or unfair computation of the amount owed, billing for defective goods, or denial of a loan because of race or sex—should know about another state agency: the **Division of Consumer Credit within the Minnesota Department of Commerce.** The address is **250 State Office Building, Saint Paul, Minn. 55155.** Under a 1974 amendment to previous state laws, banking organizations, real estate brokers, insurance companies, and other financial institutions are explicitly forbidden to discriminate in granting loans, selling property, or renting property. Marital status, as well as sex, race, religion, creed, color, national origin, and "status with regard to public assistance or disability" are all mentioned as criteria that cannot be used.

Minnesota has a law that will come in handy if you're about to have some home repairs or improvements done, and maybe even if you've already had them done. It deals with that old thorn in the homeowner's side, the mechanic's lien. (See page 95 for an explanation of what a mechanic's lien is, if you don't already know.) Contractors must supply homeowners at the beginning of a job with forms under which the contractor, not the homeowner, will be liable for any sums specified in these liens. The contractor must also tell the homeowner who his subcontractors on the job are.

On the mobile-home front, Minnesota recently required that mobile-home dealers be licensed. It has also enacted a law governing the conduct of landlords in moble-home parks. It forbids the charging of entrance fees (aside from the rent) to let a tenant come into a park, and it requires at least sixty days' notice for an eviction.

When it comes to tenants' rights in general (whether in trailer parks or apartments), Minnesota still lags behind some of the highly urban states. It does have a law flatly banning evictions by a landlord in retaliation for a tenant's making a complaint to government authorities. And it has another law requiring a landlord promptly to return security deposits when tenants' leases expire. But, as regards getting your landlord to make repairs or improve apartment conditions (other than those itemized in building and health codes), your best bet is to join with other tenants in an organization.

In the realm of drugs, it may be helpful to know that Minnesota requires drugstores to post the prices of sixty frequently prescribed drugs. Out-of-store advertising isn't permitted, but the law requires the quoting of drug prices over the phone to consumers who have prescriptions.

Though employment agencies do not rank among the businesses that inspire the most complaints (either nationwide or in Minnesota), I have often felt this is because consumers expect so little from them. Minnesota has taken the unusual and promising step of regulating these agencies, whose actions so directly affect people's hopes and economic welfare. Every employment agency in the state must be licensed by the Department of Labor and Industry, which is housed in the Space Center, 444 LaFayette Road, Saint Paul, Minn. 55101. Agencies must prominently display their licenses at their main offices. If an agency merely takes your name down, chats with you about your ambitions, and promises to call you when anything turns up, it can't charge you a fee. It must actually scare up a lead for you before it's considered to have performed a service that merits payment. The company can't send you off on a wild goose chase to Jones Widget, Inc., either: If it sends you to a place that has no job openings, it must reimburse you for your wasted transportation costs. (That rule applies only if the wild goose chase was the agency's fault. If Jones Widget asked them to send somebody out there, the agency is off the hook.) An agency is also required to tell you—assuming it knows—if the place it sends you for an interview has workers on strike. Some people would be glad to play the role of strikebreaker; others wouldn't dream of being a scab. The point is that the job-seeker ought to have an idea of what kind of situation he or she's getting into.

Mississippi

In 1974 Mississippi became the forty-seventh state to enact an Unfair and Deceptive Trade Practices Act. (This left only Alabama, Georgia, and Tennessee without such an act, and Georgia passed one in 1975.) Mississippi's law lists eleven specific types of business conduct that are banned as unfair or deceptive. However, unlike the previous forty-six state laws, Mississippi's does not include any general "catchall" prohibition on deceptive or unfair business conduct. This leaves room for ingenious operators to squeeze through loopholes in the law, with fairly good chances of evading successful prosecution.

The act allows state law enforcement officials to seek court orders mandating restitution to consumers who have been harmed by deceptive practices. The courts, besides ordering restitution, can revoke a business's charter or license to do business in the state. As an individual, you can also bring suit under the act (though not in the form of class actions). If you win, the law allows the court to award you reasonable attorney's fees in addition to the rest of the verdict.

One somewhat unusual feature of the act is that district and county attorneys, as well as the state Attorney General's office, are designated as enforcement agents. This means that, in a sense, every district or county attorney in the state is now a consumer-protection official. Thus you can take your problems to an official close to home if you want to.

Or you can follow the standard route and take them to the **Consumer Protection Division, Office of Attorney General, P.O. Box 220, Justice Building, Jackson, Miss. 39205.** The chief of the Consumer Protection Division says that his office is able to resolve successfully about 48 per cent of the cases it receives without the need for litigation. If you lump in those cases where the agency goes to court on behalf of consumers and wins, the success rate would doubtless go above 50 per cent. But, of course, cases that go to court take longer. Waiting time on the average complaint is said to be about four weeks.

The number of complaints received by the Consumer Protection Division is quite small—perhaps in the neighborhood of 1,500 a year. This once again proves Dorfman's Law—that the number of complaints received by any agency is proportional to people's expectations that the agency will actually be able to help. This doesn't mean you shouldn't try to use the Consumer Protection Division. You should. The agency has a staff of about twelve, a budget of $189,000 or so, and a sincere desire to help. Its main problem has been a lack of consumer-protection laws to enforce, which has made its task roughly comparable to that of a snow-plowing firm in Ecuador. Neither has too much to work with.

As an indication of the lack of a consumer orientation among Mississippi lawmakers, consider the situation with regard to prescription drug advertising. This is an issue that has probably attracted more attention from the consumer movement than it deserves, in comparison with other pressing problems like auto repairs and hospital costs. But it serves as a good barometer of how strong the consumer movement is in any given state. In many states, drugstores have now been required to post prescription prices, and advertising restrictions have been struck down. In Mississippi (at least at this writing) it's still illegal for drugstores to advertise on the basis of low prices.

The ten problem areas that currently produce the most complaints on the part of Mississippi consumers are (1) auto repairs and sales, (2) home repairs and improvements, (3) mobile homes, (4) real estate and land sales, (5) mail-order houses, (6) appliances, (7) furniture and home furnishings, (8) mortgages, franchises, finance, and insurance, (9) travel vacation contests, and (10) advertising. Advice on coping with almost all of these problems is contained in Part III.

With regard to real estate and land sales problems, there's another state agency consumers should know about. It's called the **Mississippi Real Estate Commission,** and you'll find it at **754 N. President, Jackson, Miss. 39201.** It has five members—all of them, strangely enough, real estate brokers. These five people have the power to revoke the licenses of other brokers who make false promises to customers, engage in untruthful advertising, receive kickbacks, or otherwise act in a deceptive or fraudulent way.

Missouri

In Missouri, as in almost every state, home improvements and repairs rank near the top of the list of consumers' complaints. They rank third here, after automobile problems and deceptive business practices. Missouri is a bit unusual, though, in that there's some action going on to help homeowners cope with this almost universal problem.

First, there's been action taken to curb that old devil, the mechanic's lien, the claim a subcontractor slaps on you, the homeowner, when your contractor hasn't paid him for all labor or materials. Under threat of a $500 fine, a contractor is required to give you a notice before doing any home repairs or improvements. In bold type, the notice warns you about the possibility that a mechanic's lien might be filed against you. It continues: "To avoid this result, you may ask the contractor for 'lien waivers' from all persons supplying material or services for the work described in this contract. Failure to secure lien waivers may result in your paying for labor and material twice."

Second, in Kansas City, the City Office of Consumer Affairs sponsored a project called HOMEE, designed to "resolve communication problems between the local home improvement industry and the buying public." (The Kansas City Chapter of the National Home Improvement Council was co-sponsor.) The program involved competition among home improvement contractors in eight categories of home remodeling. A TV special with an academy awards-type format was used to present awards to the winners and to disperse information and buying tips.

Third, if you live near Kansas City, you may be able to take advantage of a course in home improvement, co-sponsored by the University of Missouri and the City Office of Consumer Affairs. At last report, the course ran five sessions and was administered by the Communiversity program of the University of Missouri at Kansas City.

Progress on other consumer-protection fronts hasn't been marked by comparable innovation, unfortunately. But Missouri consumers do have two statewide agencies and two local ones to offer them some help if they've been chiseled.

Your bedrock resource is the **Consumer Protection Division, Office of Attorney General, Supreme Court Building, Jefferson City, Mo. 65101.** It has branch offices at **431 Missouri Office Blg., 615 East Thirteenth St., Kansas City, Mo. 64106;** and **705 Olive St., Suite 1323, St. Louis, Mo. 63101.** The Consumer Protection Division (CPD) says it's able to help 70 to 75 per cent of the people who complain to it. The average waiting time is said to be a week and a half—an unusually short wait, compared to what's reported in most states.

Besides the CPD, there's another state agency, recently created, that also has broad-gauge consumer-protection powers. So use one as a backup for the other, or try both. The new agency is the

Department of Consumer Affairs, Regulation and Licensing. It's at **P.O. Box 1157, Jefferson City, Mo. 65101.** (There are no branch offices.) As its name implies, a contact with this agency makes special sense if you feel you've been victimized by someone in a state-licensed profession.

If you live in Greene County, you might get some help from the **Consumer Fraud Prosecution Unit, Greene County Prosecutor's Office, County Courthouse, Room 206, Springfield, Mo. 65802.** However, its strengths seem to be prosecution and education, rather than getting redress for individual consumers.

For complaints involving Kansas City citizens or businesses, try the **City Office of Consumer Affairs,** whose imaginative efforts in the home repair field were noted earlier. It's at **City Hall, 11th floor, Kansas City, Mo. 64106.**

After autos, deceptive practices, and home repairs, the complaints that irritate Missouri residents the most seem to be in the areas of (4) housing and real estate, (5) mail-order houses, (6) mobile homes, (7) advertising, and (8) furniture. Specific advice on handling each of these complaint categories will be found in Part III.

Montana

Montana is new at the consumer-protection game, but it seems to be getting off to a good start. The state consumer-protection agency, created in 1973, has been given just about every legal power it could want. And—by its own account—it's doing very well, solving about 80 per cent of the complaints it receives. What's more, the time the average consumer spends waiting for action on a complaint is said to be only about two weeks. Statistics like this would be the envy of many a more industrialized state.

The agency we're talking about is the **Consumer Affairs Division, Department of Business Regulation.** You can get in touch with it at **805 North Main St., Helena, Mont. 59601.** It consists, at last report, of exactly three people and runs on an annual budget of about $50,000. These figures can be misleading, though, as can the small number of complaints received (fewer than 1,000 in 1974). When you see how big Montana looks on a map, it's easy to forget that it's one of the smallest states in population (about 700,000 people). Per capita, Montana's consumer-protection staff and complaint total are comparable to those in larger states.

Ranking complaints in order, by type, is a little iffy, since complaints here are measured in the tens, not in the thousands. Nevertheless, the Consumer Affairs Division has attempted a ranking. Here it is, juggled somewhat to fit this book's categories: (1) auto repairs and sales, with about two-thirds of the complaints on the repair side, (2) appliance purchase and repair, (3) credit problems, including billing procedures, overcharges, and the actions of credit bureaus, (4) mobile homes, (5) nondelivery of merchandise, (6) magazine and record clubs, (7) mail-order houses, (8) home repairs and improvements, (9) freight shipments, and (10) hearing aid sales and service.

You'll find virtually all these problems discussed in detail in Part III. Nondelivery of merchandise is treated under the headings "Delivery of Merchandise" and "Unfair Business Practices." Freight shipments as such aren't discussed, but some of them presumably consist of household goods, so the section on moving should be applicable. And some of the tips discussed in connection with moving logically carry over to other types of shipping.

A couple of laws recently passed in Montana merit mention, for they may save you considerable trouble. Montana was among the last states to enact a three-day "cooling-off period" on door-to-door sales (that is, you have three days to change your mind and cancel the purchase, without penalty). But Montana made up for its lateness by passing a good law: It applies to all purchases over $25, and there's no penalty connected with cancelation. If you have occasion to take advantage of this law, remember to make your cancelation in writing. And it wouldn't hurt to send it by certified mail, return receipt requested.

Another new law sets forth strict rules on landlords' handling of tenants' security deposits. This gives you a lever to keep your landlord from hanging onto your money long after your lease has expired and you've left. The law applies to mobile-home parks as well as apartment buildings.

A third law recently passed requires trade or vocational schools to be licensed by, and follow the guidelines of, the Department of Business Regulation. It would be a good idea to check with the department (at the address above) before enrolling in any vocational course.

For certain types of disputes, there are some other agencies that may come in handy. For complaints involving utilities or transportation, contact the **Montana Consumer Counsel, 330 Fuller Ave., Helena, Mont. 59601.** Then there are two county agencies that may be particularly helpful on local disputes. They are the **Consumer Protection Division, Lewis and Clark County Attorney's Office, County Courthouse, Helena, Mont. 59601;** and the **Missoula County Attorney, County Courthouse, Missoula, Mont. 58901.**

Nebraska

Nebraska in 1974 straggled onto the list of states that have an Unfair and Deceptive Trade Practices Act. Along with the entry of fellow latecomer Mississippi, this brought the total of states having such a law to forty-seven. Nebraska's lateness seems particularly ironic, because "unfair and deceptive business practices" constitute one of the top-ranking categories of consumer complaints in the state.

Nebraska consumers are also bothered by auto repairs and sales, appliances and the people who fix them, home repairs and improvements, land sales, and insurance. Advice on coping with each of these problem areas will be found in the last section of this book.

Unfortunately, a standard part of that advice is often: "Complain to your state consumer-protection agency." In Nebraska, I don't know whether to recommend that course. My ability to evaluate the agency's responsiveness is hindered by its failure to return my questionnaire. The fact that it was one of a very few state agencies that didn't return the questionnaire, despite two written invitations to do so and three long-distance telephone calls, makes me wonder about . . . well, the agency's responsiveness.

Part of the problem may well have been lack of staff. A federal publication lists the staff total for the Nebraska consumer-protection agency as "two (part-time)." But if lack of staff caused my letters and phone calls to go unanswered, the same thing could happen to your complaint.

Try anyway. My doubts may be unfounded, and the mere fact that you've written a state agency lends some additional clout to your communications with the company you're fighting. The address is **Consumer Protection Division, Department of Justice, State Capitol, Room 2119, Lincoln, Neb. 68509.**

If you happen to live in Douglas County, see if you can get help from the **Consumer Fraud Division, Douglas County Attorney's Office, Omaha-Douglas Civic Center, Eighteenth and Farnam Streets, Room 909, Omaha, Neb. 68102.** This county agency has a staff of about eleven people and a budget of about $90,000. With those resources, they should be able to do a job for you.

Meanwhile, prepare to use unconventional tactics, media, voluntary groups, and/or the courts. This last route is made more palatable by the fact that Nebraska law now allows a court to award you reasonable attorney's fees, along with other damages, if you prevail. Private citizens are also authorized to bring antitrust suits and to collect damages when they've been harmed by price-fixing or monopolistic practices under the state's newly revamped antitrust laws.

Two bright spots on the consumer-protection front deserve mention. The state recently passed the Uniform Residential Landlord-Tenant Act, which sets forth minimum responsibilities of both parties and provides recourses for both if the other defaults on those responsibilities. That means tenants no longer are legally bound to pay rent if their landlord is failing to provide the basic services that make the quarters livable. Withholding of rent, however, should be done only in consultation with a tenants' group, a lawyer, or both.

Nebraska also passed recently a three-day "cooling-off period" for door-to-door sales. This means you can change your mind about a purchase by notifying the company that sold you the goods—in writing—within three business days of the original transaction. Though Nebraska was among the last states to enact such a law, it did a good job with the legislation. The law applies to most purchases over $25. It requires the merchant to return any down payment you've made within ten days (and you're required to return all goods you received within twenty days). Door-to-door salesmen must give you written notice of the law when the sale is made. If they normally conduct business in Spanish, they must also provide a copy of the notice form in that language.

Nevada

Nevada may be the state where consumers find it easiest (and perhaps most pleasant) to lose their money. It's worth noting that neither gambling nor prostitution ranks among the most common consumer complaints here.

As a matter of fact, according to state tallies filed with the federal Office of Consumer Affairs, the number one consumer problem in Nevada is that universal curse, auto repairs and sales. After that come (2) food and drugs, (3) furniture, (4) mobile homes, (5) landlord-tenant problems, (6) sales practices and promotions, (7) warranties, and (8) appliances. You'll find advice on dealing with each of those problems in Part III of this book. Most items will be found under the same headings, and for (6), see Unfair Business Practices.

In the auto area, Nevada, like most states, is still groping for the beginnings of a cure. On some issues, though, Nevada has consumer-protection laws in force that are worth knowing about. For example, it's mandatory in Nevada for pharmacies to quote prices on prescription drugs. They must do so even over the phone, and even if you don't have a prescription. So it's not difficult for you to shop for the best price on a prescription—and you'd be surprised how much money you can save in many cases.

In some parts of the state, land sales have been a major problem. But a strict new law has been passed to govern the sale of subdivided land. It's administered by the state **Real Estate Division, 215 E. Bonanza Road, Las Vegas, Nev. 89101.** All salesmen must now be licensed, and intentional misrepresentation or deceit in subdivision sales is now a felony. For the purposes of this law, a "subdivision" is any piece of land that over the course of time will be divided into thirty-five or more parcels or lots.

In general, no matter what type of consumer problem you run into in Nevada, the place for you to turn (if complaints directly to the company prove unavailing) is the **Consumer Affairs Division, Department of Commerce.** It's located in the **Collet Building, Suite 219, 1111 Las Vegas Boulevard, South, Las Vegas, Nev. 89104.** The Consumer Affairs Division has that great boon, a tool-free number for incoming calls: **800-992-0900.** In addition, there's a branch office, in the **Nye Building, 201 S. Fall St., Carson City, Nev. 89701.**

Don't get the Consumer Affairs Division mixed up with the Consumer Protection Division of the state Attorney General's office. The latter is mainly a prosecution arm. If the Consumer Affairs Division thinks your complaint merits prosecution, it will forward the facts to the Attorney General's office. But it's the Consumer Affairs Division that is equipped to help you get redress on your individual complaint. And equipped rather well, I might add. The agency claims that it's able to resolve 90 per cent of disputes promptly and fairly. About 70 per cent of the time the consumer wins, about 20 per cent the business wins, and about 10 per cent of the cases go unresolved. The average wait for a consumer needing help is said to be only "one day to two weeks."

There are also two county agencies that may be of use, especially on disputes involving local merchants. In Clark County, it's the **Consumer Protection Division, Clark County District Attorney's Office, County Courthouse, 200 E. Carson, Las Vegas, Nev. 89101.** In Washoe County, it's the **Consumer**

Fraud Unit, Washoe County District Attorney's Office, County Courthouse, South Virginia and Court Streets, Reno, Nevada 89501.

New Hampshire

The ten most common consumer complaints in New Hampshire are about (1) automobile repairs and sales, (2) home improvements and repairs, (3) mail-order houses, (4) mobile homes and mobile-home parks, (5) land sales, (6) contests, (7) credit problems, including billing and collection practices, (8) service stations, (9) advertising, and (10) magazines. You'll find specific advice for coping with all of these problems—except for service stations—in Part III. It turns out that service station complaints mainly come back to that old nemesis, auto repairs. It's only the type of ripoff that differs. Dealers usually deal with in-state residents, who are more likely to complain about warranty coverage or perhaps workmanship. Gas stations deal more often with out-of-state residents, who are more likely to complain about overcharging or unauthorized repairs.

Motorists of both varieties can take heart from a bill recently passed by the New Hampshire legislature. All repair shops are now required to give estimates and are prohibited from exceeding the estimates by more than 10 per cent without the customer's written permission.

Some of the people who fall victim to fast-talking home-repair vendors or to magazine sellers may benefit from the three-day cooling-off period mandated by another new state law. Under it, you can cancel any sale that wasn't made at the seller's principal place of business, if you change your mind—and notify the seller in writing—within three business days. The law applies to both cash and credit sales, and there's no penalty for exercising your rights under it.

For mobile-home dwellers, the state has set down some rules that limit the power of mobile-home park owners. Entrance fees are banned. Park rules must be stated in writing. And, most important, the landlords' powers to evict people at will have been curbed: Eviction now can take place only for one of six valid reasons, stated in the law.

With regard to land sales, the state's consumer-protection agency not only takes complaints but also functions as a kind of quasi-court, to hear and resolve complaints. The law applies only to subdivided land, with a subdivision being defined as a piece of land that is (or will be) divided into fifty or more lots. Don't despair, though, if you've been gypped while buying a piece of land that isn't part of a subdivision. You may still be able to get redress under the state's Unfair and Deceptive Trade Practices Act, that general umbrella that is a consumer's last—and sometimes best—resort.

Credit problems should be diminished somewhat, at least on the collection end, by another state law just passed. It limits the techniques debt collectors may use to squeeze money out of consumers. Among the banned practices are impersonating a government agency, sending documents that falsely purport to be court documents, and calling debtors repeatedly and at inconvenient hours. These techniques, especially the court documents ruse, have been widely used in New Hampshire, according to Richard Wiebusch.

Wiebusch heads the state agency that constitutes your basic resource when you want to lodge a complaint against a company. It's the **Consumer Protection Division, Office of Attorney General, Statehouse Annex, Concord, N.H. 03301.** By its own estimate, the agency resolves some 75 per cent of the complaints it receives successfully, from the consumer's point of view. The average time a consumer has to wait for resolution of a problem is one to two months, Wiebusch reports. But some complaints will be solved in less than a week; others, requiring litigation, will take a year or more.

If this wait seems too long to you, there's not much you can do about it, except to pursue nongovernmental avenues of recourse. The Consumer Protection Division has a monopoly on governmental consumer protection in New Hampshire. There are no other broad-gauge state agencies, no county agencies, and no city agencies. With a smallish staff (seven at this writing, and scheduled to increase to ten in 1976), the agency handles some 2,500 written complaints annually, and a larger volume of telephone calls (though callers are encouraged to put their complaints in writing). It would be unrealistic for you to expect fast action from this agency. But file your complaint anyway, as early in the game as possible. You can continue to use whatever other tactics you wish while waiting for your number to come up. If it turned out you solved your problem before the Consumer Protection Division got to it, that wouldn't be so bad, would it?

New Jersey

New Jersey has a history of imaginative, reformist activism in its government, most notably exemplified by Woodrow Wilson, along with a parallel, contradictory history of bungling and corruption. The most urbanized state in the nation, it has a large share of the poor and elderly, who need consumer protection the most. Faced with this challenge, the state's actions on the consumer-protection front have sometimes been strikingly imaginative and reformist, in the Woodrow Wilson mold. However, though there have been no allegations of corruption, the state's consumer-protection actions have also followed the other, bungling tradition.

What's happened in New Jersey is the erection of a large government bureaucracy dedicated to protecting the consumer. It costs more than $3 million a year to run, employs fourteen people full time and close to two hundred people part time. If your complaint reaches the right person, your chances for favorable action are better than in most states. But if it lodges in the wrong cubbyhole, you may have added another layer to your problems.

The agency to write to, on most complaints, is the **Office of Consumer Affairs, Room 405, State Office Building, 1100 Ray-**

mond Boulevard, Newark, N.J. 07102. An official of the agency estimates that the average complaint is resolved in two to four weeks. He reports some 60 per cent of them are resolved successfully, from the consumer's point of view.

Before you write, though, you may want to try to take advantage of one of the most promising innovations by the Office of Consumer Affairs: the CALA program. The point of the program is to put a "Community Affairs Local Assistance" officer in your home community. Then, you can contact your CALA officer on consumer complaints. He or she will try to mediate them. If the CALA officer's intervention isn't sufficient to solve the problem, or if the case seems to demand prosecution, then it's forwarded to the central office in Newark.

The concept is certainly a good one, and you can give it a try by calling city hall in your home town to find out who your CALA officer is (if any). At last report, there were 126 CALA officers in 98 municipalities. (There was also one CALA officer serving all of Monmouth County and one serving all of Sussex County. In Mercer and Ocean counties, the directors of the county consumer-protection agencies are also designated as CALA officers.) Working with a CALA officer should give you personal contact with someone who's working to solve your complaint and should enable you to stay posted on how your case is coming.

If you have no CALA officer, or if the complaint is one he or she can't handle, then send your complaint in writing to Newark. Wait four weeks for reply, then start prodding the state agency by phone or letter, just as you would prod a recalcitrant business.

The number one complaint in New Jersey, as in most states, is auto repairs and sales practices. The Office of Consumer Affairs receives some 3,600 complaints every year on this subject alone. It may help you avoid problems in this area to be aware of a law recently passed in New Jersey that requires all repair shops to give written estimates on repairs, stating the price as a "not-to-exceed" figure. It's illegal for repair shops to go beyond this figure without your written consent, or to perform repairs you didn't authorize *in writing*. If someone tries to gyp you, he may have a change of heart when you let him know you're familiar with your rights under this law.

After automobile problems, the most common complaints in the state involve home improvements and repairs (some 3,200 a year), and appliances (2,500 a year). You'll find advice on each of these specific problem areas in Part III.

Another problem plaguing New Jerseyans, and consumers everywhere, is billing mistakes. New Jersey has a law to help you deal with them. It requires businesses to acknowledge within thirty days any letter you send them questioning a bill. Within ninety days, they must resolve the problem by changing your bill, notifying you that the total will be corrected on the next statement, or explaining to you why their total is right and yours is wrong. Until they've done these things, it's illegal for them to try to collect the bill or to do anything to damage your credit rating, such as saying nasty things about you to credit bureaus. If a company disobeys this law, you may go to court and collect for your actual damages, plus attorney's fees, plus (in some cases) a penalty of up to twice the disputed sum, up to a limit of $100. This law doesn't apply to utilities. For complaints involving utility bills, see the **Board of Public Utility Commissioners, 101 Commerce St., Newark, N.J. 07102.**

There are several other general complaint-handling agencies in New Jersey that you should know about. If you feel you've been mistreated by any state agency (and that includes being ignored), notify the **Division of Citizen Complaints and Dispute Settlement, Department of Public Advocate, P.O. Box 141, Trenton, N.J. 08625.** This agency functions as a sort of ombudsman to see that state citizens aren't abused by their own government. It has a toll-free telephone line for incoming calls: **800-792-8600.**

For complaints involving regulated trades and professions, you can write the **Division of Consumer Affairs, Room 504, State Office Building, 1100 Raymond Boulevard, Newark, N.J. 07102.** If you don't know if the fellow who ripped you off was a member of a regulated trade or profession, just write the Office of Consumer Affairs, in Room 405 at the same address. They can always bounce your complaint upstairs if necessary.

Last, but not necessarily least, are the county and city con-sumer-protection agencies. No fewer than eight counties and two cities in New Jersey have established such offices. They may offer a route to a fast solution, especially on problems involving local merchants. The two city agencies are Belleville Office of Consumer Protection, and the Elizabeth Bureau of Consumer Protection. The county agencies are:

- Atlantic County Office of Consumer Affairs, 25 Dolphin Ave. and Shore Road, Northfield, N.J. 08232
- Bergen County Office of Consumer Affairs, 355 Main St., Hackensack, N.J. 07601
- Burlington County Office of Consumer Affairs, Grant Build-ing, Room 101, 54 Grant St., Mount Holly, N.J. 08060
- Camden County Office of Consumer Affairs, Commerce Building, Room 606, No. 1 Broadway, Camden, N.J. 08103
- Cumberland County Department of Weights and Measures and Consumer Protection, 800 East Commerce St., Bridgeton, N.J. 08302
- Mercer County Division of Consumer Affairs, County Ad-ministration Building, 640 South Broad St., Room 116, Trenton, N.J. 08607
- Ocean County Department of Consumer Affairs, 129 Hooper Ave., Toms River, N.J. 08753
- Somerset County Department of Consumer Affairs, County Administration Building, Somerville, N.J. 08876

One kind of complaint you may or may not want to take to a state agency is a landlord-tenant dispute. New Jersey tenants have more rights than tenants almost anywhere else. But most of these rights have been conferred by court decisions rather than by legislation. If your dispute with your landlord involves apartment conditions, you'll probably do better by banding together with other tenants than by writing a government agency. For expert advice on tenant organizing, contact the New Jersey Tenants Organization in Fort Lee: They're one of the country's oldest and most successful tenant groups.

If your landlord responds to your newfound militancy by trying to evict you, don't panic. Eviction can be done only by court order in New Jersey, and the eviction notice must inform you that you have a right to a court hearing. Retaliatory eviction in reaction to your filing a complaint against your landlord (say, with a local health board or building inspector) is banned; so is retaliatory eviction in response to your joining a tenants' group.

New Jersey, by the way, is one of the few states where a landlord must pay you interest if he takes a security deposit from you. That deposit is limited by law to one and a half months' rent.

New Mexico

Winston Churchill once said, "Give us the tools, and we'll finish the job." There's a converse to that statement, and it seems to apply in New Mexico: Don't give us the tools, and we can't do the job.

The consumer-protection agency in New Mexico is trying hard to protect consumers. My guess is that it succeeds about half the time. I can't give you the agency's own estimate, since it ducked the question in my questionnaire about "percentage of cases successfully resolved." I can tell you this: According to the agency's own records, only 42 per cent of the complaints filed in October 1974 had been resolved as of January 4, 1975. As of the same date, only 61 per cent of the complaints filed in June 1974 had been resolved.

That seems to mean that, if you file a complaint and wait a couple of months, there's about an even chance that your complaint will reach a resolution. And those statistics don't tell the odds on the resolution's being in your favor. But don't blame the Consumer Protection Division for this; it really isn't their fault. We spoke, with regard to Michigan, of sending the state agencies out to police the market place armed with a feather duster. In New Mexico the situation is even more extreme. You might say the agency has been sent out to do battle with a nest of rattlesnakes, armed only with bare feet. The agency lacks subpoena power; it has no official power to arbitrate complaints;

it isn't even authorized to seek court orders for restitution on behalf of aggrieved consumers.

Faced with this situation in your capacity as an aggrieved consumer, what do you do? Well, first of all, file your complaint anyway. You have virtually nothing to lose. The agency's intercession might help you. The mere fact that you've filed a complaint might make your adversary take you a bit more seriously or be more willing to compromise. Send your complaint to the **Consumer Protection Division, Office of Attorney General, Lamy Building, P.O. Box 2246, Santa Fe, N.M. 87501.**

While you're waiting for your complaint to get attention from the Division's small (seven-person), underbudgeted ($26,400) staff, you can undertake other action. You can, for example, go to court on your own behalf. In New Mexico, though, you can't count on being awarded attorney's fees, even if you ultimately prevail. So be sure to discuss fees early and thoroughly with your lawyer. You can also use county agencies, the media, voluntary organizations, and imaginative guerrilla tactics to further your cause (see tips in other chapters.) Whatever works.

The complaints that sting New Mexico consumers most often, according to records of the Consumer Protection Division, are about (1) auto repairs and sales, (2) mobile homes and mobile-home parks, (3) mail-order houses, (4) contractual agreements, (5) land subdivisions, (6) home repairs and improvements, (7) appliances and their repair, and (8) landlord-tenant problems. You'll find specific advice for dealing with most of these areas in Part III.

We mentioned county agencies earlier, in passing. If you live in Barnalillo County, Eddy County, or Valencia County, this is an avenue you should certainly try. The Valencia agency is new and something of a question mark. The other two county agencies compare favorably to the state agency in funding, staff, and even legal powers, in some ways. In Bernalillo County, it's the **Consumer Protection Division, Bernalillo County District Attorney's Office, Courthouse, 415 Tijeras, N.W., Albuquerque, N.M. 87101.** In Eddy County, it's the **Consumer Affairs Division, Eddy County District Attorney's Office, P.O. Box 1240, Carlsbad, N.M., 88220.** And in Valencia County, the fledgling agency is simply the **District Attorney's Office**, **Valencia County, Los Lunas, N.M. 87031.**

Buena suerte. Good luck.

New York

New Yorkers bristle with complaints. And New York bristles with consumer-complaint handling agencies. There are no fewer than twenty-four such agencies around the state, not even counting those that handle only a certain type of complaint. Eleven of them are city agencies, eleven are county agencies, and two are statewide.

For most New York State residents, the backbone of consumer protection is the Consumer Frauds and Protection Bureau, which is part of the New York State Attorney General's Office. The bureau thinks it is pretty hot stuff, and it's probably right, though it may not be as good as it thinks it is. "Ours was the first and is the most outstanding and productive [consumer-protection] bureau in the country," Barnett Levy, the Assistant Attorney General in charge of the bureau, wrote me. Whether or not that claim is puffery is difficult to say, since Levy refused to estimate the bureau's success rate ("very high percentage") or the average time a consumer must wait for resolution of a complaint ("difficult to average"). Best or not, the bureau is good. It has a full complement of legal powers, a budget around $1 million, and a full-time staff of seventy-three, including thirty-three lawyers and twenty investigators. You can use it by writing or visiting ("telephone complaints are discouraged") the **Consumer Frauds and Protection Bureau, Office of Attorney General, Two World Trade Center, New York, N.Y. 10047.** Or you can write or visit one of the ten branch offices around the state. The largest of these, at the **State Capitol, Albany, N.Y. 12224,** serves as a second headquarters. The other nine branches are in Auburn, Binghamton, Buffalo, Plattsburgh, Poughkeepsie, Rochester, Syracuse, Utica, and Watertown. Check your phone book—under New York State government listing in the white pages—for locations.

At last report, the Consumer Fraud and Protection Bureau was handling about 26,000 complaints a year. A second state agency, the **State Consumer Protection Board, 99 Washington Ave., Room 1000, Albany, N.Y. 12210,** was handling about 8,000 a year. Lacking many of the legal powers of the Bureau, the Consumer Protection Board is more concerned with representing consumer interests before regulatory bodies and the legislature. It is also involved with consumer education and with complaint handling, which it does through voluntary mediation. Use it as a backup agency to the bureau: It wouldn't hurt at all to send copies of your complaint letters to both.

Statewide, the complaints that irritate New Yorkers most often deal with (1) auto repairs and sales, (2) mail-order houses, (3) credit billings, (4) magazine subscriptions, (5) travel problems, (6) furniture, (7) funeral establishments, (8) air-conditioners, refrigerators, and stoves—in other words, appliances—(9) collection practices, and (10) health spas. You'll find specific advice for coping with each of these problem areas in Part III. But there are also specific state laws that can help you deal with many of them.

Take auto repairs. A 1974 state law requires all repair shops to register with the State Department of Motor Vehicles, Swan Street Building, South Mall, Albany, N.Y. 12210. Anyone engaging in "fraudulent or negligent practices" can have his registration revoked. At this writing, the Department of Motor Vehicles was setting up regional boards around the state to administer the law and to take consumer complaints against auto repair shops.

Another law, which took effect in 1975, offers you help in straightening out mail-order problems. It requires mail-order companies to ship the goods to you within thirty days of your order. If they don't, they must offer you either a substitute article or a complete refund. You get to choose which.

In the area of billing problems, New York passed a law in 1973, which has since been copied by a few other states and by the federal government. It requires a company, on receiving your protest about a bill, to acknowledge receipt of your protest within thirty days and to straighten out the whole mess within ninety days. The company can straighten things out either by making a correction or by sending you a written explanation of why its total is correct and yours is wrong.

Other legislation limits the means collection agencies can use to get money from you and requires funeral homes to provide customers with an advance itemization of funeral costs. Since these protections come from state legislation, you should probably direct your complaints in these areas to the agencies mentioned above.

However, if you live in one of the eleven cities or eleven counties that have consumer-protection agencies, you may have additional rights under local ordinances. You can find out about them by inquiring of your local agencies at the addresses given below. These agencies can also help you in many disputes—especially those in which both you and the merchant are within their geographical jurisdiction.

The largest, and probably the strongest, of these agencies is the **New York City Department of Consumer Affairs, 80 Lafayette St., New York, N.Y. 10013.** Armed with formidable legal powers, it marshals a staff of some 325 people and a budget of around $4 million. (This staff and budget total exceed those of both state agencies combined.) It has been highly innovative in consumer protection. For example, its 1973 regulation requiring the licensing of appliance and television repairmen was a pioneering step. The regulation requires these repairmen to give written estimates and to get written permission from owners before doing repair work that costs more than $15. Some people in the consumer movement feel that the department's performance has gone downhill somewhat since the departure of Bess Myerson as Commissioner. They attribute the decline to morale problems and the resignation of several skilled staff members. The department is also bound to suffer as a result of New York City's fiscal troubles. However, it remains a valuable resource for consumers.

Among the county agencies, the strongest are probably those in Nassau and Suffolk counties. Each has a budget of around $800,000 and a staff of between sixty and seventy people. Both require the licensing of home improvement and home repair contractors, and Nassau County puts out a useful booklet, *How to Avoid Home Improvement Problems*. Suffolk County, at this writing, was working on the licensing of electronic and television repairmen and hoped to go on in the future to regulate collection agencies, auto repair shops, and appliance repairmen. Nassau County gained public attention with a program designed to combat the high cost of food. The most publicity probably attended the checks on the weight of quarter-pound hamburgers in fast-food outlets. But the program also included support of the nationwide meat boycott in 1973 and checks on the fat content of ground meat in supermarkets, which resulted in four prosecutions.

The county agencies in Erie, Orange, and Westchester counties also appear to be strong. The Rockland County agency is well funded and well staffed but would probably be more effective with some broader legal powers. It's certainly worth trying, though. So are the other city and county agencies, most of which operate with relatively small staffs and modest budgets.

The ten city agencies, besides New York City's, are as follows:

- City Office of Consumer Affairs, City Hall, Room 203, Glen Cove, N.Y. 11542
- Town Consumer Protection Board, Town Hall, 227 Main St., Huntington, N.Y. 11743
- Consumer Protection Section, Town Attorney's Office, 655 Main St., Islip, N.Y. 11571
- City Department of Weights and Measures and Consumer Affairs, Police Headquarters, Roosevelt Square, Mount Vernon, N.Y. 10550
- City Consumer Affairs Committee, City Hall, New Rochelle, N.Y. 10801
- Colonie Consumer Protection Agency, Memorial Town Hall, Newtonville, N.Y. 12128
- City Bureau of Consumer Protection, City Hall, Room 206, Jay St., Schenectady, N.Y. 12305
- City Consumer Protection Board, Ramapo Town Hall, Route 59, Suffern, N.Y. 10901

- Corporation Counsel's Office, City Hall, Room 420, 233 East Washington St., Syracuse, N.Y. 13202
- Yonkers Office of Consumer Protection, Weights and Measures, City Hall, Room 316, Nepperhan Ave., Yonkers, N.Y. 10701

The eleven county offices and their addresses are:

- Consumer Fraud Bureau, Erie County District Attorney's Office, 25 Delaware Ave., Buffalo, N.Y. 14202. Also in Erie County there's the Consumer Protection Committe, Office of Erie County Executive, 95 Franklin St., Buffalo, N.Y. 14202
- Consumer Frauds and Economic Crimes Bureau, Kings County District Attorney's Office, Municipal Building, 210 Joralemon St., Brooklyn, N.Y. 11201 (interested in "complaints of a criminal nature only")
- Nassau County Office of Consumer Affairs, 160 Old Country Road, Mineola, N.Y. 11501. Also in Nassau County there's the Commercial Fraud Bureau, Nassau County District Attorney's Office. 262 Old Country Road, Mineola, N.Y. 11501
- Oneida County Consumer Advocate, County Office Building, 800 Park Ave., Utica, N.Y. 13501
- Onondaga County Office of Consumer Affairs, 635 James St., Syracuse, N.Y. 13203
- Orange County Department of Weights and Measures and Consumer Affairs, 99 Main St., Goshen, N.Y. 10924; also in Orange County: Orange County District Attorney's Office of Consumer Affairs, County Government Center, Main St., Goshen, N.Y. 10924
- Rensselaer County Department of Weights and Measures and Consumer Affairs, 399 Whiteview Road, Troy, N.Y. 12180
- Rockland County Office of Consumer Protection, County Office Building, New Hempsted Road, New City, N.Y. 10956
- Steuben County Department of Weights and Measures and Consumer Affairs, 19 East Morris St., Bath, N.Y. 14810
- Suffolk County Department of Consumer Affairs, Suffolk

County Center, Veterans Highway, Hauppauge, Long Island, N.Y. 11787

- Westchester County Office of Consumer Affairs, Office of County Executive, White Plains, N.Y. 10601; also in Westchester: County Division of Weights and Measures and Consumer Affairs, 38 Brockway Place, White Plains, N.Y. 10601; and Frauds Bureau, Westchester County District Attorney's Office, County Courthouse, 111 Grove St., White Plains, N.Y. 10601

North Carolina

North Carolina was the first state to wake up to what's been happening in small claims courts. Designed as a cornerstone of consumer protection for the little man and the average guy, the courts have become, in effect, collection agencies for businesses in many places. When consumers do come into the court as plaintiffs, they may win, but their victories all too often turn out to be hollow. In about a third of the cases the business that victimized the consumer in the first place just ignores or refuses to pay the court judgment!

In North Carolina the Department of Commerce looked into the situation and reported that most consumers were "not sufficiently sophisticated" to collect by attaching property or other means. As a result, the state passed a new law in 1974, saying the courts must not only hand down small-claims judgments but also assist in seeing that consumers actually get the money that's coming to them under the court rulings. At roughly the same time the state legislature raised the limit on the dollar amount that can be involved in a small claims dispute. It's now $500, up from $300. This is certainly a step in the right direction for consumers, since no attorney is needed in a small claims court, making it relatively inexpensive for you to obtain your legal rights. For a booklet on how to use the small claims courts— which, by the way, are located in all county seats and most major cities in the state—contact the **Consumer Protection Divi-**

sion, Office of Attorney General, Justice Building, P.O. Box 629, Raleigh, N.C. 27602.

The Consumer Protection Division is also the agency you can go to with complaints. It can intercede with the business on your behalf and sometimes mediate a solution. It can also prosecute, if it deems that course to be warranted. The toll-free number for complaints is 1-800-662-7925. James Blackburn, the head of the division, estimates that the agency achieves a successful resolution of 65 to 70 per cent of the complaints it gets. He figures the waiting time on the average complaint is thirty to sixty days.

If those results don't impress you, you'll probably have to try the small claims courts or the regular courts, or else a non-governmental type of recourse. The Consumer Protection Division is the only broad-gauge consumer-protection agency in the state, except for the Fraud Unit of the Charlotte Police Department.

Statewide, the biggest source of complaints is probably mobile homes. Blackburn led a major study of mobile-home problems in 1974. The study concluded that one of the big problems was the lack of a single government agency empowered to help mobile-home dwellers. What little government regulation there is (construction standards, rules governing the sale of new mobile homes) was diffused through different branches of the state government. So far as I know, this situation remains unchanged. What's more, North Carolina has no laws requiring licensing of mobile-home dealers, setting standards for mobile-home warranties, or spelling out the rights of tenants in mobile-home parks. Until this situation improves, mobile-home complaints should be brought to the Consumer Protection Division—but without too much hope of success.

After mobile homes, Blackburn listed (2) auto repairs and sales, (3) undelivered merchandise, primarily from mail-order houses, (4) receipt of unsolicited merchandise, and (5) appliances and their repair as the biggest areas of consumer problems in the state. Tallies by the Charlotte Police Department would suggest adding to that list home improvements and repairs, credit problems, and TV and radio sales and servicing. All of these topics are discussed in some detail in Part III.

North Dakota

The ten top complaint categories in North Dakota in 1974 and the number of complaints for each were (1) mobile homes, 471; (2) household appliances, 449; (3) motor vehicles, 307; (4) franchises, 164; (5) building and land sales, 144; (6) services, 143; (7) books and magazines, 123; (8) health and beauty aids, 123; (9) clothing, 82; and (10) food, 41.

For most of the problems listed, and for most others you're likely to encounter, there are two state agencies you can turn to. You may as well write them both. You won't be spending any time at all writing to county or local consumer-protection agencies, because there aren't any in North Dakota. So take pen, carbon paper, or copying machine in hand and write to both the **Consumer Fraud Division, Office of Attorney General, State Capitol, Bismarck, N.D. 58501,** and the **Consumer Affairs Office, State Laboratories Department, Bank of North Dakota Building, Box 937, Bismarck, N.D. 58505.**

The Consumer Protection Division is the spine of consumer protection in the state. It handles more than two thousand complaints a year. With a staff of some thirteen people (eleven of them part time) and a budget around $45,000, it brings 97 per cent of the complaints it receives to some kind of a conclusion. The average waiting time for a consumer needing help is said to be thirty-six days.

While the Consumer Protection Division has all the enforcement powers, the Consumer Affairs Office of the State Laboratories Department can sometimes resolve complaints through voluntary mediation. It also studies consumer problems, proposes rules and regulations, and has responsibilities in the field of consumer education. The laboratory facilities at its disposal enable it to make some unusual and valuable contributions in the consumer area. For example, it recently studied forty-nine antacids sold over the counter as indigestion aids and made public the results of its study. It also tested the bacterial content of hot dogs, luncheon meats, and ground beef sold in the state. Finding a wide variation (from "very good to very bad"), the office proposed formal standards to govern how many bacteria can be allowed in meat to be sold in the state in the future. The Consumer Affairs Office also publishes a monthly newsletter, *North Dakota Consumer,* which can keep you up to date on your rights and remedies and on consumer-protection activity in the state in general. You can get a single subscription free.

Be warned, by the way, that the Consumer Affairs Office is small: The staff totaled three (two full time) as of this writing. So pin your hopes for complaint help primarily on the Consumer Protection Division, and use the Consumer Affairs Office as a backup. If both fail, be prepared to fall back on voluntary organizations, media, the courts, guerrilla tactics, or whatever. If you live in the northeastern portion of the state, one group that might be of use is a voluntary organization called **Consumer Action Line Inc., Box 8281, Grand Forks, N.D. 58201.**

Ohio

Once upon a time, when consumer protection was gaining in popularity, there was an Attorney General of one political party and a Governor of the other party. At that time, consumer-protection agencies were only a gleam in Ohio politicians' eyes. But things were consummated, and the gleam eventually found its realization as—you guessed it—twins! And so Ohio is now one of several states with two consumer-protection agencies, which operate, at least in some ways, independently of each other.

"It's a two-headed monster which could probably more efficiently function as a one-headed monster," said Robert Tongren, chief of the Consumer Frauds and Crimes Section of the Attorney General's Office. "The Department of Commerce takes more complaints than we do. But, of course, we have most of the enforcement powers. If a complaint starts with them and then has to be passed on to us, the whole thing can take several months, or even longer."

There is a bright side to the existence of two agencies, though.

It does give you, as the consumer, two cracks at getting your problem resolved through the help of a state agency. And, with some merchants, it may help to have two heads of a monster snapping at them rather than one.

You'll probably want to file your first complaint with the **Consumer Protection Division, Department of Commerce, 33 North Grant Ave., Columbus, Ohio 43215**, if only because that agency has a toll-free telephone number for your convenience: **800-282-1960**. Your second complaint should go to the **Consumer Frauds and Crimes Section, Office of Attorney General, State Office Tower, Suite 1541, 30 East Broad St., Columbus, Ohio 43215**.

Perhaps spurred in part by a bit of intramural competition, both agencies have done some aggressive and thorough policing of the market place. The Consumer Protection Division did a thorough job of researching the consumer abuses in the mobile-home field. That investigation resulted in some prosecutions by its sister agency and also in the issuance of a pamphlet called *Guide to Buying a Mobile Home*. The pamphlet is still available at this writing, and single copies are free.

Meanwhile, the Consumer Frauds and Crimes Section has been tinkering with some cars and some television sets. After its consulting engineers know exactly what's wrong with the cars, they're driven into auto repair shops. After the engineers know exactly what's wrong with the TV sets, they're taken to repairmen. These carefully laid nets have resulted in some prosecutions and in some voluntary agreements to mediate future complaints (through the Better Business Bureau, for example) or to set up escrow funds to repay customers who feel they've been mistreated.

The ten areas in which Ohio consumers find themselves mistreated most often, according to the Consumer Protection Division's 1975 annual report, are (1) auto repairs and sales, (2) appliances and housewares, (3) mail-order houses, (4) home repairs and improvements, (5) furniture and carpeting, (6) mobile homes, (7) door-to-door sales, (8) personal services, such as health spas and dating services, on which payment is made in advance for future services, (9) clothing and jewelry, and (10) toys, hobbies, sports, and pets. The number of complaints received in 1974 ranged from 1,735 in the automobile category to

195 in category (10). You'll find suggestions for dealing with most of these problem areas in Part III.

For some additional help, aside from the two state agencies, you may be able to turn to one of the four county or seven city agencies scattered around the state. It will come as no surprise that the largest of these, with a staff of about thirty and a budget around $300,000, is the Cleveland agency. It may come as a surprise, though, that there's no agency in Cincinnati. You can use these agencies if you live within their jurisdiction or if your ill-fated transaction took place there.

The four county agencies are in Franklin, Greene, Lake, and Montgomery counties. The **Consumer Fraud Division** in the **Franklin County Office of Prosecuting Attorney** can draw on a staff of nine, and a budget of $400,000. Its address is **Hall of Justice, S. High St., Columbus, Ohio 43210.** The Greene County agency, which is new and something of a question mark, is the **Greene County Consumer Services Office, c/o Chamber of Commerce, Xenia, Ohio 45385.** In Lake County, where the agency consists of a director plus volunteers, write the **Lake County Consumer Protection Council, Prosecuting Attorney's Office, Lake County Courthouse, Painesville, Ohio 44077.** In Montgomery County, a staff of three mans the **Fraud Section, Montgomery County Office of Prosecuting Attorney, County Courts Building, 41 North Perry St., Suite 308, Dayton, Ohio 45402.**

The seven city agencies are as follows:

- City Division of Weights and Measures, and Consumer Protection, 69 North Union St., Akron, Ohio 44314
- City Consumer Protection Commission, 919 Walnut Ave., N.E., Canton, Ohio 44704
- City Office of Consumer Affairs, City Hall, Room 119, 601 Lakeside Ave., Cleveland, Ohio 44114
- Program Administrator for Consumer Affairs, City Department of Community Services, 220 Greenlawn Ave., Columbus, Ohio 43223
- City Bureau of Consumer Affairs, 101 West Third St., Dayton, Ohio 45402
- City Consumer Protection Agency, 565 North Erie St., Toledo, Ohio 43624

- Division of Weights and Measures, and Consumer Protection, City Department of Health, City Hall, Youngstown, Ohio 44503

You'll have to judge for yourself the effectiveness of these city agencies. I can tell you, though, that in my opinion the award for the most original mode of operation goes to Toledo. There, five law students from the University of Toledo work as complaint handlers for the agency, taking care of about 80 per cent of the complaints received. For advice, the students regularly huddle not only with senior agency officials but also with two or three members of the law school faculty. This arrangement costs the taxpayers nothing, but the students receive academic credit for their work.

Oklahoma

In its 1974 report to the Governor of Oklahoma and the "honorable members of the Oklahoma legislature," the state Attorney General's office gave a statistical rundown on its recent activities. Complaints were being received at the rate of about 1,300 a year. Of that total, about 20 per cent were shipped off to other state or federal agencies. Another 4 per cent were still pending. The rest had been decided—51.5 per cent as "satisfactory to the consumer," and 48.5 per cent as "unsatisfactory to the consumer."

These odds may not strike you as overwhelmingly favorable. But following the advice in this book might help you land among the satisfied sector. To file a complaint with the Attorney General's office, write the **Assistant Attorney General for Consumer Protection, Office of Attorney General, State Capitol Building, Room 112, Oklahoma City, Okla. 73105.**

There's another state agency that might be able to help you called the **Department of Consumer Affairs.** It's located in the **Jim Thorpe Building, Room 460, Oklahoma City, Okla. 73105.** I can't tell you much about its activities or powers, unfortunately, since it didn't answer my letters or phone calls (nor did it, apparently, file requested information with the federal Office of Consumer Affairs). But you may find the agency more responsive than I did, so it's probably worth dropping them a line. This is especially true since you probably won't be spending any time writing city and county agencies. There are no consumer-protection agencies as such on the city level in Oklahoma. And there's only one county agency—the **District Attorney for LeFlore County, County Courthouse, Poteau, Okla. 74953.**

The complaints that prompt Oklahomans to write most often to the Attorney General's office are about (1) auto repairs and sales, (2) home furnishings, (3) home improvements and repairs, (4) mail-order houses, (5) mobile homes, (6) credit problems, (7) publications, (8) television, radio, and stereo, (9) real estate, and (10) landlord-tenant problems. You'll find specific advice for dealing with each of these complaint categories, by the way, in Part III.

The problem is that, no matter how diligently state agencies try to help you with these problems, they're at a disadvantage in Oklahoma compared with many other states. And that goes back to those "honorable members of the Oklahoma legislature" who just haven't passed too much in the way of significant consumer-protection legislation.

A few examples should illustrate the point. The legislature has given the Attorney General's office the power to prosecute businesses that gouge consumers, but no official powers to mediate for the redress of individual consumers' grievances. You might think that means consumers would be forced to go to court on their own behalf. But if they do, they're handicapped, because Oklahoma is one of twelve states where individuals aren't authorized to bring suit under the state Unfair and Deceptive Trade Practices Act.

While some states have passed laws encouraging advertising and price competition among pharmacies, Oklahoma still lets its state Board of Pharmacy prohibit advertising and discourage even the quotation of drug prices over the phone. While some states have passed laws requiring minimum warranties on mobile homes and limiting the powers of mobile-home park landlords, Oklahoma hasn't. In fact, it only recently became one of the forty-six states that have construction standards for mobile homes.

One area where Oklahoma is ahead of most states is in its institution of a revolving fund for antitrust enforcement. This means that, whenever a business is found guilty of a price-fixing or monopolistic offense, a portion of the penalty it pays will go into a special fund. That fund is used to finance future antitrust prosecutions.

Most consumers would applaud that step. But preventing price-fixing and encouraging competition are only partial steps toward the maintenance of a fair market place. Until Oklahoma takes more steps, consumers there will need both persistence and imagination to defend their rights.

Oregon

Oregon has a wealth of consumer-protection legislation, and two state agencies to help you see that it's enforced. Most of the legal powers are vested in the **Consumer Protection Division, Office of Attorney General, 1133 S.W. Market St., Portland, Ore. 97201.** The CPD, as we'll call it for short, successfully prosecutes about 63 per cent of the cases it gets. In many of the remaining cases, the complaint the CPD received wasn't really valid in the first place. But restitution to the consumer occurs in only about 29 per cent of the cases. The **Consumer Services Division, Department of Commerce, Salem, Ore. 97310,** is specifically charged with helping consumers get restitution: It gets directly involved in mediating many disputes.

When you have a complaint, it makes sense to write both agencies. Their powers complement each other; and by writing to both, you'll also be increasing the pressure on your corporate adversary to reach a fair settlement.

Some complaints, of course, should go to specialized agencies. The Consumer Services Division publishes a leaflet called *Where to Go for a Specific Complaint*. Single copies are free to state residents. So take a moment right now to send for it. It may save you a lot of trouble some day. While you're at it, you may also want to request the agency's latest listing of consumer-oriented documents available from state and federal sources.

When you do launch a complaint, there's a pretty good chance it will fall into one of the ten areas that bother Oregon consumers the most: (1) auto repairs or sales, (2) advertising, (3) gasoline sales, (4) mobile homes, (5) magazines, (6) food, (7) appliances, (8) records and tapes, (9) clothing, and (10) landlord-tenant problems. You'll find advice on dealing with most of these problem areas in Part III.

There are also a few specific state laws it may help you to be aware of. With regard to gasoline sales, for example, the CPD has promulgated a rule prohibiting the tie-in of gasoline sales with the sale of other goods or services. The rule applies only to gas stations. Your local hamburger joint can still give you free gas as an inducement to buy a hamburger if it wants to. Gas stations may still offer premiums, but it can't require you to buy any other goods or services as a condition for getting gas. This rule becomes especially important during gasoline shortages, of course.

In the realm of advertising the CPD has conducted an innovative program in cooperation with the state's newspapers. Whenever a paper gets a "business opportunity" ad that seems a little bit fishy to it, it's asked to forward a copy of the ad to the CPD. The CPD then writes the business that placed the ad and asks it to furnish the names and addresses of corporate officers, a financial statement, and other relevant documents. If the business doesn't respond, the CPD lets the newspaper know, and the newspaper usually responds by refusing to run the ad thereafter.

On the mobile-home front, the state requires the licensing of mobile-home dealers. But it has not gone as far as some states in protecting mobile-home dwellers. It hasn't passed a law spelling out the rights of tenants in mobile-home parks, and it hasn't set up any standards for compulsory warranties on the homes.

In terms of tenant protection, Oregon lags behind the most progressive states, but it is ahead of most. The state passed a watered-down version of the Uniform Residential Landlord-Tenant Act. Tenants' rights to make needed repairs and deduct the cost from rent were deleted in the Oregon version of the act. But other key tenant protections were put through. These include a ban on retaliatory eviction (in response to a tenant complaint about the landlord to a government body, or to a tenant's joining a tenants' group); limitations on how long a landlord may keep a tenant's security deposit; and establishment of the principle that a tenant's obligation to pay rent is dependent on the landlord's maintaining the building in livable condition.

It's worth noting some complaints that didn't make the list of the top ten in Oregon. One is credit problems—which happened to be eleventh but ranks much higher in most states. The fact that debt collectors are regulated in Oregon probably has something to do with that. Similarly, radio and television repair complaints rank relatively low. They're handled by a separate agency, the Television Service Advisory Board, which is part of the Department of Commerce (same address as the Consumer Services Division).

In 1974 the state legislature determined that "vast tracts of marginal and submarginal lands in Oregon and other states" were being "subdivided and sold to the public as investments and potential residential and commercial property." The legislature also found that such practices were largely uncontrolled in Oregon at the time. To remedy the situation, it required that all sellers of subdivided land file extensive information with the state Commissioner of Real Estate. From this information, the Commissioner compiles* a public report, which must be furnished to prospective buyers before they actually sign a contract. Misleading and deceptive acts by land sellers were made punishable by fines up to $10,000 and jail terms up to three years. These protections are administered by the Real Estate Division of the Department of Commerce (same address again).

In Oregon, as in most states, utility problems are the province of the Public Utility Commission (PUC). But the PUC in Oregon has promulgated some unusually strong consumer-protection regulations. For example, if a utility requires you to post a security deposit, it must pay you 6 per cent a year in interest on it. What's

---

* In practice, the report on some out-of-state lands may be compiled by state officials in that state, who in effect trade reports with Oregon officials.

more, it must refund the deposit immediately when you discontinue service or when you've gone through twelve consecutive billing periods without having been late in payment more than twice. If a utility wants to shut off your service, it must give you five days' notice, along with notification that the consumer can appeal to the PUC. All bills must contain enough information so that you can see how they were computed. If a bill involves a meter reading, you have a right to request a check on the accuracy of the meter—and to get one within ten days! If you make this request more often than once a year, you can be charged for it. But if a check reveals that your meter really was wrong by more than 2 per cent, you can get a refund of the fee. And if the meter was off, you're entitled to an adjustment—of your bill, not just the meter.

Other examples of progressive state laws and regulations could be cited, but I think the point is made. Your job as a consumer is simply to inform yourself of the rights available, to use those rights intelligently, and to find the right person to complain to when necessary.

In addition to the state agencies already mentioned here, and the ones in that leaflet you've already sent away for (right?), there are two county agencies that may be of help to you if you live within their jurisdiction or have quarrels with businesses that do.

They are the **Consumer Protection Service, Jackson County Office of District Attorney, County Courthouse, Medford, Ore. 97501;** and the **Consumer Protection Department, Multnomah County Office of District Attorney, 600 County Courthouse, Portland, Ore. 97204.**

Pennsylvania

See if you detect a correlation among these three items:

Item one: Whenever a welfare recipient in Pennsylvania gets a public assistance check in the mail, he's likely to find inside a card containing some consumer tips.

Item two: The standard complaint form of the main state consumer agency in Pennsylvania is available in Spanish as well as English.

Item three: After 5 P.M., when the branch offices of the state consumer-protection agency close, calls to those branches are automatically put through at no extra charge to the central Harrisburg office, which remains open until 9 P.M.

To me, those three items all bespeak the actions of an agency that is innovative, intelligent, and making a genuine effort to increase its availability to the people it is meant to serve. That agency is the **Bureau of Consumer Protection, Office of Attorney General, 23A South Third St., Harrisburg, Pa. 17101.** By this praise I certainly don't mean to imply that the agency is perfect. Far from it. Its rate of successful resolutions on complaints is probably between 50 and 75 per cent, by estimate of its director, Joel Weisberg. The average waiting time for a consumer needing help is probably longer than it should be (Weisberg said there were "no figures available" to tell what that average wait might be). And the Bureau probably never even hears about some complaints that it *would* receive if it had a toll-free telephone number for consumers to call. All these faults aside, the agency is well worth using. You can send complaints to the bureau's main office, at the address above, or to any of the eight branch offices scattered around the state. (Addresses of the branch offices appear on page 150). If you don't live near Harrisburg, using a branch office may increase your chances of having in-person or telephone contact with someone handling your case.

While the bureau is the main complaint agency for the state, complaints regarding food should be to the **Division of Consumer Affairs, Department of Agriculture.** Its main office is at **2301 W. Cameron St., Harrisburg, Pa. 17120.** And it has seven branch offices around the state, in Meadville, Linden, Tunkhannock, Evans City, Altoona, Summerdale, and Lansdale. Check your phone book for addresses and phone numbers.

There are also local consumer-protection agencies in no fewer than seven counties and three cities. These are listed on pages 150–51. This means that, if you happen to live in Philadelphia or Pittsburgh, for example, or have a quarrel with a business there, you could seek help from a city agency, a county agency, a state agency, or all three. One caveat: The city agencies seem to me quite understaffed compared to the potential demand for their services. This seems less true of the county agencies, in general.

Statewide, the complaints that are most likely to send Pennsylvanians scrambling for a sharp pen are about (1) auto repairs and sales, (2) home improvement and repair contractors, (3) records and tapes, (4) miscellaneous store purchases, (5) television, radio, and stereo, (6) clothing, (7) furniture, (8) appliances, (9) books and magazines, (10) landlord-tenant problems. You'll find advice on coping with most of these problem areas, by the way, in Part III of this book.

A couple of notes should be made about that top ten complaint list. First, the tally was kept by the Bureau of Consumer Protection, which in 1974 received 3,500 complaints on category number one (autos), and 750 complaints on category number ten (landlord-tenant). The records and tapes category, which accounted for 1,200 complaints, probably included a great many complaints from out-of-state residents about record clubs headquartered in the state. In particular, the bureau stated in 1974 that it had received hundreds of complaints about the Record Club of America, many of them to the effect that prepaid merchandise was not received months after it was ordered. In August 1974 the bureau announced that the club, while admitting no wrongdoing, had agreed in the future to offer its members a refund, credit, or alternate selection if it couldn't fill an order within thirty days.

In the realm of landlord-tenant problems, Pennsylvania tenants should be aware that state statutes give them more rights than are enjoyed by tenants in a vast majority of states. For example, a legal rent strike procedure exists in Pennsylvania. This remedy, however, is best used in consultation with a lawyer, a tenants' association, or both.

Though door-to-door sales do not rank among the top complaints in the state, they should be mentioned here because of a peculiarity in Pennsylvania law. Like many states, Pennsylvania provides a three-day cooling-off period during which you can change your mind about an item you bought from a door-to-door salesman. The purchase (most purchases over $25, that is) can be canceled by writing the seller within three business days of the time of the sale. The peculiarity is this: Pennsylvania law does not require the seller to tell you about the cooling-off period. You have to know about it yourself. If you decide to use this law, by the way, it would be wise to keep a carbon of your letter and to send the original by certified mail, return receipt requested.

Speaking of mail, here's a list of addresses you might be needing. First, the branch offices of the Bureau of Consumer Protection:

- 133 N. Fifth St., Allentown, Pa. 18102
- 919 State St., Erie, Pa. 16501
- 25 South Third St., Harrisburg, Pa. 17101
- 342–44 N. Broad St., Philadelphia, Pa. 19102
- 300 Liberty Ave., Pittsburgh, Pa. 15222
- 1835 Centre Ave., Pittsburgh, Pa. 15219
- 129 North Washington Ave., Scranton, Pa. 18503
- 36 North Main St., Wilkes-Barre, Pa. 18701

Here are the names and addresses of the seven county consumer-protection agencies:

- Allegheny County Bureau of Consumer Affairs, Jones Law Building, 12th floor, Fourth and Ross Streets, Pittsburgh, Pa. 15219
- Bucks County Department of Consumer Protection, Administration Annex, Broad and Union Streets, Doylestown, Pa. 18901
- Delaware County Office of Public Information, Toal Building, Second and Orange Streets, Media, Pa. 19063
- Lackawanna County Department of Transportation, Environmental and Consumer Affairs, News Building, 8th floor, Scranton, Pa. 18503
- Consumer Protection Commission, Lancaster County District Attorney's Office, County Courthouse, Lancaster, Pa. 17602 (staffed entirely by volunteers)
- Montgomery County Department of Consumer Affairs, County Courthouse, Norristown, Pa. 19404

- Economic Crimes Unit, Philadelphia County Office of District Attorney, No. 5 Penn Center Plaza, 22d Floor, Sixteenth and Market Streets, Philadelphia, Pa. 19103

And here are the names and addresses of the three city consumer-protection agencies:

- Monessen Bureau of Consumer Affairs, Municipal Building, Third and Donner, Monessen, Pa. 15062
- Mayor's Office of Consumer Services, City Hall, Room 143, Philadelphia, Pa. 19107
- City Office of Consumer Advocate, City-County Building, Room 517, Pittsburgh, Pa. 15219

Rhode Island

The ten categories of complaints that the Attorney General's office in Rhode Island receives most often are (1) automobile repairs and sales, (2) home repairs and improvements, (3) swimming pools, (4) asphalt paving companies, (5) appliances, (6) mail-order houses, (7) finance companies, (8) real estate, (9) insurance, and (10) travel problems. While the top of the list stays fairly constant, the bottom is in flux. Moving companies and carpeting, for example, sometimes edge their way into the top ten. A large number of complaints are also received about utilities. You'll find specific advice for dealing with most of these complaint categories in Part III.

On most of these complaints, and most others, there are two state agencies you can turn to for aid. One is the **Consumer Affairs Division, Office of the Attorney General, 250 Benefit St., Providence, R.I. 02903.** It claims to handle the average complaint within a week and to resolve 90 per cent of its cases successfully. That doesn't mean there's a 90 per cent chance you'll get your money back, but it does suggest the agency is well worth using. The second recourse agency is the **Rhode Island Consumers' Council, 365 Broadway, Providence, R.I. 02902.** It doesn't have some of the legal powers that the Attorney General's office has, but it can often solve complaints through voluntary mediation.

If your complaint concerns a utility, you'd probably do best to take it straight to the Rhode Island Public Utilities Commission, 169 Weybosset St., Providence, Rhode Island 02903. You'll notice that all of your recourse agencies are in Providence. There are no branch offices and no consumer-protection agencies as such on the city or county level. That's not as bad as it might sound, though. After all, every place in the state is within 50 miles of Providence.

In the number one complaint field—autos—the state has recently passed a couple of pieces of legislation that may come in handy for you. One attempts to increase your chances of getting decent warranty repair work done by requiring manufacturers to reimburse dealers fairly for warranty repairs. Another regulates auto body shops. Any chicanery you run into in a body shop should be reported to the Automobile Body Repair Shop Commission, a newly formed entity with the power to revoke any shop's license. The five-member commission (which consists of two representatives of the body-shop industry, one representative of the insurance industry, one representative of the public, and one representative of the Department of Business Regulation) will also have the power to arbitrate disputes between body shops and insurance companies. This could help keep you from getting involved in a squeeze where you have to use the repair shop your insurance company suggests or else end up paying a big slice of the bill yourself at a shop of your choice.

Another useful law to know about in Rhode Island concerns merchandise you order at a store, to be delivered later. If the store doesn't make good on delivery within thirty days, it must inform you of your right to a full refund. Or, if you prefer, you can negotiate a new delivery date, select new goods, or take a credit to your account in lieu of a refund. The important thing is that the choice is yours.

And, while we're at it, here's one more tip. If you have a mortgage or similar loan and want to pay it back early, state law requires the seller to let you; he can't charge you an interest penalty for prepayment. In fact, if yours was one of those long-term contracts where most of the interest is paid at the beginning, you may even be entitled to a partial refund.

South Carolina

There's a new agency in charge of handling consumer complaints in South Carolina. Perhaps the best thing about it is that it's easy to reach. Pick up the phone and dial **800-922-1594.** Your call goes through toll-free. When you have occasion to write, it's the **Department of Consumer Affairs, 600 Columbia Building, P.O. Box 11739, Columbia, S.C. 29211.** If you have occasion to visit, the Columbia Building is at 1200 Main St.

It's difficult to say exactly what kind of results you'll achieve. The agency is new enough so that its record so far may not be too revealing. From the time it started functioning in November 1974 through June 1975, it had received some 1,371 complaints. Of these, it had resolved 633. According to Stephen A. Graham, a complaint analyst, "Not all of these have been resolved to the satisfaction of the consumer, but many of them have." Most complaints, Graham said, are processed within a week of the time they're received.

The complaints received most often are related to (1) auto repairs and sales, (2) mobile homes, (3) mail-order houses, (4) home repairs and improvements, (5) appliances, television, and radio, (6) home furnishings, (7) finance and loan companies, (8) repair shops and rental shops, (9) advertising, and (10) credit billing. You'll find specific advice for dealing with most of these types of complaints in Part III of this book.

Perhaps in response to the many complaints received about mobile homes, South Carolina has passed laws regulating both manufacturers and dealers. These laws are administered by the South Carolina Manufactured Housing Board.

If your complaint seems to call for prosecution or other legal action, the Department of Consumer Affairs will probably turn it over to the Assistant Attorney General for Consumer Protection,

Office of Attorney General, Hampton Office Building, P.O. Box 11549, Columbia, S.C. 29211. The Attorney General's office is no longer soliciting complaints from individual consumers, however.

One other agency in the state may be of use to you, not so much in handling particular complaints as in providing you with information or letting you have a voice in political decisions that affect consumers. It's the **Office of Citizens Service, Office of Governor, State House, P.O. Box 11450, Columbia, S.C. 29211.**

South Dakota

In 1974 all of the consumer-protection functions of the South Dakota state government were transferred to a new agency, the Department of Commerce and Consumer Affairs. It's a little early to predict how successful the new agency will be. Its secretary, James V. Guffey, says, "Every case is resolved to some extent, be it in the form of completely solving the case or advising the consumer to seek private counsel." He could not offer a percentage figure on cases successfully resolved. In response to my question about the average waiting time for consumers needing help, Guffey wrote, "We attempt to answer each consumer within 24 hours. This is our goal, and we endeavor to meet this type of schedule in every circumstance."

To make contact with the agency, write **Division of Consumer Protection, Department of Commerce and Consumer Affairs, State Capitol, Pierre, S.D. 57501.** There's also a branch office at **Courthouse Plaza, Suite 2, Sioux Falls, S.D. 57102.** The agency began operations with a staff of five people and an annual budget of $62,000, though of course those figures are subject to change.

In its early months of operation, the complaints received most often by the department concerned (1) mail-order houses, (2) retail stores, (3) mobile homes, (4) home repairs and improvements, (5) auto repairs and sales, (6) credit, (7) miscellaneous, and (8) housing and real estate. You'll find advice on dealing with each of these areas in Part III.

Members of a number of professions and occupations (including mobile-home dealers) are licensed in South Dakota. You can find the appropriate licensing board through the Department of Commerce and Consumer Affairs, which supervises all twenty of them.

One specialized agency worth noting is the South Dakota Real Estate Commission, which supervises the sale of subdivided land. In case you're thinking of buying some land or have bought some recently, there's a state law you should be aware of. It provides that, if you buy land without seeing it and then, within four months of the sale, go to look at it and are horrified, you can cancel the purchase. You must make your demand for cancellation within twenty days of the time you view the property. This admirable measure parallels the "cooling-off period" for door-to-door sales now common in many states. However, this is one instance where you should feel more than a bit embarrassed if you have to take advantage of the law. It's better to hold from the beginning to the adage, "If a piece of land is worth buying, it's worth traveling to see."

As it happens, South Dakota also has a cooling-off period for door-to-door sales. You can cancel most purchases from a door-to-door salesman within three days if you think better of it by sending the business notice in writing (best send it certified mail, return receipt requested, keeping a carbon for yourself). As in many states, the law applies to most purchases over $25. But there are two unusual features to South Dakota's law. You have to know about it yourself, since the salesman isn't obliged to tell you. And the three-day limit extends to fifteen days in the case of home study, correspondence, trade school, or self-improvement courses.

Tennessee

"The state of Tennessee," a state official wrote me rather plaintively, "is the only state in the union that does not have consumer-protection legislation. The only thing we can really do is try to help as best we can." The official, Trudy L. Smith, is Consumer Protection Coordinator in the state's Office of the Attorney General, which receives about 500 consumer complaints a year. She estimates that the agency successfully resolves about 20 per cent of those cases. The average waiting time for a consumer seeking help is three to four weeks.

William C. Koch, the Assistant Attorney General in charge of consumer complaint handling, described Tennessee as "the only state in the union without a state-level consumer-protection office." His office, he said, is working with state legislators on a bill to set up such an agency, but "the earliest date for passage would be sometime in the spring of 1976."

Actually, these two officials may be overstating the case—ever so slightly. As their comments bear witness, the Attorney General's office *is,* in effect, a consumer-protection agency. It lacks only the name—and an Unfair and Deceptive Trade Practices Act to enforce. Tennessee is not quite the only state without such an Act: Alabama also lacks one. But Alabama does have a separate agency devoted specifically to consumer protection.

Until Tennessee does pass a basic consumer-protection bill, the powers of state government to help you are limited. But there are two state agencies that stand ready to try. The **Office of the Attorney General** is located in the **Supreme Court Building, Room 419, Nashville, Tenn. 37219.** And there's also the **Division of Consumer Affairs, Tennessee Department of Agriculture, P.O. Box 40627, Melrose Station, Nashville, Tenn. 37204,** which serves as a clearinghouse for complaints. The Department of Agriculture even has a toll-free number to call with complaints: **800-342-8385.** Though it lacks legal powers to help you, the Department will see that your problem reaches the right cranny in the state government structure. And it may be able to nudge a merchant toward an accommodation through goodwill and voluntary mediation.

Most of the complaints received by the Attorney General's office in 1974 fell into these five categories: (1) vacation giveaways, (2) mail-order houses, (3) home repairs and improvements, (4) songwriting companies, and (5) auto repairs and sales. You'll find specific advice for dealing with most of these areas in Part III.

Now for a couple of tidbits of good news. While you have little protection in many areas, you have a lot if you're discriminated against in the realm of credit on the grounds of sex or marital status. You can go to court, and if you win the minimum award to you (penalty to the business) is $100. The maximum is $1,000. And the creditor who discriminated against you must pay your attorney's fees and the court costs. In this particular area, class action suits are also legal.

The other tidbit of good news concerns a handy little cardboard device that can help you compare unit prices (in this case, price per ounce) of different items when you're shopping. The device is called "The Comparison Shopper," and at last report you could get one free by writing the Department of Agriculture at the address above.

Texas

Consumer protection throughout Texas isn't bad. But if you must get cheated, try to do it in Dallas. Consumer protection there is truly superior.

In all, there are eleven broad-gauge consumer-protection agencies in the state. Two are statewide, five are county agencies (serving nine counties), and four are city agencies. The backbone of protection throughout the state is the **Antitrust and Consumer Protection Division, Office of Attorney General, P.O. Box 12548, Capitol Station, Austin, Tex. 78711.** The stream of complaints it handles probably adds up to about 10,000 a year. The agency estimates that it successfully resolves about 75 per cent of these cases and that the average waiting time for a consumer needing help is about four weeks.

Besides the main office in Austin, the Antitrust and Consumer Protection Division maintains six branch offices around the state. Using them may increase your chances of personal or telephone contact with the person handling your case. (Addresses of the branch offices are given on page 161.)

The second statewide agency that may be able to help you with a complaint is the **Consumer Affairs Office, Department of Agriculture, 113 San Jacinto Boulevard, Austin, Tex. 78701.** It doesn't have the strong legal powers of the Attorney General's office, but it can often win you a settlement through voluntary mediation.

Statewide, the problems that most often trouble Texans fall into these categories: (1) auto repairs and sales, (2) landlord-tenant relations, (3) home improvements and repairs, (4) distributorships, (5) radio, television, records, and stereo, (6) credit problems, (7) mail-order houses, (8) mobile homes, (9) general merchandising, and (10) insurance. You'll find suggestions for dealing with most of these problem areas in Part III.

A couple of these categories have specialized agencies to deal with them. For credit problems, contact the **Office of Consumer Credit, 1011 San Jacinto Boulevard, P.O. Box 2107, Austin, Tex. 78767.** Insurance problems go to the **State Board of Insurance, State Insurance Building, 1110 San Jacinto Boulevard, Austin, Tex. 78786.**

In general, the statewide agencies seem to be doing a good job administratively. But they are somewhat hampered by the legislative climate, which isn't among the most progressive when it comes to consumer-oriented legislation. In Dallas the situation is different. The city has passed a variety of tough and imaginative consumer-protection measures.

Take that constant consumer nemesis, auto repairs. In Dallas you must be given an estimate of repair costs before any repairs are made. The actual costs can't exceed the estimate by more than $10 or 10 per cent (whichever is larger). If you leave your car with a repair shop and the shop can't give you an estimate right then, it must give you an itemized schedule of any charges you may be liable for. These include the fee for making an estimate, if any; the charge for releasing your vehicle to you in a disassembled state if it is not repaired; the charge for putting your car back together if it is not repaired; storage charges; towing charges; and any other charges you might incur. You are not liable for any costs except those specified on this schedule, until you are given an estimate and authorize the shop to go ahead.

Take another common problem, electronic repairs. This would include repairs on the items in category (5), such as TVs and stereos. The Dallas electronic repairs ordinance runs parallel to the auto repair ordinance. Electronic repair shops, like auto repair shops, must be licensed by the City Department of Consumer Affairs. They must give estimates before any repairs are done. If you leave, say, a radio or television at a repair shop, and the shop can't give you an estimate right then, it must give you a list of possible charges. These include service charges; pickup and delivery charges; charges for making an estimate; storage charges; charge for restoring the equipment to its original condition in the event it's not repaired; hourly labor charge or flat labor charge; and any other charges you may incur, except for parts. Again, you're not liable for any charges other than those on this list until you actually get the total estimate and authorize the shop to go ahead. And again, the actual charges can't run more than 10 per cent over the estimate. Similar rules apply to electronic equipment repairs made in your home.

Take one more area—door-to-door sales. If you don't want to be disturbed by salesmen, you can place a sign on or near your front door saying "No Solicitors." The sign should be weatherproof, and at least three inches by four inches. It's illegal in Dallas for door-to-door salesmen to disturb you if you post such a sign. And even if you don't have a sign, it's illegal for them to come knocking before 9 A.M., after 9 P.M., or on New Years, July 4, Labor Day, Thanksgiving, or Christmas. If you buy something from a door-to-door salesman but later regret it, you can cancel the sale by notifying the company in writing within three business days. That three-day cooling-off period isn't unusual as a matter of state law. In fact, Texas as a whole has such a law. But Texas's law, like most state statutes, applies only to purchases over $25. The Dallas door-to-door ordinance applies to most contracts over $5.

These ordinances and others like them are enforced by an agency that is alert, active, and aggressive. It's the **City Department of Consumer Affairs, City Hall, Room 108, Dallas, Tex. 75201.** One example of its approach is a leaflet it passes out. "Who cares if you gets cheated?" the leaflet asks, and answers in bold type, "We do!" It goes on to say, "Consumer Affairs will handle your consumer complaint by telephone at (214) 744-1133.

You will not be required to come to City Hall in person or file a written complaint." To my way of thinking, this shows that someone has finally realized that much business in the final quarter of the twentieth century gets done on the phone or not at all. Also impressive is what you see when you flip the leaflet over. Its entire message is repeated in Spanish.

The Dallas agency has another thing going for it: cold cash. Its annual budget is around $505,000, enough to support a staff of forty-three. That means the city agency is roughly equivalent in cash and staff to the Antitrust and Consumer Protection Division, which serves the whole state. And the Dallas agency is drawing complaints at the rate of 12,000 a year. That's a higher complaint total than I estimate the Attorney General's office handles. This demonstrates once more the truth that a successful agency seems to draw complaints out of the woodwork. People who once wouldn't have thought of sticking up for their rights start to do so when it becomes a bit more convenient, and when they can see definite chances of success.

The other local agencies in Texas aren't as strong as Dallas's, but they may be a substantial help to you—particularly in resolving disputes with local merchants. The other three city agencies are:

- Consumer-Vendor Affairs Office, City Attorney's Office, Municipal Building, Austin, Tex. 78767
- Office of Consumer Affairs, City Department of Human Resources, 1800 University Drive, Room 218, Fort Worth, Tex. 76107
- Office of Consumer Services, City Department of Human Resources, Press Building, Suite 108, 600 Hemisfair Way, San Antonio, Tex. 78205

The five county offices and their addresses:

- Consumer Fraud Division, Bexar County Office of Criminal District Attorney, San Antonio, Tex. 78205
- Consumer Fraud Division, El Paso County Office of District Attorney, City-County Building, Room 401, El Paso, Tex. 79901 (this office also serves Culberson and Hudspeth counties)

- Consumer Fraud Division, Harris County Office of District Attorney, 301 San Jacinto Boulevard, Houston, Tex. 77002
- Consumer Fraud Division, Tarrant County Office of District Attorney, New Criminal Courts Building, 300 West Belknap St., Fort Worth, Tex. 76102
- County Office of District Attorney, County Courthouse, Box 171, Hempstead, Tex. 77423 (this office serves Waller, Austin, and Fayette counties)

The branch offices of the statewide Antitrust and Consumer Protection Division are located at

- 2405 Cedar Springs, Suite 155, Dallas, Tex. 75201
- City-County Building, El Paso, Tex. 79901
- Consumer Center, 201 E. Belknap St., Fort Worth, Tex. 76102
- 369 One Main Plaza, Houston, Tex. 77002
- 806 Broadway, Lubbock, Tex. 79401
- 100 Dwyer Ave., San Antonio, Tex. 78204

Utah

In 1974 the complaint most often received by the Utah Attorney General's office dealt with the purchase of silver. A major investigation was undertaken, and at least one company was sued by the state after 351 people complained that they thought they'd been bilked on purchases of the precious metal.

After silver, the complaint heard most often concerned money-making schemes, which usually took the form of pyramid plans. In principle, these schemes resemble the old-fashioned chain letter: Those who get in early can make money, but everyone else gets gypped. With a pyramid plan, you usually sign up as a "distributor" for a product (it hardly matters what the product is), and you're supposed to make most of your money, not by selling the product, but by recruiting "subdistributors." In practice, you usually wind up with a heavy financial loss (since you pay for the privilege of being a distributor and for a big supply of merchandise). You also usually wind up with a big pile of unsold wares.

After silver purchases and pyramid plans, the leading areas of consumer complaints were (3) health spas, (4) real estate and land development schemes, (5) automobile dealers, new and used, (6) deceptive advertising, (7) auto repairs, (8) mail-order houses, (9) vocational schools, including modeling schools, and (10) door-to-door sales, particularly of magazines, photos, and cookware.

Utah does have a law concerning door-to-door sales, but it gives you only partial protection. If you buy something *on credit* from a door-to-door salesman and later decide you made a mistake, you can cancel the sale by sending notice to the company in writing within three business days. It's advisable to keep a carbon of your letter and to send the original by certified mail, return receipt requested. There's a small penalty for canceling out, but it's worth it, compared to the cost of buying an item you really didn't need in the first place.

You'll find advice on dealing with each of the ten problem areas mentioned above in the Part III of this book. If you want help from a state agency, there are three to choose from. On problems in any way involving credit, write to the **Uniform Credit Code Office, Department of Financial Institutions, 10 West Broadway, Suite 331, Salt Lake City, Utah 84101.**

For other problems, you can write either or both of two agencies: the **Division of Consumer Affairs, Trade Commission, Department of Business Regulation, 330 East Fourth South, Salt Lake City, Utah 84111**; and the **Consumer Protection Division, Office of Attorney General, 236 State Capitol, Salt Lake City, Utah 84114.** Both agencies have good legal powers to help you, although Utah has less on the books in the consumer-protection field than many states do. The Consumer Protection Division estimates that it successfully resolves 55 per cent of the complaints it gets and that the average waiting time for a consumer needing help is three weeks.

One more remedy you might want to consider in some situations is a class action suit, that is, a lawsuit in which you join together with other people as plaintiffs. Utah is one of the eighteen states that currently allow class actions, though it puts limits on their use. The advantages of a class action suit include the pooling of information about the abuses encountered and the pooling of funds to hire a lawyer to conduct your case in the most effective way possible. If you win in court, there's a chance that you'll get back some or all of your attorney's fees as part of the award.

Vermont

Mail-order houses give Vermont consumers more headaches than any other single consumer problem, according to the tally kept by the state Attorney General's office. In 1974 there were 190 complaints about mail order houses, 125 about motor vehicle repairs, and 105 about home improvements or repairs. Appliances and furniture also accounted for a sizable number of complaints. You'll find advice for coping with each of these types of problems in Part III of this book.

Despite its conservative reputation, Vermont has some innovative consumer-protection measures on the books. If you buy a used car, for example, the dealer is required to give you the name and address of the previous owner, should you request it. He also must give you a written statement telling you whether the mileage shown on the car's odometer is correct or not. Naturally, the statement almost always says the odometer reading is right. But the Attorney General's office believes odometer tinkering is still widespread in Vermont. In 1974 it sued three used-car dealers for alleged tampering and was investigating several others.

Another law provides that a store can't make you pay an overdue charge unless it's disclosed in advance. Many stores were charging 1 per cent or 1.5 per cent of the total bill as the monthly fee for late payment. But state officials ruled that in many cases such fees violated the state interest ceiling of 8.5 per cent a year. (One per cent a month, of course, is 12 per cent a year. The 8.5 per cent ceiling doesn't apply, however, to charge accounts, formal installment contracts, motor vehicle purchases, and purchases of income-producing items.)

Like most states, Vermont provides a three-day cooling-off period for door-to-door sales. You can cancel a purchase by sending written notification to the seller within three business days. But Vermont's law is unusually good in that it applies to most purchases of more than $5.

Despite such protections, you're bound to run into a problem sometime that requires outside help. The basic consumer-protection agency for the state is the **Consumer Fraud Division, Office of the Attorney General, 200 Main St., P.O. Box 981, Burlington, Vt. 05401.** It says it's able to resolve successfully about 60 to 70 per cent of the complaints it receives. The average waiting time for a consumer needing help is said to be only one week.

If you live in Chittenden County, or if your ill-fated transaction took place there, you may be able to get some help from the Economic Crime Division, Chittenden County State's Attorney's Office, 39 Pearl St., P.O. Box 27, Burlington, Vt. 05401. For complaints involving radio or TV repairs, you may want to contact the Radio and Television Technicians Licensing Board, c/o the Licensing and Registration Division, Office of the Secretary of State, Admans Building, Montpelier, Vt. 05602.

Virginia

Virginia has recently reshuffled its government agencies in an attempt to handle consumer complaints efficiently. Its legislature has also been entertaining proposals to require the licensing and regulation of auto repair shops, electronics repairmen (especially radio and television repairmen), and debt collection agencies.

This book catches the Old Dominion with its agencies newly shuffled and its regulation proposals in midair. You can see how things turn out by watching the newspapers or by inquiring of the two agencies that now bear the chief responsibility for consumer protection in the state. One of them—the one you should go to first with most complaints—is the **Office of Consumer Affairs, Department of Agriculture and Commerce, 825 East Broad St., Richmond, Va. 23219.** If you're complaining because you think you've been mistreated by a state agency, you can call the Office of Consumer Affairs on a special toll-free hot line: **800-552-9963.** Otherwise, you can write or use the regular phone number listed in the directory. The Office of Consumer Affairs also has a branch office, at **8301 Arlington Boulevard, Fairfax, Va. 22030.**

The other agency to watch is the recently created State Commission for Professional and Occupational Regulation. It has drawn up proposals for the licensing of the businesses mentioned above plus some others. And if those proposals go through the state legislature, this agency will be the one granting, suspending, or revoking the licenses. It has made public its plans for requiring auto repair shops to give customers carefully itemized bills, to carry liability insurance, and to give written estimates in advance whenever the customer so requests.

The Office of Consumer Affairs reports that so far it is resolving successfully "over 50 per cent of all complaints" that it receives. It was unable to provide an estimate of the average time a consumer has to wait for resolution of a complaint. Before the office gets involved, it tells consumers to contact not only the merchant involved in the transaction but also the manufacturer, when there is one. It prefers to work from written complaints rather than telephoned ones, and it has a standard complaint form to be "filled out, dated, and signed."

Complaints most frequently received by the Office of Consumer Affairs fall into these ten categories: (1) auto repairs and sales, (2) retail stores, (3) mail-order houses, (4) home repairs and improvements, (5) credit, (6) food, (7) utilities, (8) real estate, (9) television sets and other electronic appliances, and (10) landlord-tenant relations.

You'll find advice on coping with each of those ten complaint categories in Part III. But specific comments are in order about a few of them. Categories (1), (5), and (9) are directly affected by the pending regulation proposals. Utilities complaints are probably best taken straight to the **Virginia State Corporation Commission, Blanton Building, P.O. Box 1197, Richmond, Va. 23209.** In the realm of landlord-tenant relations, tenants recently acquired a number of rights when Virginia adopted the Uniform Residential Landlord-Tenant Act. Among other things, Virginia tenants may now make needed repairs and deduct the cost from rent in certain circumstances. In general, the best way to assert your rights as a tenant is in conjunction with a tenants' association, a lawyer, or both.

Some other pieces of recent Virginia legislation merit mention. If you have a billing dispute with a creditor, he must respond to your protest of a bill within thirty days and resolve the dispute within ninety days. Otherwise, he forfeits all rights to the amount in dispute.

Like many states, Virginia allows you to cancel a door-to-door sale by notifying the seller in writing within three business days of the transaction. Virginia's law is a good one in that it applies to most sales in excess of $15, and there's no penalty to you for exercising your right of cancellation.

To inform Virginians of these and other rights, the Office of Consumer Affairs has prepared a series of fliers called *There Is a Law in Virginia*. Back issues of these may still be available.

Some further help to you in coping with the jungle of the market place may come from one of the three county and four city consumer-protection agencies scattered around the state. Some of these agencies may be especially effective in helping you resolve disputes with local merchants. The three county agencies serve Arlington, Fairfax, and Prince William counties, with the Fairfax County agency being particularly strong. Their addresses are as follows:

- Arlington County Office of Consumer Affairs, 2049 Fifteenth St., North Arlington, Va. 22201
- Fairfax County Department of Consumer Affairs, Erlich Building, Suite 402, 4031 University Drive, Fairfax, Va. 22030
- Prince William County Office of Consumer Affairs, Garfield Administration Building, 15920 Jefferson Davis Highway, Woodbridge, Va. 22191

The four city agencies serve Alexandria, Newport News, Norfolk, and Virginia Beach. Of these four, the Virginia Beach agency is the oldest, best funded, and best staffed. The addresses are:

- City Office of Consumer Affairs, City Hall, Room 104, 125 N. Royal St., Alexandria, Va. 22134

- City Office of Consumer Affairs, City Hall, 2400 Washington Ave., Newport News, Va. 23607
- Division of Consumer Protection, City Department of Community Improvement, City Hall Building, Room 804, Norfolk, Va. 23501
- City Bureau of Consumer Protection, Municipal Center, City Hall, Virginia Beach, Va. 23456

Washington

Next time you weary of this volume's deathless prose, do not turn on the TV or go to the bathroom. Instead, pick up your telephone. Dial **800-552-0700**. That's the toll-free line of the Consumer Protection and Antitrust Division of the state Attorney General's office. If there's a complaint that's been bothering you (of the consumer variety, that is), now's the time to unleash it. But even if you have no pending complaints, dial the number and ask for the *Consumer's Dozen Educator's Handbook*. It's a small volume that will give you a rundown on Washington's consumer laws and how you can use them.

That toll-free line comes in handy, but there may be times when you'll want to write the agency. Here's the address: **Consumer Protection and Antitrust Division, Office of Attorney General, 1266 Dexter Horton Building, 710 Second Ave., Seattle, Wash. 98104.** If you don't live near Seattle, you may maximize your chances of having personal or telephone contact with the person handling your complaint by using one of the three branch offices. They're at **Temple of Justice, Olympia, Wash. 98504; 1305 Old National Bank Building, Spokane, Wash. 99201;** and **116 South Ninth St., Tacoma, Wash. 98402.**

With three branch offices and a toll-free line, this consumer-protection agency would seem well on the way to being accessible and responsive. I hope it is, but I don't know, because it's one of the handful of state agencies that didn't return my questionnaire, despite two letters and two phone calls. The last time I called, a senior agency official said he would send the information right away, but he never did. This, I hope, is not at all predictive of the treatment you'll get when you go to the agency for help with a complaint. It had better not be, since the Consumer Protection and Antitrust Division is the basic complaint-handling agency for the state.

A second recourse agency handles primarily complaints and inquiries concerning food, agricultural products, and poison prevention. It's the **Office of Consumer Services, Department of Agriculture, 406 General Administration Building, Olympia, Wash. 98504.** There are branch offices in Seattle and Yakima.

If you live in Seattle, or if your unfortunate transaction took place there, you'd certainly be well advised to make use of the **City Department of Licenses and Consumer Affairs, Municipal Building, Room 102, 600 Fourth Ave., Seattle, Wash. 98115.** With a staff of fifteen, a budget well over $100,000, and fairly comprehensive legal powers, this agency should stand a good chance of being able to untangle a tangled transaction.

Two other local agencies might be of use. In King County, there's the **Fraud Division, King County Prosecutor's Office, C517 King County Courthouse, 516 Third Ave., Seattle, Wash. 98104.** And in the city of Everett, there's the **City Weights and Measures Department, City Hall, 3002 Wetmore Ave., Everett, Wash. 98201.**

The most common complaints in Washington, judging by reports filed by the Attorney General's office with the federal Office of Consumer Affairs, concern (1) mail-order houses, (2) retail stores, (3) auto repairs and sales, (4) landlord-tenant relations, (5) home repairs and improvements, (6) television, radio, and stereo equipment and repair, (7) medical treatment, and (8) mobile homes. Advice for grappling with each of these types of complaints will be found in Part III.

West Virginia

It would be an understatement to say that West Virginia is behind the times when it comes to consumer protection. On the other hand, it is probably a decade or two in advance of where it was only a couple of years ago.

In 1974 West Virginia became one of the last states to pass an Unfair and Deceptive Trade Practices Law and to designate a consumer-protection agency. The agency designated to handle most kinds of complaints is the **Consumer Protection Division, Office of Attorney General, State Capitol Building, Charleston, W.Va. 25305**. Since it started functioning in September 1974, the agency has attracted a real outpouring of complaints—close to 1,000 a month, according to its director, James S. Arnold. Speaking frankly, Arnold said, "Half the stuff we get in here to handle is bullshit. Particularly in the credit area, people have no concept of what their rights and obligations are." He figures, though, that his agency is able to reach a fair settlement in about 90 per cent of the cases, and that this means a consumer victory about 55 to 60 per cent of the time. The average waiting time for a consumer needing help, by the director's estimate, is about four weeks. However, "A couple of problem areas are very hairy and tend to take longer—especially those involving motor vehicles and mobile homes."

Complaints concerning the *safety* of mobile homes should go to the **Consumer Protection Division, Department of Labor, 1900 Washington St. East, Charleston, W.Va. 25305**. This agency has also been charged with handling a few other odd types of problems, involving weights and measures, and the safety of bedding and upholstery. Complaints concerning food and agricultural products should go to the **Consumer Protection Division, Department of Agriculture, State Capitol, Room E-111, Charleston, W.Va. 25305**.

Those agencies are pretty much the ballgame, and as you can see, the ballgame is pretty much played in Charleston. There are no branch offices. There are no county offices. There is one city office of consumer protection, but it too happens to be in Charleston, and its staff and budget are tiny. That's the **City Consumer Protection Department, P.O. Box 2749, Charleston, W.Va. 25330**.

The six categories that are most likely to produce complaints from West Virginians, according to Arnold, are the following:

(1) home improvements and repairs, (2) auto repairs and sales, (3 and 4) tie between mail-order houses and mobile homes, (5) credit problems, excluding debt collection, and (6) debt collection. You'll find advice on coping with each of these problems in Part III.

Construction standards were just passed for mobile homes in 1974 (those are the ones the Department of Labor enforces), which enabled West Virginia to join the list of forty-six states that have such standards. But mobile-home dwellers here are still without any of the protections enjoyed by their counterparts in some other states, such as licensing of mobile-home dealers and manufacturers, laws requiring certain minimum warranties on mobile homes, and laws spelling out the limits to the power of mobile-home park landlords. The plight of mobile-home dwellers is thus emblematic of the situation of consumers in general in this state. They've made a little progress, but there's a long way to go.

Wisconsin

Wisconsin has an arrangement that exists in no other state that I know of. Some eight state agencies that receive consumer complaints of one kind or another feed their information into a common computer bank. Sharing this information enables the agencies to use their resources more effectively and to pick industries that need investigation—or companies that need prosecution—with some accuracy.

The ten types of complaints that topped the data bank's list in 1974 concerned (1) used cars, (2) home improvements and repairs, (3) auto repairs, (4) new cars, (5) mail-order houses, (6) appliances, (7) food, (8) landlord-tenant relations, (9) furniture and home furnishings, and (10) general merchandising.

You'll find advice on handling most of those types of complaints in Part III. If you need government help, there's plenty available in Wisconsin. The state has three strong statewide consumer-protection agencies.

First, there's the **Office of Consumer Protection, Department of Justice, State Capitol, Madison, Wis. 53702.** This office receives some 15,000 complaints a year. The Assistant Attorney General in charge, James D. Jeffries, told me his estimate was that 50 per cent of the complaints were successfully resolved. (Frankly, I think this is one of those rare cases where a public official may be erring on the side of modesty). Complaints are acknowledged within three days, and work begins on them within two weeks, Jeffries said. But actual resolution probably takes four to six weeks, on the average. If you live closer to Milwaukee than to Madison, you may want to use the branch office to file a complaint: It's at **819 N. Sixth St., Room 520, Milwaukee, Wis. 53203.**

A second, at least equally good, place to take a complaint is the **Bureau of Consumer Protection, Trade Division, Department of Agriculture, 801 West Badger Road, Madison, Wis. 53713.** While in many states the Department of Agriculture handles only food-related matters, in Wisconsin its a strong and broad-gauge agency. In fact, it's this bureau that promulgates consumer-protection rules and regulations in Wisconsin. At this writing, the bureau was on the verge of issuing regulations requiring the licensing of auto repair facilities. Among other things, the regulations would require auto repair shops to provide customers in advance with written estimates on repair work. By the time you read this, these rules may have taken effect. You can find out by calling, writing, or visiting the bureau. Besides the main office mentioned above, there are branch offices at **1727 Loring St., Altoona, Wis. 54720; 1181A Western Ave., Green Bay, Wisconsin 54303;** and **8500 West Capitol Drive, Milwaukee, Wis. 53222.**

Your third potential recourse is the **Governor's Council for Consumer Affairs, 16 North Carroll St., Room 415, Madison, Wis. 53702.** Although not primarily a complaint-handling agency, it claims to resolve successfully some 85 per cent of the complaints it gets, with an average waiting time of two to three weeks. It can't hurt to write all three state agencies. Oddly, there are at the moment no consumer-protection agencies as such on the county or city level in Wisconsin.

Wisconsin has passed a number of items of powerful consumer-protection legislation. We'll touch here on a couple of laws that you should know about. The state motor vehicle code requires that used-car dealers tell you about any significant mechanical or structural defects in a car before you sign a contract to buy it. This doesn't eliminate the need for you to have your own mechanic check a car out. But it does give you an added measure of protection—plus a stronger case if it turns out the dealer has concealed something he ought to have warned you about.

Home repair and home improvement contractors in Wisconsin are required to furnish you with waivers of lien, so you won't get stuck with a mechanic's lien against you if the contractor fails to pay one of the subcontractors. Also, in virtually every case, Wisconsin law requires that there be a written contract between you and the contractor. This contract must spell out exactly what's to be done, what materials will be used, the total cost including any finance charges, and the time when the work is to be completed.

Minimum standards are set for the construction of mobile homes sold in the state, and both mobile-home manufacturers and mobile-home dealers are licensed. There's also a law limiting the power of landlords in mobile-home parks.

For door-to-door sales, there's a three-day cooling-off period. You can change your mind and cancel the sale by notifying the company, in writing, within three business days of the sale. Most states have a law along these lines, but Wisconsin's is a relatively good one. It applies to most cash purchases over $25, and to most credit purchases regardless of the amount involved. The salesman must tell you about the law or give you notice of it, and there's no penalty for exercising your right to cancel.

As you can see, you have at least a fighting chance as a consumer in Wisconsin. The laws are there, the agencies are there. The rest is just a question of having the initiative and persistence to use them.

Wyoming

The consumer-protection movement originated as an urban phenomenon, and it took a while to reach places like Wyoming. In 1973, though, the state legislature here passed an Unfair and Deceptive Trade Practices Law. The agency charged with administering that law (and, therefore, with handling your complaints) is the **Consumer Affairs Division, Office of Attorney General, Capitol Building, Cheyenne, Wyo. 82002.**

The division, when you come right down to it, consists of three people. It has no separate budget but simply functions as a segment of the Attorney General's office as a whole. What's more, its powers were left fairly limited by the state legislature. It can't issue subpoenas or hold hearings. Technically speaking, it can't arbitrate consumer complaints, only prosecute them. But, human nature being what it is, informal arbitration or mediation occurs here and in other states where the law doesn't expressly provide for it.

The agency being as new as it is, having no branch offices, and having no toll-free telephone line for complaints, it's not surprising that the number of complaints coming in is small—fewer than 1,000 a year. What is surprising is the agency's rather good success rate with the complaints it does get. William Hill, the Assistant Attorney General in charge, estimates that 75 per cent of complaints are resolved successfully. The average waiting time for a consumer needing help is three to four weeks. Creditable results like that are bound to bring an increased number of complaints to the agency in the future. Maybe yours will be among them.

In 1974 the complaints most frequently received dealt with (1) mobile homes and mobile-home parks, (2) auto repairs, (3) appliances and appliance repairs, (4) home repairs and home improvements, (5) auto sales, (6) door-to-door sales, (7) advertising, and (8) mail-order houses. You'll find advice on dealing with each of these problems in Part III of this book.

It must be said that there aren't too many specific statutes on the books to help Wyoming consumers. Take the state's number one consumer problem, mobile homes. Wyoming is one of four states that haven't established minimum construction standards for mobile homes. Nor does it limit the power of mobile-home park landlords, as several states do, or require the licensing of mobile-home dealers, as many states do.

Or take that number six problem, door-to-door sales. Wyoming is the only state that doesn't have a three-day cooling-off period, allowing you to cancel a sale within three days if you think better of it. There is, however, a federal law in this area. Wyoming residents should read the passage on door-to-door sales in Part III of this book and take advantage of the federal rule.

One place where Wyoming is ahead of most states is that it does allow class action suits. These are suits in which you join together with other plaintiffs who have been similarly harmed. These suits can be a highly effective tool in some cases. It's not only that there's strength in numbers, but also pooling information can greatly strengthen your case. And it doesn't hurt to pool funds to hire a top-notch lawyer. So, if you find you've been victimized along with several other people, consider a class action. If, so far as you know, you're a lone victim, see what you can do on your own to strike back, then try the Consumer Affairs Division in Cheyenne.

PART III

Complaint Encyclopedia

Where to Go with What Complaint— Advice for Solving Fifty of the Most Common Consumer Problems

This section is devoted to helping you cope with specific problems, as they come up. In it, we discuss fifty of the most common consumer problems. They're listed alphabetically to aid you in finding the advice you need when you need it.

But how, you ask, do I know what the fifty most common consumer problems are? Good question. The answer is that I'm partly guessing. But my guesses are not shots in the dark. My aim is assisted by two guidance systems. The first is my compilation of answers from questionnaires I sent to consumer-protection agencies in all fifty states. In forty-four states, at least one key agency answered. In some states more than one agency did. Officials in each state told me what's bothering consumers in their jurisdiction. (You'll find many of the answers reproduced in Part II of this book, "Consumer Protection, State by State.") The patterns in many states displayed similarities, and so I was able to determine which problems are the most serious and the most widespread nationwide. To those I have devoted special attention. But this list of fifty includes virtually every kind of problem that showed up in my state-by-state survey.

My second guidance system in selecting the fifty problems for treatment here is my own experience over several years as an author and journalist interested in consumer affairs. At times I've written about people's complaints. At times I've written about efforts to solve them. At times I've been trying to solve them myself. Eventually one gets a feeling for the ways in which people are being victimized in the market place.

In my research, I've also developed something called a GRIPE index. GRIPE happens to be an acronym, but you'd need to pour several drinks into me to find out what the letters stand for. The important thing about the index is that it measures both the universality of a consumer problem and its seriousness. It does this in a very simple way. If a complaint ranks number one in any given state, it gets ten points; if it ranks number two, it gets nine points, and so on. (The number ten complaint in each state gets one point.) The more widespread a given complaint is, the higher its GRIPE index will be. And the more serious it is in the states where it is among the leading complaints, the higher its GRIPE index will be. The consumer complaint with the highest GRIPE index is automobile repairs. The complaint with the second highest index is automobile sales. A complete tabulation follows on pages 180–81.

Of course, no matter what the statistics say, the problem most important to you is the one you're faced with right now. You'll probably find it in the list that follows.

Advertising. The slightly misleading ad is the mosquito of the market place. The downright false ad is its wasp. If you've been bitten or stung, there are a number of places you can turn for help.

Your goal may be either or both of two things: fair treatment for yourself and a halt to the deception. Decide in advance which of these goals is more important to you, and pursue your strategy accordingly. If your primary goal is to get your money back or to get the article you *thought* you had coming to you, then hold off on writing government agencies immediately. You can use the threat of writing to them to strengthen your bargaining position.

Here's an example of how to use that dangling sword. A doctor I know on Long Island saw an ad for a cabinet to hold medical supplies. Pictured clearly in the ad was a cabinet with four drawers. Prominently displayed was a price. The doctor sent away for the cabinet, writing out a check for the amount shown. To his surprise, the cabinet that was delivered had only two drawers. He pulled out the ad and scanned it carefully. In tiny print at the bottom was a notice that the price quoted was for a two-drawer model, and that the model pictured could be had for a somewhat higher price. "The difference in price was peanuts to me," the doctor said. "But here I had spent my time ordering a cabinet that wouldn't hold all my supplies. I was fuming." He called the company and pointed out that the ad clearly conveyed the impression that the four-drawer model could be bought for the price shown in large type. The company had a choice, he said. It could send the four-drawer model immediately, at no extra charge, or it could take its chances on how legal officials would view the fine print in its ad. The company chose not to take that chance: The next day it sent out a delivery man, who dropped off the larger cabinet and took the two-drawer model away.

The dispatch shown by the cabinet company may have been partly the result of the threat that was hanging over its head. If the doctor had already filed a complaint with a government agency, the company might have taken a more defensive stand.

On the other hand, your main concern may be to stop the company from engaging in deceptive advertising in the future. If that's the case, write a protest letter to the head of the company. Send a copy of that letter, along with a covering note, to some or all of the following:

(1) *The regional office of the Federal Trade Commission.* You'll find the address of the office nearest you in Chapter 3. The FTC's duties specifically include the investigation of false and deceptive advertising. And for the FTC to have jurisdiction, the firm you're complaining about need *not* be an interstate firm; it only has to be big enough to "affect" interstate commerce. The FTC's staff is limited, however. There's a tendency for it to file complaints away. Then, if enough complaints accumulate against one firm, it launches an investigation. When it does move against a firm, the FTC can trot out big guns, including the threat of a $10,000-a-day fine. Under the gun, many firms sign "consent orders" agreeing to drop the disputed ads. At times the FTC has also required "corrective advertising." This means the company has to run new ads, disclaiming what it had said in previous

THE COMPLAINTS THAT BOTHER CONSUMERS MOST

Type of Complaint	GRIPE Index
Automobile repairs	428
Automobile sales	364
Home improvements and repairs	285
Mail-order houses	259
Mobile Homes	188
Appliances and appliance repairs	151
Furniture and home furnishings	110
Credit	97
Landlord-tenant problems	91
Real estate	88
Advertising	43
Retail stores	39
Publications (magazines, books etc.)	37
Door-to-door sales	34
Utilities*	32
Debt collection	31
Houses	28
Television, radio, and stereo	27
Repairmen	26
Travel	26
Insurance*	25
Health spas	24
Clothing	19
Distributorships	19
Food	13
Electricians	13
Swimming pools	12
Vocational schools*	11
Precious metals	10
Buying clubs	9
Waterproofing of basements	9
Washing machines	9

Type of Complaint	GRIPE Index
Paving of driveways	9
Short weight, measure, or count	8
Service stations	8
Records and tapes	8
Contests	8
Songwriting companies	7
Hospitals	7
Franchises	7
Hearing aids	6
Carpeting	6
Recreational vehicles	6
Professional services*	6
Rentals	6
Unsolicited merchandise, receipt of	5
Funeral establishments	4
Nursing homes	3
Mortgages	3
Motorcycles	3
Cosmetics	3
Termite inspection	2
Encyclopedias	2
Moving companies*	1
Pets	1
Inheritance schemes	1
Air conditioners	1
Hobbies	1
Toys	1
Jewelry	1
Dating services	1

* Problems marked with an asterisk are more serious than this tabulation would suggest, because complaints about them are normally heard by specialized agencies rather than broad-gauge consumer-protection agencies.

ones. One bread maker, for example, had to disclose that its "diet bread" didn't have fewer calories per ounce than other breads; it was merely sliced thinner.

(2) *The National Advertising Review Board,* a self-regulatory agency sponsored by the advertising industry and the Council of Better Business Bureaus, Inc. It handles complaints about national advertising only. It has no legal powers and can't penalize a company for false advertising—only persuade it to stop. But the NARB, as it sometimes calls itself, has surprised skeptics by taking a tough stance against misleading advertising, even if the ad's wording left a technical loophole through which the advertiser could wriggle out. For example, NARB got Hardee's Food Systems to stop using the term "charco-broiled," which implied (though it did not state) that the food was broiled over charcoal. In fact it was grilled on ceramic briquets. You can write the National Advertising Review Board at 850 Third Ave., New York, N.Y. 10022.

(3) *Your local Better Business Bureau.* This is a good place to take complaints about local advertising. Often the BBB can lean on the business to shape up. And, in any case, your complaint will be logged as part of a file used to warn people who call the BBB to check out a firm's reputation. In some communities, the local Chamber of Commerce, rather than the BBB, performs this function.

(4) *Your state consumer-protection agency.* If an ad was fraudulent, or distinctly misleading, this agency offers the best chance that legal action will be taken against the company. If there's more than one consumer-protection agency in the state, copies of complaints involving false advertising should be sent to the state Attorney General's office. See Part II of this book for names and addresses of your state agencies.

(5) *The advertising manager of the newspaper, magazine, TV station, or radio station where you saw or heard the advertisement.* Some of the media have established "advertising acceptability" departments to review such complaints and to keep out ads from undesirable businesses. By making this complaint, you may help limit the exposure the ad gets in the future.

In making any complaint, of course, accurate records count. Advertising complaints are an area where many consumers find it difficult to come up with the necessary documentation. But try to put yourself in the position of one of the five complaint-handling agencies we just listed. What can they do for a complainant who says, "A few weeks ago, I heard an ad on the radio. The impression it gave was that the product could be used for cutting your hair as well as trimming your hedges." Instead, your complaint should go something like this:

> On August 11, around 8:30 or 9:00 A.M., I heard an ad on WQZY radio for a product called The Miraculous Mower. The ad said this product "will trim your hedges, and can also be used for cutting your hair." When I purchased the product, I found that it scarcely dented my hedges but did considerable damage to my scalp. This advertisement is, in my opinion, misleading and deceptive. I would appreciate your investigating it as soon as possible and notifying me of the results. I have enclosed a copy of my protest letter to Mr. Kenneth Malicious, president of Miraculous Mowers, Inc., which proved to be the manufacturer of the item in question.

Of course, if the ad was in a magazine or newspaper, a copy of the ad itself should be included in your letter. It's a good idea to get in the habit of saving these until you've used the product and are sure you're satisfied with it. But if you haven't yet formed the habit of saving ads, you can trudge over to the library, find the ad again, and make photocopies. Or you may be able to get a copy of the ad from the firm itself.

Now you're familiar with two approaches, one for "getting yours," and the other for seeing that the advertiser "gets his." There's no reason why you can't begin with the first approach, then move on to the second after you've taken care of your personal problem. Some people might call this biting the hand that just placated you. But, if you're angry enough about the deception, you may feel perfectly justified in doing just that. Fiorello LaGuardia, a celebrated mayor of New York, is said to have remarked, "One thing that qualifies me for this job is my monumental ingratitude."

Age Discrimination.   See Discrimination.

Air Conditioning.   See Appliances and appliance repairs.

Airlines.   See Travel.

Annuities.   See Insurance.

Apartment-Location Services.   See Rentals.

Apartments.   See Landlord-tenant problems.

Appliances and Appliance Repairs.   (See also Stereo, audio, and audio-visual equipment and repairs.) You say that your refrigerator's insides feel like a Florida beach? That your dishwasher or clothes washer is reluctant to trouble the dirt? That your dryer looks as if it's trying to do the latest dance step? Or maybe the trouble is with a trash compactor, humidifier, dehumidifier, freezer, oven, hot water heater, waste disposer, air conditioner, or range. All of these qualify as major appliances. Complaints about any of them may be sent to MACAP, the Major Appliance Consumer Action Panel, 20 North Wacker Drive, Chicago, Ill. 60606. MACAP was set up in 1970 as a self-policing (and public relations) measure by the major appliance manufacturers. In its first five years, the organization has received some 7,000 complaints. It claims about 90 per cent of them were resolved to the satisfaction of the consumer.

Upon receiving a complaint, MACAP asks the retailer and the manufacturer to tell their side of the story within two weeks. Then it makes a "strong recommendation" for a solution. Bess Myerson, the capable former head of the New York City Department of Consumer Affairs, has said that the two-week deadline is sometimes breached and that some consumers find MACAP to be too lenient toward the manufacturer and the retailer. Nevertheless, she views MACAP as a remedy worth using and says the panel "has expedited an impressive number of consumer complaints." Complaints to MACAP should include the appliance's brand name, model, and serial number; your name, address, and phone number; the date and place you bought the appliance; the name and address of the repair service that was sent out, if it's different from the store's name; and a description of what went wrong and the unsuccessful attempts to fix it.

Of course, you shouldn't try MACAP until you've complained in writing to both the retailer and the manufacturer without positive results. If MACAP fails to come up with a solution you consider fair, you can still complain to your state agencies (see Part II). You might also go to small claims court and sue the retailer from whom you bought the appliance.

Controversies involving defective major appliances always tend to be drawn-out affairs. To save you a little time along the way, here are the addresses of some major appliance manufacturers:

- Admiral Corp., 3800 West Cortland, Chicago, Ill. 60647 (Ross D. Siragusa, Jr., president)
- Amana Refrigeration, Inc., Amana, Iowa 52203 (George C. Foerstner, president)
- Frigidaire Division, General Motors Corp., 300 Taylor, Dayton, Ohio 43401 (Harold W. Campbell, general manager)
- General Electric Co., 570 Lexington Ave., New York, N.Y. 10022 (Reginald H. Jones, chairman of the board)
- Hotpoint division, General Electric Co., Appliance Park, Louisville, Ky. 40225 (W. B. Clemmens, manager)
- Kelvinator, Inc., 1545 Clyde Park, Southwest, Grand Rapids, Michigan 49509 (Thomas I. Dolan, president)
- KitchenAid Dishwasher Division, Hobart Manufacturing Co., Troy, Ohio 45373 (David Meeker, president)
- The Maytag Co., 403 West Fourth St., Newton, Iowa 50208 (Daniel Krumm, president)
- Norge Division, Fedders Corp., Edison, N.J. 08817 (E. Hart, vice president)
- Westinghouse Electric Corp., Westinghouse Building, Gateway Center, Pittsburgh, Pa. 15222 (C. E. Hammond, president of consumer products division)
- Whirlpool Corp., Benton Harbor, Mich. 49022 (John Platts, president)

So far, we've been talking about major appliances. With small appliances, MACAP doesn't come into play. State agencies, small claims courts, and voluntary consumer organizations are usually the best pressure points to use on small-appliance complaints.

If your problem doesn't concern the appliance itself but the repair outfit that was sent to fix it, the dispute assumes a more local character. A city or county consumer agency might be the best place to take this type of complaint. A Better Business Bureau might also be quite effective on a complaint of this kind. After that, small claims courts, state agencies, voluntary consumer groups, and unorthodox tactics are the avenues worth pursuing.

Audio Equipment.   See Stereo, audio, and audio-visual equipment and repairs.

Automobile Repairs.   Car repairs are without any question the nation's number one consumer complaint. Federal statistics, as well as my own GRIPE Index computations, bear this out. So, if you've got auto repair headaches, you're not alone.

To discuss the problem intelligently, we've got to break it into three parts. There are mechanical repairs for a car under warranty. There are mechanical repairs for a car that's not under warranty. And there are body repairs. Each of these three situations poses a different challenge and demands a different strategy on your part.

If your car is under warranty, your basic problem will most often be to avoid the "sunshine treatment," also known as the "sunbath" and the "parking-lot treatment." By whatever name, it's the procedure whereby the dealer takes your car in, does nothing to it, and proclaims it fixed. Dealers do this because their payment for warranty work doesn't come from you; it comes from the manufacturer. The manufacturer isn't going to hear the squeal in your brakes or see your broken windshield wipers. It's going to see only an invoice from the dealer claiming that those things were fixed.* So there's little incentive for the dealer to do quality repair work. In addition, dealers claim—apparently with

---

* A few dealers have even set up rackets, bilking manufacturers by billing them for thousands of dollars in phony, completely nonexistent, repairs.

truth—that manufacturers don't reimburse them adequately for warranty repairs. So the incentive for good work is twice reduced.

Of course, you might be lucky enough to find a dealer whose pride and desire for repeat business make him furnish good service under warranty—even if it means running his warranty repair operations at a loss. But if you have found this man, you're probably not reading this passage.

Whenever you buy a new car, you should keep meticulous records of everything that goes wrong with it and of the servicing it gets. You'll need these records if you have to write complaint letters, or (if worst comes to worst) if you get involved in a lawsuit. Your first complaint should always go to the dealer. Find out who's in charge and deal only with him, if you want to avoid an endless runaround. If, after you deal with the top man at the dealership, your car still doesn't satisfy you, write to the manufacturer.

In their book *What to Do with Your Bad Car: An Action Manual for Lemon Owners,* Ralph Nader, Lowell Dodge, and Ralf Hotchkiss suggest that all complaints to the manufacturer should be addressed to the president or chairman. Copies should always go to the dealer and to the manufacturer's zone or regional office. The zone officer's address will normally be in your owner's manual. If not, you can get it from the dealer. This procedure should help keep your complaint from being bucked up and down the line. But it's the zone office that will probably end up dealing with your complaint.*

The addresses of the big four American auto makers are:

- American Motors Corp., 14250 Plymouth Road, Detroit, Mich. 48232 (William V. Luneberg, president)
- Chrysler Corp., P.O. Box 1919, Detroit, Mich. 48231 (John J. Riccardo, president)
- Ford Motor Co., The American Road, Dearborn, Mich. 48121 (Lee Iacocca, president)

---

* Without telling its dealers, Ford Motor Company recently had a policy of adjusting certain rust complaints at the zone level for consumers who took the trouble to go that far.

- General Motors Corp., General Motors Building, Detroit, Mich. 48202 (E. M. Estes, president)

If the manufacturer doesn't help you reach a prompt and fair solution, you can try several other recourses. The most drastic— revoking acceptance of your car—should be done only if the car is a total lemon, and only in consultation with a lawyer. According to Nader, Dodge, and Hotchkiss, the way to do it is to write a letter (keeping a copy, of course, and sending it by certified mail, return receipt requested) as follows: "In accordance with Section 2-608 of the Uniform Commercial Code, I am hereby revoking my acceptance of [the car, whose model and serial number you give], purchased from you on [date] for the sum of [amount of money paid]." You should go on to describe the defects that you can't live with and that the dealer and manufacturer have been unable to rectify. Then you should demand return of the purchase price of the car. Naturally, the dealer will refuse to take it back. But you should note the mileage at the time you return the car to him. If, later, the total on the odometer is significantly higher, that may help you prove the dealer has "exercised dominion" over the vehicle. To show that you mean business, you should cancel your insurance on the car and your registration. Notify the dealer in writing that you've done these things. If you're making payments on the car, the whole procedure becomes even more complex. Get detailed advice from your lawyer and be sure that any finance company or bank involved gets a copy of all communications you send the dealer. Do not assume, by the way, that a car must be almost brand-new for you to revoke acceptance of it. An Alabama man once revoked acceptance on a car he'd had for nearly a year, after driving it some 20,000 miles. A court upheld his action, saying that it was only the constant promises from the dealer that everything would be straightened out that caused the man to keep the car so long.

Revoking acceptance of a car is, to repeat, an extreme measure. You're more likely to want to pursue a somewhat more conventional route. You can—and should—complain to your state consumer-protection agency (see Part II). Send a copy of your complaint to the state department of motor vehicles. At the same time, you can try to get the complaint before some kind of arbitration board. Many Better Business Bureaus provide arbitration services. If your local BBB is one of them, see if it will let you sit in on some proceedings, so you can form an opinion of the leanings or biases of the arbitrators. The decision of a BBB arbitration panel is legally binding. But the panel can't arbitrate unless both parties agree in advance. If your dealer doesn't agree, you can try to bring pressure on him through the state automobile dealers' association. If you don't know where to find your state association, write the National Automobile Dealers Association, 2000 K St., N.W., Washington, D.C. 20006.)

The National Automobile Dealers Association is also a co-founder, along with other trade groups and the federal Office of Consumer Affairs, of the AUTOCAPs—Automobile Consumer Action Panels. AUTOCAPs try to mediate complaints. If negotiating fails, they assemble a panel consisting of representatives of both dealers and consumer groups to hear your case and hand down an opinion. That opinion carries considerable weight, but it's not legally binding.

At last report, there were AUTOCAPs in seven locations, each administered by an automobile dealers association:

- In *Colorado,* the Metropolitan Denver Automobile Dealers Association, Suite 101, 70 W. Sixth Ave., Denver, Colo. 80204
- In the *District of Columbia,* the Automotive Trade Association, National Capitol Area, Suite 505, 8401 Connecticut Ave., Chevy Chase, Md. 20015
- In *Florida,* the Orlando Automobile and Truck Dealers, Suite 221, 1350 Orange Ave., Winter Park, Fla. 32789
- In *Maryland,* see District of Columbia listing
- In *Ohio,* the Cleveland Automobile Dealers Association, 310 Lakeside Ave., N.W., Cleveland, Ohio 44113
- In *Oregon,* the Oregon Automobile Dealers Association, Box 14460, Portland, Ore. 97214
- In *Pennsylvania,* the Pennsylvania Automotive Association, Box 2955, Harrisburg, Pa. 17105

- In *Utah,* the Utah Automobile Dealers Association, Box 1019, Salt Lake City, Utah 84101
- In *Virginia,* see District of Columbia listing

If none of these locations are near you, you can write the National Association of Automobile Dealers to see if any new AUTOCAPs have started up in your area.

So far we've been talking about repairs while the car is still covered by its warranty. Now let's say the warranty has expired. We're in a different ballgame now, because *you're* paying for the repairs. In most cases your concern now becomes not that the repair shop is doing too little, but that it's doing too much—or at least charging you for too much.

You'll notice that we've switched to saying "repair shop" instead of "dealer." Once the warranty expires, you're free to go to any shop you choose. Naturally, an advance inquiry to the BBB and some consultation with neighbors or co-workers could save you from making a costly error in your choice. As a rule of thumb, repair shops on local streets depend more on repeat business than do those on crowded highways. This means they might have more incentive to do a careful, workmanlike job. As a rule, repair shops that give written estimates are more to be trusted than those that don't.

In some states—California, Connecticut, Maryland, New York, and Rhode Island, at this writing—repair shops are licensed. You can look at the license, which must be displayed on the premises, and jot down the number and the name of the state agency to whom you can complain if you encounter any irregularities. Some major cities (New York, Dallas, and Washington, D.C., for example) also license repair facilities. Where shops aren't licensed, your best recourses are your state consumer agencies and local Better Business Bureaus. In some places there are also voluntary consumer groups that take a special interest in auto repair problems. Among these groups:

- Automobile Owners Action Council, Suite 236, 733 Fifteenth St. N.W., Washington, D.C. 20005
- Consumers Education and Protective Association, 6048 Ogontz Ave., Philadelphia, Pa. 19141 (known for its willing-

ness to use picketing, CEPA was founded in Philadelphia but is now also active in Baltimore and several other cities)

- Lemons, Inc., Greater Metro Foundation, 1821 University Ave., St. Paul, Minn. 55104
- Tulane-Loyola Auto Consumer Complaint Center, Human Relations Institute, P.O. Box 5039, Tulane University Station, New Orleans, La. 70115

There's one more thing you should do without fail. Complain to your state consumer-protection agency or agencies. Send a copy of your complaint to the state department of motor vehicles. You're more likely to get action from the former than the latter, but there's no sense in neglecting any avenue of recourse with a complaint as annoying as auto repairs.

Speaking of annoyance, there are few things more disheartening than the sight of the crumpled steel when your car's been hit. This brings us to the third and last area of auto repair problems: body shops. The problem here is that, as with warranty work, we have a three-cornered waltz. In this case, the third party is the insurance company, which will probably be footing a good part of the bill for the body work. The insurance company will probably suggest a place you can go to have the work done. It's legal for it to do this in almost all states. The adjuster will tell you that the shop does good-quality work, is fast, and possibly has even agreed in advance to charge the fee determined by the adjuster. Consumer advocates almost always advise people against going to these shops. They might, of course, be fine. But there's a temptation for them to do high-volume, low-quality work. In exchange for a steady stream of business from the insurance company, they may keep prices at bargain-basement levels—but then your car may look as though it's been fixed at a bargain basement.

So, *you* make the decision as to what body shop to use. As with repair shops, take recommendations from friends and check with the Better Business Bureau. Get an estimate from the shop of your choice. Typically, the insurance company will say the figure is too high. Let the company try to bargain with the shop. The shop is not about to take a loss, so any figure it agrees to is probably fair. But if the insurance company and the shop can't reach agreement, you should offer to get other estimates—again from body shops of *your* choice. If the insurance company reaches an impasse with two or three body shops, it's time to start writing letters. Send one to your state insurance department and one to your consumer-protection agency.

The insurance company may give you a check early in the game in the amount it thinks is fair. That's fine, but don't cash the check yet. Cashing it often constitutes your agreement to the amount of the settlement. Instead, hold on to the check until after all the repair work is done to your satisfaction and the final bill is submitted. Then, if the check still seems like a fair settlement, go ahead and cash it.

If you're not satisfied with the quality of repairs at the body shop you chose, you can't really expect the insurance company to ante up more money to pay for additional repairs. Instead, you should insist that the shop do the work right at the price you originally agreed on. In this kind of a dispute with a body shop, your recourses are the typical ones for local complaints: city, county, and state agencies; small claims courts; the Better Business Bureau (including its arbitration service); and voluntary consumer organizations.

Automobile Sales. Most complaints about newly bought cars concern their mechanical condition. The best way to make sure a car is delivered to you in the condition you want is to refuse to accept it—or pay for it—until everything is just right. This, however, requires steely self-control and an alternate mode of transportation. If you take the car with some defects remaining to be corrected, sit down right away and send a letter to the dealer, keeping at least one photocopy (not just a carbon copy, since this letter may have to be reproduced later). The letter should say something to this effect:

> I today purchased from you, at a cost of [amount], a [year, make, and model] with the serial number [whatever]. On delivery, it had three defects of which I was immediately aware. Paint on the right front door was chipped. The glove compartment opens and closes only with extreme difficulty. And an ordinary AM radio was installed instead

of the AM-FM unit I had ordered. You will recall our discussion of this morning, in which you said all these defects would be remedied as soon as possible. Please advise me when I can bring the car in for the necessary adjustments. I would appreciate your selecting a date before [a specified time]. I appreciate your prompt attention to these matters, and will let you know if any other defects manifest themselves.

Every time another defect does show up, write the dealer again, taking the opportunity to remind him of any previous defects that haven't been corrected yet. Your letters won't necessarily bring you any faster service than phone calls would. Indeed, you may want to supplement them with phone calls. But your letters will create a written record, which will be invaluable in any subsequent disputes.

Most other complaints in the car sales field revolve around what are politely termed "misunderstandings." The best way to avoid these is to get everything in writing in the first place, including (1) the delivery date, (2) the exact list of options you're buying, (3) the list of things the dealer will do to make the car ready, often known as "dealer prep," (4) the terms of the financing, if you're doing it through the dealer, and (5) the exact cost, including options, dealer preparation charges, shipping charges, and financing. The dealer should sign a statement to the effect that there will be no other charges.

Nailing things down that way will help keep last-minute charges from cropping up. Protective undercoating, for example, is a favorite way for dealers to tack on a few more dollars. But it's often included on the dealer preparation checklist, which means you supposedly have already paid for it. Anyway, undercoating—other than what's done at the factory—is usually unnecessary, according to Consumers Union. If a dispute comes up, it's still not too late to ask to see a copy of the dealer preparation checklist. There's certainly no reason you should pay twice for the same item.

Financing is another area in which consumers often have complaints against car dealers. But the complaints typically concern oral misrepresentation, which is difficult to prove. For example, dealers sometimes quote seemingly low interest rates, when the actual Annual Percentage Rate is much higher. If you have a complaint of this type, send it to your state consumer-protection agency, the Better Business Bureau, and the Federal Trade Commission (which administers the Truth in Lending Act). The BBB can warn other potential victims, and the other two agencies might launch an investigation if they get enough complaints. But don't expect any help for yourself if you've signed a contract. You'll just have to make the payments. If you can't make them, see the entry on "Debt collection" for a description of your rights.

In the used-car realm, your rights are effectively limited to whatever is spelled out in any warranty or written agreement you've gotten from the seller.* If you feel you've been gypped, tell the Better Business Bureau, your state and local consumer agencies, and voluntary consumer organizations. By doing this, you'll be helping to protect future victims, but again you usually can't expect much help for yourself. Of course, if the odometer's been tampered with, that's a different matter. Your state agencies will then be interested in prosecution, and you have a good court case for getting your money back.

Complaints about auto dealers should be taken, by and large, to the agencies mentioned in the entry on "Automobile repairs." These include state consumer-protection agencies (see Part II), your state automobile dealers association, voluntary consumer groups, AUTOCAPs, BBB arbitration panels, and your state department (administration, division) of motor vehicles.

Bait and Switch Tactics.   See Unfair business practices.

Banks.   Folklore usually credits bankers with hearts of granite and minds that see only dollar signs. That never was quite true, and lately bankers have been working hard to change their image.

---

* When buying a used car, it's a good idea to request a written statement from the seller to the effect that he knows of no hidden damage to the car or mechanical defects in it. You should also test-drive the car; have it inspected (for a fee) by your own mechanic; and take it, if possible, through a state inspection line (if your state has them). You should also talk to the car's previous owner, whose name and address the seller always knows, whether he admits it or not.

So take your first complaint straight to a top-level official of the bank itself. It's not as hopeless as you may think. But if your appeal or protest fails, and you still think you have a legitimate complaint, there are plenty of government agencies to turn to.

All fifty states have agencies that regulate state-chartered banking institutions. About two-thirds of all banking institutions are state chartered; the rest are federally chartered. You'll find the address of your state banking agency at your local library. Normally you'll be looking for the "Department of Banking," "Division of Banking," "Commissioner of Banking," or "Superintendent of Banking." In Indiana and Utah, look for the "Department of Financial Institutions"; in Missouri, the "Director of Finance"; in Montana, the "Department of Business Regulation."

Almost every banking institution—whether state chartered or federally chartered—is regulated by some federal agency or other. There's a whole team of such agencies. To find the right one, the information below will serve in lieu of a scorecard.

Your first step in seeking help is to be sure what type of banking institution you're dealing with. There are three basic types, each regulated by a different set of authorities. First, there are commercial banks. Owned by stockholders, they have broad powers to make business and commercial loans, and they are permitted to offer checking accounts. A commercial bank will typically have the words "bank" or "trust" in its name. Second, there are savings institutions. These include savings and loan associations and (in seventeen states) mutual savings banks. Ostensibly owned by their depositors in most cases, savings institutions must make most of their loans (by law) in the mortgage field. They are allowed to pay slightly higher rates of interest on savings accounts than commercial banks, but they are not allowed to offer checking accounts.* Third, there are credit unions. These are cooperative associations (usually joined through work or a fraternal or religious organization), which perform banking functions for their members. Being unconcerned with maximizing profits, they typically pay higher rates on savings, and charge lower rates on

* In an increasing number of states, notably Massachusetts, New Hampshire, and New York, savings institutions are finding ways around this restriction.

loans, than other banking institutions do. But they offer few ancillary services.

If the institution you're having a problem with is a national commercial bank (you can tell, because it will have the word "national" in its name), send your complaint to the Comptroller of the Currency, United States Department of the Treasury, Washington, D.C. 20220. There are about 4,700 national banks.

Most of the nation's 14,535 or so commercial banks are state chartered, but almost all of them are still answerable to federal authorities. About 1,000 state-chartered banks are members of the Federal Reserve System (as are all national banks, automatically). To launch a complaint against one of these "in-between" banks, write the Federal Reserve Board at Twentieth St. and Constitution Avenue, N.W., Washington, D.C. 20551. Or contact one of the twelve Federal Reserve Banks scattered around the country. They're in Boston, New York City, Philadelphia, Cleveland, Richmond, Atlanta, Chicago, St. Louis, Minneapolis, Kansas City, Dallas, and San Francisco. Check the white pages of a telephone book under "Federal Reserve Bank" for the address and phone number. By the way, if your bank is state chartered, the only easy way to tell whether it's a member of the Federal Reserve System is to ask.

For the remaining state-chartered commercial banks, complaints can usually be sent to the Federal Deposit Insurance Corporation (FDIC). You can tell if your bank is insured by the FDIC by walking into the lobby. You'll probably see signs all around saying, "Each depositor insured up to $40,000 by the FDIC." If that's the case, go ahead and write to the Division of Examination, FDIC, 550 Seventeenth St., N.W., Washington, D.C. 20429. If your bank is one of those rare birds not insured by the FDIC, your only recourse is your state department of banking.

If your problem is with a savings institution, you have to determine whether the institution is federally chartered. (If it is, the word "federal" will appear somewhere in its name.) If so, send your complaint to the Federal Home Loan Bank Board, 101 Indiana Ave., N.W., Washington, D.C. 20552. If not, but if it carries federal insurance, send your complaint to the Federal

Savings and Loan Insurance Corporation (FSLIC) at the same address. Again, almost all savings institutions have their deposits insured by the FSLIC, and you can tell simply by walking into the lobby and looking around.

If your problem is with a credit union, you again must determine whether it's a federally chartered one. Once more, the word "federal" will appear in its name if it is. If so, send your complaint to the National Credit Union Administration, Office of Examination and Insurance, 2025 M St., N.W., Washington, D.C. 20456. If not, your state banking department is the place to go.

Basement Waterproofing. See Home improvements and repairs.

Billing. (See also Credit problems, Debt collection.) Basically, there are three nasty things people can do to you when they're billing you for a product or service. They can bill you for the wrong amount. They can bill you so late—or demand payment so early—that you don't have enough time to pay the bill. And they can use methods of calculating your bill that, while technically correct, are unfavorable to you. But you have remedies for each of these problems.

Let's say you get billed for the wrong amount. The time-honored continuation of this scenario is for you to write back that the bill is wrong; your creditor ignores your letter (or letters) and keeps dunning you for payment in an increasingly insistent fashion. I know one fellow, a highly intelligent and urbane editor, who grew so exasperated at this phantom correspondence that he started sending the dunning letters back with obscene messages scrawled on them in red ink. His messages mainly suggested that the company should take its bill and store it in an interior portion of its anatomy.

You may not be driven so far. A few states, starting with New York, have required creditors to respond to billing protests within thirty days and to straighten them out within ninety days. Now, thanks to the Fair Credit Billing Act, that's also the law nationwide.* Remind your creditors of this, if you get involved in a

* The federal law applies basically to credit card issuers. Some state laws also apply to other types of billings. You can check with your state consumer agencies to be sure.

protracted dispute over a billing error. And if you need help in enforcing the law, start with the regional office nearest you of the Federal Trade Commission. By the way, if a creditor fails to resolve a billing dispute—either by correcting his bill or by explaining to you why he's right and you're wrong—within ninety days he forfeits his right to the disputed amount, up to $50. In ᷉ome states, he forfeits the entire amount, period.

What about the bill that comes on September 12 and demands payment by September 13, or perhaps even by September 11? That problem, too, is largely solved by the Fair Credit Billing Act. It's now the law of the land that a bill must be sent and postmarked at least fourteen days in advance of the time finance charges become due.

One area where many consumers remain in the dark is in comprehending how their bill is calculated. On most charge accounts, you're billed 18 per cent a year, or 1.5 per cent a month. But 1.5 per cent of *what?* Most consumers don't know. "My balance, I suppose," they would say. But there are many ways of calculating the balance. The very best, from the consumer's point of view, is the "unpaid balance" method, also known as the "previous balance less payments" method. If you had a $200 balance at the start of a billing period but have since paid in $100, you would be charged interest only on the remaining $100 under this method. That means your finance charge for the month would probably be $1.50. The finance charge would be the same even if you've meanwhile charged the purchase of a $50 table.

The worst method, from the consumer's viewpoint, is the "previous balance" method. With it, you'd be charged interest on the whole $200, so your finance charge would probably be $3.00. The previous balance method is now outlawed in a number of states, but there are still plenty of places where it's used. Once you get in the habit of checking to see what kind of computation methods are used on your bills, you can outlaw it from your personal financial domain.

Two in-between methods, in terms of their favorability to you, are the "adjusted balance" method and the "average daily balance" method. With the adjusted balance method, your finance charge takes account of both payments and purchases you've made since the last statement. So, in the situation described above, your balance would be $150. (That's $200 to start with, minus the $100 payment, plus the $50 for purchase of the table.) Your finance charge would probably be $2.25.

With the average daily balance method, the balance on which you pay your interest is, as the name implies, the average of the balances you maintained on each day of the billing cycle. How favorable this method is to you depends on whether you are charged interest on a purchase starting the moment you buy it, or whether you get a "free ride" until after you've been billed for the purchase. This free ride period has been one of the main features making the use of credit cards worthwhile. But some card issuers have started doing away with it.

Let's say you have an account using the average daily balance method, a thirty-day billing cycle, and no free ride period. You start the cycle with a $200 balance, as before. You make a $100 payment, which is received on the tenth day of the billing cycle. Then you buy that $50 table on the twentieth day of the billing cycle. Your average daily balance would be $150. (This is reached by taking the total you owed each day and dividing by thirty. You owed $200 for ten days, $100 for ten days, and $150 for ten days, which works out to an average of $150.) Your finance charge would probably be $2.25.

But suppose you made your payment on the second day and didn't buy your lamp till the twenty-eighth day? Then your average daily balance would be only $108.33, and your probable finance charge would be only $1.62. On the other hand, if you bought the lamp on the second day and didn't make your payment till the twenty-eighth day, your average daily balance would be $238.33, and your probable finance charge would be $3.57.

Now suppose there *is* a free ride period, so you are not charged interest on a purchase until after you have been billed for it and have had a reasonable time to pay the bill. Then it doesn't matter when you buy the lamp. If you pay the bill on the tenth day of the billing cycle, your average daily balance would be $133.33, and your probable finance charge would be $2.00.

These examples are intended to help you decipher your own bills, so you can tell if you're being charged correctly. They're also intended to drive home the point that *it does matter* what balance method is used. Your finance charges varied by more than 57 per cent in the examples we cited. So it's important to ask the question, "One and a half per cent of *what?*" Call or write the credit department of your credit card issuers and keep asking questions until you're satisfied. Many stores and credit card issuers, by the way, have been quietly changing in the last couple of years to balance methods that help *their* balance sheets and hurt yours. Such a change is often accompanied by the mailing to you of an "explanation" full of fine print and incomprehensible language. If you understood the preceding passage, you're less likely to toss such a notice into the wastebasket now: You're more likely to understand it or challenge it. And if someone switches the rules of the credit game on you in midstream, there's no reason why you shouldn't switch credit cards.

One more billing problem should be mentioned here. If you have a bank card or a general-purpose charge card, you may use it sometime to buy merchandise that proves defective. When your bill comes, you may be in a quandary as to whether or not to pay. Your quarrel is with the merchant, not the card issuer. But if you pay, you rightly fear you may never see your money again. The answer, since the passage of the Fair Credit Billing Act, is *don't pay* the disputed portion. See the entry on "Credit problems" for further details.

Bonds.   See Securities.

Book Clubs.   See Buying clubs.

Builders.   See Home improvements and repairs; Houses.

Business Practices.   See Unfair business practices.

Buying Clubs.   "I can get it for you wholesale." That time-honored claim is the whole basis of buying clubs. By being a member, it is claimed, you can get cars, books, records, coins, magazines, or general merchandise at prices well below what you'd normally expect to pay. By the time you add in the membership fees or shipping charges, this claim may turn out to be wishful thinking. But even if it is true, you may end up with merchandise you wouldn't normally have bought. In that case, the savings are real in a bookkeeping sense but all too illusory in the pocketbook.

Before joining a buying club, it's wise to inquire about (1) annual or one-time membership fees, (2) the number of items, or dollar volume, you're required to purchase, (3) mailing, shipping, or handling charges that may come up, (4) "negative option" plans, and (5) the sending of merchandise "on approval."

A negative option plan is an arrangement by which you'll be sent the club's selection of merchandise unless you specifically request not to be sent it. FTC regulations require that you be given at least ten days to decide whether you want a particular selection. Even so, over a period of time, the effect of a negative option plan is often to cause you to "order" merchandise you never would have gone out and bought.

Merchandise that is sent on approval theoretically can be accepted or rejected by you. But if you reject it, you sometimes have to ship it back at your own cost. Some buying clubs send items "on approval" without making it clear in advance exactly what you're going to receive or how you can return it if you don't want it. Sometimes the term "on approval" isn't explained, so that the consumer doesn't realize until too late that he's expected to pay for the merchandise, even though he may not specifically have ordered it.

If you've already joined a buying club, but one or more of these key conditions weren't made clear to you when you joined, you may be able to bow out and get some or all of your money back. Send a complaint letter to the president of the club, explaining your desire to withdraw from the club, to get a refund, or both. Send a copy of your letter to your state consumer-protection agency (see Part II). If the club operates by mail, send a copy also to the Postal Inspector in Charge at the nearest regional office of the U.S. Postal Service.

Carpeting. CRICAP, the Carpet and Rug Institute Consumer Action Panel, folded in 1975 for lack of financial support. Set up in 1973, it was more or less modeled after MACAP, which is described under the heading "Appliances and appliance repairs."

If your initial complaints to the retailer and manufacturer have proved fruitless, though, you can still write CRICAP's sponsor, the Carpet and Rug Institute, at P.O. Box 2048 (Holiday Drive), Dalton, Ga. 30720.

If the institute can't bring your problem to a satisfactory solution, you should decide who you think is really at fault, the retailer or the wholesaler. If it's the retailer, complaints to the Better Business Bureau, your local consumer-protection agency (if there is one), and your state consumer-protection agency are in order. Perhaps you can press the retailer to have your dispute arbitrated by a Better Business Bureau panel. Or you can go to small claims court.

If you figure it's the manufacturer who's really to blame, and the Carpet and Rug Institute hasn't been able to help, send a complaint letter to the consumer-protection agency in the manufacturer's state, as well as to your own state agency.

Cars.   See Automobile repairs; Automobile sales.

Clothing.   Most garments now come with permanent care labels attached. If you don't follow the label's instructions, and your garment rips, deteriorates, puckers, or otherwise self-destructs, you don't have much of a case. But if you have given it proper care and no more than reasonable wear, and if one of these things *still* happens, that's another story. Fixing the garment is probably impossible at this point, so what you're after is either a replacement or a refund. (Decide in advance which one you want, and then stick to your guns.)

There may be three parties involved besides you—the store, the manufacturer, and a dry cleaner. Your goal is to keep your complaint from turning into a triple runaround, with each party blaming the other. Try standard complaining first. If a runaround develops, an organization that can help pin the blame where it belongs is the International Fabricare Institute, P.O. Box 940, Joliet, Ill. 60434. It can inspect a garment and render an opinion as to whether it was damaged by inept cleaning or defective to start with. Try to have your local Better Business Bureau forward the garment to the institute rather than do it yourself. While you're at it, you might as well give the BBB a crack at resolving your complaint.

Condominiums. The offer looked simply too good to pass up. The condominium unit wasn't too costly. The annual maintenance fees were modest. Financing was available. The condominium was in a resort area, so you figured you could make up a good portion of its cost by renting it out during the tourist season. The prospect of owning your own home and having a tax shelter (through mortgage interest payments) to boot, appealed to you.

Only, a few troubles cropped up. The maintenance fees, low the first year, have gone up substantially. The developer retained title to the swimming pool, golf course, and parking facilities, and is charging you stiff fees for the use of each. You found out that if you rent your unit out when you go on vacation, you'll have to put a large portion of the income into a pooled fund. The proceeds will be shared by all the unit owners, and the developer will get a cut. And you learned there's nothing in your contract guaranteeing you any compensation if the developer decides to gut the whole place ten years from now and put up a shopping center. It turns out the developer still owns the land.

Well, the troubles described are a conglomerate of extremes. It's unlikely that *all* of them would happen to you. And if you were lucky, or skillful, when you bought your condominium unit, your contract protected you against all of these problems.

If you do have a problem, the best way to solve it is almost certainly by acting in concert with other members of the owners' association at your condominium development. Any problem you have is almost certainly shared by others. Your bargaining power and your ability to afford legal advice or the costs of any necessary litigation will be much greater if you're acting together than if you're acting separately. In addition to seeking legal advice, you and the other owners should draft a letter to your state consumer-protection agency (see Part II), and to the Federal Trade Commission (see pages 32–35). Condominium laws are currently being revised on both the state and federal levels, so you'll need up-to-date advice to see just what your possible remedies are. The general trend is to increase the rights of unit owners and to limit the ability of developers to hold long-term leases and milk the property for every last drop of profit.

Contests. See Unfair business practices.

Contractors. See Home improvements and repairs.

Correspondence Schools. See Vocational schools.

Cosmetics. If there's a fly in your ointment, direct your complaint to the Food and Drug Administration, whose regional offices are listed on pages 37–38. The FDA is responsible for seeing that cosmetics are pure. It's also responsible for seeing that as few people as possible suffer allergic reactions to them. To this end, the FDA requires that all cosmetics sold after September 3, 1976, bear a label listing the ingredients. It took strong lobbying by the consumer movement to bring this step about. But the step will have been wasted if people fail to report any allergic reactions they suffer.

If you have a complaint about a personal care product but are not sure whether the product qualifies as a cosmetic, report it to the FDA anyway. The term cosmetic, as used here, includes not only perfume, lipstick, and eye shadow, but also such items as toothpaste, hair dye, and soap—pretty much any chemical composition that you can apply in any way to your body.

If your problem with a cosmetic concerns its failure to get the right person to fall into your arms, direct your complaint— subtly—to that person.

Credit Problems. (See also Billing; Debt Collection; Discrimination.) Some states have special offices designed to help consumers deal with credit problems. The entry for your state in Part II will tell you if your state is one of them. If so, make that agency your first recourse. If not, the place you'll need to go to seek help depends on what type of problem you have.

If you're turned down for a loan, you have a right to know why. In particular, you have a right to know whether the company that refused you the loan obtained a report on you from a credit bureau. (Such reports constitute what people think of as their "credit rating.") Credit bureaus are private firms that make money by collecting information on people and passing it on to banks, loan companies, insurance companies, and employers. They share information with each other, and they keep extensive files. (The largest credit bureau, Retail Credit Company, recently had files on some 48 million Americans.)

If a credit bureau's report was a factor in a decision to deny you a loan, the bank or loan company must tell you so. It must also give you the name and address of the bureau where it got the report. You can then go there and find out what's being said about you. You can't actually see your file, but you have an employe read you what's in it. (This is one of those strange legislative compromises that sometimes get hammered out in Congress. The idea was to try to give you some protection while also concealing the identity of credit bureaus' informants.)

If you think the information in your file is wrong, say so. Say so in person, then go home and say so in writing, in a letter to the credit bureau, with a copy to the place that refused you the loan. Under the Fair Credit Reporting Act, the bureau must re-investigate your situation. If, after that, it still thinks its report is correct, you have the right to have your own written version of the facts placed in your file. The bureau must give your state-ment, along with its own report, to anyone who asks it for infor-mation on you in the future. Complaints about credit bureaus should go to the regional office of the Federal Trade Commission (see Chapter 3 for locations).

If you think you've been turned down for a loan because of discrimination (on grounds of race, sex, marital status, national origin, or religion) file a complaint with the appropriate banking agency and with the authorities listed in the entry under "Dis-crimination."

If you succeeded in getting a loan, but feel its terms were misrepresented to you, get in touch with the Federal Trade Com-mission or the appropriate banking regulatory agency (see "Banks"). Also notify your state credit agency or consumer-pro-tection agency (see Part II). The Truth in Lending Act requires that loan terms be accurately spelled out in writing and that the interest rate always be expressed as an Annual Percentage Rate.

Now we come to an entirely different problem but one that still falls in the credit realm. What do you do when you're billed for defective merchandise or services? If the bill comes from the merchant with whom you have the dispute, pay only the part you believe you owe. Write him a letter explaining why you don't believe you owe the rest. Spell out exactly what he would have to provide (such as replacement merchandise or redoing a poor job) to get the rest of the money. If you can't conceive of any circumstance in which you would pay the disputed amount, be forthright and say that. Keep a copy of the letter and of all other documents relevant to the dispute. Read the entry under "Debt collection" so you'll know your rights in the event he starts collection proceedings against you. If you think you're likely to wind up in court, consult a lawyer. And remember that you always have available to you the alternative strategy of paying up, then going to small claims court to sue the merchant. In general, though, you're better off having the money in your own hands. Then *they* have to sue *you*. And, if you're in the right, they're not too likely to do so, though they may threaten.

But suppose the bill is not from the merchant who sold you the defective goods or services, but rather from a third party. This can easily happen; indeed, it happens every day. You might have bought something from a merchant on the installment plan. Then the merchant may have sold your debt to a separate firm, such as a finance company. The finance company traditionally couldn't care less whether your freezer works or whether the car you bought doesn't run. It had a piece of paper saying you owe it $111 a month (or whatever). It paid good money to buy that debt, and it planned to collect. The fact that the debt arose through your buying something that proved to be a lemon didn't concern it in the least. Meanwhile, if you went to the merchant, he was conspicuously unconcerned with fixing your problem. After all, he'd already gotten his money by selling your contract to the finance company.

This frustrating situation stemmed from a legal tradition called the "holder-in-due-course" doctrine. It holds that, when the holder of an IOU (a debt) passes that collectible debt on to a third party (the holder in due course), the new holder has a right to collect, regardless of any disputes surrounding the original transaction.

As of May 14, 1976, this whole situation is changed—thank goodness. The Federal Trade Commission has passed a rule (called "preservation of consumers' claims and defenses") that in effect abolishes the holder in due course doctrine. If a third party seeks to collect a debt from you, and if the goods or services you purchased were defective, you can tell the third party so. If he sues you to collect the money, you can use the defectiveness issue as a valid defense in court. The traditional fine print in which you waive your rights to this defense is henceforth illegal and invalid. In short, there's no longer any legal way in which you can be compelled to pay for defective goods. This new rule, incidentally, makes it more important than ever for you to keep copies of your complaint letters to merchants concerning defective merchandise.

The same type of situation arises when you use a bank credit card or a general purpose credit card to buy goods or services that turn out to be defective. If you pay the bill, you have the strong feeling you'll never see that money again. If you don't pay it, you're worried, because, after all, it wasn't the card issuer's fault that the merchandise was bad. What should you do?

Answer: You should pay that portion of the bill that you legitimately owe, but not the portion that involves defective items. Under the Fair Credit Billing Act, you may send a letter to the card issuer explaining why you're paying only part (or none) of the bill. The card issuer then has three choices. It can swallow the loss. It can get involved in mediating the dispute. Or it can return the debt to the store to collect. In almost all cases, card issuers will choose the third option.

Technically, your right to assert this credit card remedy applies only to purchases involving more than $50 and to cases where the merchandise was bought within 100 miles of home, or within your home state. In practice, however, you should probably ignore these restrictions, at least for as long as possible. That way, the credit card company becomes your *de facto* ally in your dispute with the merchant, providing some needed leverage. If you pay up without a fight, you've forfeited a lot of your bargaining power.

If you have a problem exercising your rights under the Fair Credit Billing Act, make contact with the appropriate banking authority, if a bank credit card is involved, or the Federal Trade Commission. For other problems involving the holder-in-due-course doctrine, call upon the FTC, your state credit agency (if any), or your state consumer-protection agency.

Credit Unions.   See Banks.

Dating Services.   See Unfair business practices.

Debt Collection.   (See also Billing; Credit problems.) If someone's trying to collect money from you that you don't believe you really owe, you'll find advice under "Billing." If you do indeed owe it and just can't pay it, this passage is intended for you.

There are basically four ways a creditor can seek to collect a debt from you: through threats, through a lawsuit, through garnishment, and through repossession. If the business to which you owe money is legitimate, the only threat it can make is use of the other three methods.

If the business is not legitimate—if, for example, you made the mistake of borrowing money from a loan shark—your recourse agency is the police. You should go to them as quickly and as discreetly as possible.

If a bill collector uses threats, harassment tactics, or abusive language, you should call the police and write to your state consumer-protection agency, your state Attorney General's office (if it's distinct from the consumer agency), and your local consumer-protection agency (if there is one).

If a bill collector calls so repeatedly on the telephone as to constitute harassment, of if he calls at late hours, complain to the telephone company. Such practices are illegal under the rules of the Federal Communications Commission. And the FCC has delegated to the telephone company the task of taking action against those kinds of tactics. (If the phone company ignores you, complain about the phone company to the state Public Utilities Commission).

If a bill collector sends you what purports to be a court form (but isn't), or if a bill collector impersonates a government agency, notify your state consumer-protection agency.

So far, we've been talking about things bill collectors can't legally do. Now, let's talk about the things they *can* do—lawsuits, garnishment, and repossession. The best way to stave off a lawsuit is to pay as much as you can, *regularly,* and to communicate honestly with your creditors in writing about your difficulty in paying their bills. If you do this, they may threaten to sue you, but they're unlikely actually to do so. If you are sued, your creditor can win a court judgment forcing you to pay up. If that happens, you might have to sell your assets, such as a house, car, or furniture, in order to meet the debt. Or, alternatively, you could declare bankruptcy.

Declaring bankruptcy is not the end of the world. It is a legal proceeding—a fairly simple one, in many states—under which you pay what you can to your creditors and are released from what then remains of your debts. The advantage is that you'll be free of your debts. The disadvantage is that your credit rating will carry the record of the bankruptcy for at least fourteen years. This means you would find it difficult if not impossible to get credit cards or loans, difficult to get insurance in some cases, and perhaps difficult to get a new job.

But the advantages of bankruptcy should not be shrugged off too lightly. Not only are your debts canceled out, giving you a fresh start, but you are allowed to keep certain minimum items to make that fresh start possible. What you are allowed to keep varies according to state law. In some states you can keep clothes, Bibles, school books, and a few hundred dollars in cash or property. In the most generous state, California, you can keep up to $20,000 equity in a house, up to $1,000 in savings ($1,500 if it's in a credit union), and a $500 interest in a car. Many states also exempt the tools of your trade and property that's jointly owned with your spouse (if the debts are yours alone, and not your spouse's).

Before you even consider bankruptcy, you should be aware

that there are certain types of debts it can't wipe out. These include most debts owed to the government (taxes and fines), as well as alimony or child support. They also include "secured debts," in other words, loans for which you've put up property as collateral. The classic example is a mortgage loan.

Bankruptcy is also a potential shield against the other two tactics in the debt collector's repertoire, garnishment and repossession. But it's not the only shield against these tactics.

Garnishiment, sometimes called "wage attachment," means a creditor goes to your employer and demands to be paid a slice out of your salary before you are. This tactic is legal, *but* there's a limit on how big a slice can be taken. Federal law says a creditor can't take more than a quarter of your *after-tax* earnings. It also says you can't be left with less than thirty times the U.S. hourly minimum wage as your weekly take-home pay. Some state laws offer you further protection in terms of how big a slice a creditor may legally take. So if you find someone has started taking a slice out of your paycheck, inquire of your state consumer-protection agency immediately as to what your rights are.

With repossession, as its name implies, the company that sold you something takes it back because you've fallen behind in your payments. This, too, is legal. In most states it's legal even without any warning to you. (Many a debtor has come home to find his car has been jump-started and driven away by a creditor.) If something of yours has been repossessed, do not wait a minute in seeking help from your state consumer-protection agency (or specialized consumer-credit agency, where one exists) *and* from a lawyer. I know a lawyer is the last thing you think you can afford when you're in debt, but you may be able to get excellent advice from a Legal Aid lawyer, whose services are paid for out of public funds.

Though creditors in most states don't have to warn you before they repossess something, they *do* have to tell you how, when, and where they plan to sell it again. In some states you can try to buy the item back, in others not. (Do you begin to see why I say you should consult a lawyer?) But whether or not you're allowed to bid, you should try to be present when the item is sold, or at least keep close tabs on what happens to it. Many merchants will strike up a deal with somebody and sell the merchandise at an artificially low price. Then, you're out your merchandise and may still owe the merchant the difference between what he resold the item for and what you owed him on it when it was repossessed.

By way of illustration, suppose you bought a $3,000 car, paid $1,000 on it in monthly installments, and then fell behind. The merchant could repossess the car, sell it for $500 (perhaps getting more under the table), and still claim that you owed him $1,500. You may be out both the merchandise and the money. Note, though, that in some enlightened states the merchant can have either your money or his goods back, but not both. Because the laws vary from state to state, and because some states are in the process of reforming their laws, it's imperative that you get quick, sound advice. Hence the injunction to contact both a state agency and a lawyer.

One more right you have in the debt collection area also concerns repossession. If the repossessed goods are sold for *more* than you owed—if, for example, that car was resold for $2,100— then the merchant who repossessed your goods owes *you* money. In practice, however, few debtors collect this money, mostly because they don't know they have it coming. You know, however. And that knowledge could enable you to eke a small consolation payment out of your financial setback.

Deceptive Advertising.   See Advertising.

Deceptive Business Practices.   See Unfair business practices.

Dehumidifiers.   See Appliances and appliance repairs.

Delivery of Merchandise.   (See also Mail-order houses.) The store told you your new furniture (or whatever) would be delivered in two weeks. Now it's been five and a half weeks, and still no sign of it. When you call the store to complain, you're told your merchandise should be in shortly. There was a little problem at the supplier's end.

What you do depends on how much you want this particular merchandise and on whether anyone else carries it. If this store is the only one around carrying the very item you want, you'll have to grit your teeth and wait till the merchandise arrives. Meanwhile you can file a complaint with the Better Business Bureau to warn other consumers. If your heart isn't set on this particular item, you can cancel the shipment. This usually creates a furor. If the store refuses to accept your cancellation, you can turn for help to a state or local consumer-protection agency, a voluntary consumer group, or the media. Cancellation works best as a strategy when you haven't yet paid for the goods. If you *have* already paid, you may need to go to small claims court to get your money back. Of course, you're on much stronger ground when canceling an order (or demanding the speed-up of delivery) if you have a written commitment of when the merchandise was supposed to be delivered. Always try to get a delivery date written on the sales slip at the time of purchase.

At least one state, Rhode Island, provides that missing a delivery date by more than thirty days automatically entitles the customer to cancellation of the contract with a full refund, if that's what he wants. In Rhode Island the customer may also select a different but comparable item instead of the original one, or cancel the contract and take a credit toward future purchases. Though I don't know of any other state with a comparable law, there may be some. Your state consumer agency can advise you of the law in your own state.

Discrimination.   For any kind of complaint about discrimination, especially if race is involved, write the U.S. Commission on Civil Rights, 1405 I St., N.W., Washington, D.C. 20425. The commission may not be able to handle your complaint, but it will usually have a good idea where to forward it. For complaints involving job discrimination, write the Equal Employment Opportunity Commission, Room 1246, 1800 G St., N.W., Washington, D.C. 20506. Also contact your state department of labor. For complaints involving sex discrimination, the local chapter of the National Organization for Women can often be helpful.

If you feel you were discriminated against by a bank or finance company, notify your state department of banking and your state consumer credit agency, if there is one. If an insurance company discriminated against you, write or call the state insurance department. As a general rule, on any complaint involving discrimination send a copy of your complaint to your state consumer-protection agency. Send additional copies to your political representatives, from aldermen to U.S. Senators. Your representatives are often keenly interested in such problems, and they may be able to get you quick results in terms of a solution.

Dishwashers. See Appliances and appliance repairs.

Distributorships. See Unfair business practices.

Doctors and Dentists. See Medical treatment.

DOOR-TO-DOOR SALES. Any stereotype you have of door-to-door salesmen has to be wrong, at least some of the time. There are more than 2 million people involved in selling goods and services door to door. Some of them just have to be honest. And some of them just have to be crooks.

If you give in to a persuasive pitch and regret it later, you can take advantage of a three-day cooling-off period law. A Federal Trade Commission regulation, which applies nationwide, gives you three days to cancel a purchase. FTC regulations require the salesman to give you a "notice of cancellation" when you buy anything costing $25 or more. To cancel a sale, all you have to do, legally, is fill out this notice and send it in within three business days of the time the sale took place. Personally, I recommend going a little bit beyond the law and making a photocopy of the notice of cancellation. Also, I recommend sending it by certified mail, return receipt requested. When the seller gets it, he must refund any money you've already paid. If he doesn't, he can theoretically be fined up to $10,000 for violating the FTC rule.

Note that the FTC rule applies only to sales of $25 or more. It does not apply if you're purchasing insurance, real estate, securities, or supplies you use for work. If you feel your rights under the FTC rule have been violated, you can write to "Cooling Off," Federal Trade Commission, Washington, D.C. 20580. Or you can write to the FTC regional office nearest you (they're listed in Chapter 3).

Many states have their own three-day cooling-off period laws, and some of them are better than the FTC rule, in the sense of having lower dollar limits. Many of these state laws are described in Part II. To assert your rights under a state law, send a letter canceling the sale within three business days. Again, keep a copy and send the letter by certified mail. If you have problems, contact your state consumer-protection agency. There is, of course, no reason why you can't use both a state law and the FTC rule. That may sound like overkill, but, if you've just been talked into buying a $300 vacuum cleaner you didn't need, you can use all the help you can get.

Even after the three-day limit has passed, complain if you feel you've been gypped. Write to your state consumer agency, with a copy to The Direct Selling Association, 1730 M St., N.W., Washington, D.C. 20036.

Draperies. See Furniture.

Drugs. All complaints concerning drugs should go to the Food and Drug Administration. The FDA's headquarters are at 5600 Fishers Lane, Rockville, Md. 20852. Its district offices (of which there are nineteen around the United States and in Puerto Rico) are listed on pages 37–38. Be sure to keep all containers you have of the drug, whether they're empty, partly empty, or full.

You may be able to spare yourself the painful possibility of making a drug-related complaint by reminding your physician whenever you're taking two or more medications and asking about their compatibility. Remember that many over-the-counter drugs are quite potent and that your doctor may not be aware if you're taking one of them on a short-term basis at the time he gives you a prescription. (No over-the-counter medication should ever be taken on a long-term basis except under a doctor's supervision. The OTC remedy may provide just enough relief to mask a serious symptom that should be getting medical attention.)

If your complaint concerns a pharmacy, take it to your state board of pharmacy. You'll usually find the board by looking in the phone book for your state's capital city. But be sure also to file a copy of the complaint with your state's consumer-protection agency, especially if the complaint concerns a pharmacy's pricing practices. State boards of pharmacy have often been stanch opponents of price advertising and even of price disclosure.

Electric Companies.   See Utilities and utility bills.

Encyclopedias.   To borrow someone else's phrase about insurance salesmen, encyclopedia salesmen "pander to your best instincts." Of course you want your kids to have the best in life, do well in school, and have their souls opened to the wonders of knowledge. But that doesn't necessarily mean you should buy any particular encyclopedia—or any encyclopedia at all if you can't afford it. Some wonderful soul- and mind-opening goes on in public libraries.

In 1971 *Consumer Reports* magazine did a report on "Encyclopedia Sales Frauds" that remains timely. Among the abuses mentioned were the insistence that prospects sign a contract immediately,* the offering of illusory "free" volumes, the posing of salesmen as school employes, and the offer of a supposedly low price in exchange for a family's serving as a demonstration center or source of testimonials for an encyclopedia. In January 1975 a Federal Trade Commission administrative law judge said that the Encyclopaedia Britannica has made a practice of using deceptive methods to recruit salesmen and of training them to use deceptive methods to enter prospects' homes. (That ruling was subject to appeal and did not constitute a final ruling of the FTC.)

Since most encyclopedias are sold door to door, the rules regarding three-day cooling-off periods may be helpful here. See the entries on "Door-to-door sales" and "Unfair business practices" for some recourse tips. In general, send complaints about encyclopedia sales practices to your state consumer-protection agency, your state Attorney General's office (if the two

---

* This was sometimes said to be necessary to avoid a repeat trip by a salesman. Some prospects were told the volumes would cost $50 more if the salesman had to make another trip.

are different), and the nearest regional office of the Federal Trade Commission.

Environmental Problems.   See Pollution.

False Advertising.   See Advertising.

Finance Companies.   See Credit problems.

Food.   (See also Short weight, measure, or count.) Wrap whatever's left of food you suspect was contaminated in two plastic bags and refrigerate it to preserve the evidence. Call the appropriate agencies without delay. I'm assuming that we're talking about something more serious than milk that's gone sour. In nonserious cases, just go to the store manager and demand your money back. If he refuses, your best recourse is probably not to shop there again. If that store is the only convenient one for you, you can complain to the Better Business Bureau, local consumer agency (if there is one), or state consumer agency.

Your city or county board of health is the first agency to call if you suspect the contamination may pose a health hazard. In some places this agency will have the power to investigate. Elsewhere, it may refer you to another agency, usually the state board of health.

If a meat or poultry product was involved, you should get in touch with your state department of agriculture or the U.S. Department of Agriculture (USDA). It's often difficult to know which one you should call. If you still have the little blue stamp that tells who inspected the meat, contact that agency. If you don't, then you should probably make contact with both agencies to be on the safe side. However, don't bother with the state agency if you live in Colorado, Kentucky, Minnesota, Missouri, Montana, Nebraska, Nevada, New Jersey, North Dakota, Oregon, Pennsylvania, or Washington. In those states all meat and poultry inspection responsibilities have been ceded to the federal government. If a poultry product is involved, don't bother with the state agency in Arkansas, Georgia, Idaho, Maine, Michigan, South Dakota, Utah, or West Virginia either, for the same reason. If you live in New York, you can call your state agriculture department with complaints about meat, but call the USDA with complaints about poultry.

If you think the food product may have been contaminated when it left the food processor (if, for example, you find contamination in a just-opened can or box of a food product), you should notify the nearest regional office of the Food and Drug Administration as soon as possible. The offices are listed on pages 37–38. The FDA has the power to order food-product recalls. The most famous instance of a recall recently involved a fatal case of botulism poisoning from canned mushrooms. But the FDA makes large numbers of recalls involving various degrees of urgency. For its supervision of the market place to be effective, it depends on citizen complaints.

Franchises. See Unfair business practices.

Fraud. See Unfair business practices.

Freezers. See Appliances and appliance repairs.

Funeral Parlors. The Federal Trade Commission has proposed (but, at this writing, has not yet formally adopted) a trade regulation rule that would "require disclosure of price and other information and prohibit various exploitative, unfair, and deceptive practices by the nation's 22,000 funeral homes." The FTC said a rule was needed because it had "reason to believe that bereaved buyers are in an especially vulnerable position and that their vulnerability has been exploited by undertakers through a variety of misrepresentations, improper sales techniques, nondisclosure of vital information and interferences with the market." By the time you read this, the FTC rule may have become law. You can check by looking at newspaper clippings in your local library or by asking the nearest FTC regional office (they're listed on pages 34–35).

The rule would prohibit funeral directors from

- Picking up or enbalming corpses without getting the family's permission first
- Requiring those who opt for an immediate cremation to purchase a casket, or refusing to have inexpensive containers

available for those who choose cremation. (Because cremation can cut funeral and burial costs drastically, perhaps 75
per cent, if the cremation is combined with a simple memorial service instead of the standard funeral, this is an
extremely important provision.)
- Falsely telling people that the law or public health requires
  embalming, a casket, or a burial vault
- Profiting on cash advance items, such as obituary notices,
  flowers, and cemetary charges (These will have to be
  furnished by the funeral home at cost.)
- Making untrue claims about the watertightness or airtight-
  ness of caskets or burial vaults
- Using bait-and-switch tactics (see "Unfair business practices")
- Disparaging a customer's concern over price
- Refusing to provide price information (In fact, funeral
  homes would have to provide fact sheets, price lists, and a
  memorandum recording exactly what items a customer
  selects and what their prices are. Any funeral home that
  advertises would be required to include in its ads the fact
  that price information is available, and the phone number
  people can call to get it.)

Once this trade regulation rule becomes law, your primary
recourse agency on funeral complaints will be the FTC. In the
meantime some states have laws regulating the funeral industry.
Some of them are mentioned in Part II. By the way, according
to the Continental Association of Funeral and Memorial Societies,
only two states, Michigan and Massachusetts, require a casket
for cremation. If a funeral director anywhere else tells you that
state law requires one, he's lying. In some places the crematorium
may choose to require one. But four states—California, Maryland, Minnesota, and New Mexico—expressly permit cremation
without a casket.

A good source of information on funerals and low-cost alterna-
tives is the Continental Association of Funeral and Memorial
Societies, Suite 1100, 1828 L St., N.W., Washington, D.C. 20036.

Furniture. In November 1973 major furniture manufacturers set up the Furniture Industry Consumer Advisory Panel (FICAP) to handle complaints that can't be resolved between the consumer and the retailer or manufacturer. It mediates disputes informally. If necessary, it also assembles a seven-member panel (consisting of one city consumer-protection official, two home economists, a housewife, a home furnishings retailer, a marketing man, and a furniture industry expert) to hear cases in a more formal manner. Judging by press reports I've seen, FICAP (High Point, N.C. 27260) is doing a good job of handling about 400 complaints a year. But it seems to be getting only a small fraction of the cases, judging by the large number of furniture complaints that showed up on my state consumer agency questionnaires. By all means try FICAP if your complaints to the seller and manufacturer seem to be falling on deaf ears. If FICAP fails, some appropriate next steps would be small claims court or letters to the state consumer-protection agencies in both your state and the manufacturer's state.

If your problem concerns home furnishings, such as draperies, rather than furniture *per se*, a smaller amount of money may be involved. It may be useful on these complaints to focus on the merchant rather than the manufacturer, using small claims courts or pressing for Better Business Bureau arbitration. If you wish to bring pressure to bear on the manufacturer, perhaps a letter to the National Curtain, Drapery, and Allied Products Association, 271 North Ave., New Rochelle, N.Y. 10801, would do some good. A letter to the consumer-protection agency in the manufacturer's home state might again prove useful here.

Gas Companies.   See Utilities and utility bills.

Gold.   See Precious metals.

Health Spas.   A better body is something most of us would like to have, and a lot of us seek to acquire one by joining a health spa. So far, fine. The problem is that most health spa contracts require you to pay in advance for all, or a large part, of the cost of a series of shape-up sessions. Some spas then keep a very healthy grip on your money, even if you get sick, move away, or decide after one session that exercise isn't your cup of tea after all.

A typical story was told to me by a woman in Chicago: "I

enrolled my daughter at a health club, but my daughter changed her mind, as teenagers tend to do. I called the club, and a girl there told me I should just tear up my copy of the contract. Well, because she was so charming, I assumed she was truthful as well. Months later I found they had gotten a judgment against me. And shortly thereafter there was a garnishment against my wages."

In another variation on this theme, new health spas sometimes take large deposits or fees from customers before they even open. Then, sometimes, they never do open, or their opening is repeatedly delayed. Meanwhile, they have the consumer's money and the consumer doesn't.

To remedy this situation the Federal Trade Commission has proposed (but, at this writing, not yet formally adopted) a rule that would limit deposits with unopened health spas to 5 per cent of the total contract price. The rule would also require all health spas to give pro rata refunds if a customer canceled out without completing the number of sessions specified in the contract. The spa would be allowed to keep no more than 5 per cent of the total contract price as a penalty for cancelation. Suppose, for example, that you signed up for ten sessions at a price of $100. If you decided, after the second session, that you didn't care for the spa, you could cancel and be entitled to a refund of $75.

By the time you read this book, the proposed FTC rule may have become law. You can find out by checking newspaper clippings at your library or by asking the nearest FTC regional office (see pages 34–35). Besides the FTC, you should report complaints about health spas to your state consumer-protection agency.

Hearing Aids.   For many people a hearing aid can be a blessing. But the way they're advertised and distributed isn't. Some sellers suggest that a hearing aid is the right solution for any hearing problem. But certain types of problems can't be corrected with a hearing aid. And some overzealous dealers have even gone so far as to try to sell hearing aids to people with normal hearing, according to a 1974 study by a Public Interest Research Group in Queens, New York.

The Federal Trade Commission has also been investigating apparent antitrust violations in the hearing aid industry. Several manufacturers allegedly force their distributors to carry one brand only. And exclusive territories are allegedly assigned for dealers, so price competition within brands is virtually eliminated. What's more, dealers are said to be discouraged from offering even replacement parts on other models, so effective servicing of hearing aids is hampered. If you run into any of these problems, call the nearest regional office of the Federal Trade Commission (see pages 34–35).

Under a proposed FTC regulation that may have become law by the time you read this book, you would have the right to a thirty-day trial period if you buy a hearing aid. This would go a long way toward curbing the abuses mentioned earlier. If you decided to return the device, you would have to pay a cancellation fee, but it would be only a small fraction of the total cost. The FTC can advise you whether the rule has gone into effect.

Complaints regarding hearing aids should go to the Food and Drug Administration (which is considering regulating the devices' manufacture and distribution), as well as to the FTC and your state consumer-protection agency.

Heating. See Home improvements and repairs; Utilities and utility bills.

Home Furnishings. See Carpeting; Furniture.

Home Improvements and Repairs. This area generates more complaints than any other except automobiles. The phrase "home improvements and repairs" can cover a multitude of sins, and often does! Among the types of work that may be involved are roofing, siding, painting, driveway paving, basement waterproofing, termite inspection or extermination, remodeling, installing swimming pools, and room additions. The number of things that can go wrong is limitless; the ways in which you can be gypped are virtually endless. The vast majority of troubles can be avoided, though, by choosing a reputable, well-established contractor from your local area and by drawing up a complete contract that specifies exactly what is to be done, the exact materials to be used, a completion date, the exact cost, and the time or times when payment is due. The contract should also include protection against mechanic's liens (see below), a provision for cleanup of the work area, and a prohibition against changes in the contract terms unless made in writing and signed by both you and the contractor. Separately, the contractor should give you written assurance that all his workers on the project, whether they're with his own firm or subcontractors, are covered by workmen's compensation insurance.

Of course, if you've already got problems in the home repair or home improvement realm, all of those tips may sound like advising the farmer after his animals have fled through the open barn door. So let's see what we can do about getting the animals back.

To begin with, a few states have laws that require home improvement or repair contractors to give you some of the protections we talked about. In Wisconsin, for example, contractors are legally obligated to provide written contracts before any work is done. In several states contractors are obligated to warn homeowners about mechanic's liens. A mechanic's lien is a judgment (legal claim) against a homeowner's property that can be obtained by a subcontractor or supplier of materials if he isn't paid by the contractor. That means that if you pay your contractor and he goes broke or skips town without paying his subcontractors, you could end up paying for the same work twice. Several states require the contractor to give the homeowner a complete list of all subcontractors and material suppliers. This gives the homeowner a chance to get lien waivers (agreements not to file a mechanic's lien) from them or to demand that the contractor do this. In Wisconsin the contractor is obliged to obtain lien waivers for the homeowner whether the homeowner asks for them or not. Few states are as progressive as Wisconsin in this area, but check with your state consumer-protection agency to see what protections you have or had coming to you. If your contractor violated the law, this gives you an extra bargaining chip in trying to get some of your money back from him.

When you communicate with your consumer-protection agency,

be sure to find out if home improvement and home repair contractors are licensed in your state. If so, get the name and address of the licensing board and file a detailed complaint with it. At the moment this remedy is available in only a minority of states, but the trend seems to be in the direction of more licensing. In some states contractors are required to post a large bond with the state, just in case some abused consumer has to be compensated someday. You might be that consumer.

Another possible source of help is a trade association. The ones listed below are affiliated wtih the National Home Improvement Council, whose headquarters are at 11 East Forty-fourth St., New York, N.Y. 10017. They vary considerably in how far they can or will go in mediating complaints. But at the least they're an avenue worth checking.

- Boston area: Eastern Massachusetts Home Improvement Council
- Buffalo, New York, area: Home Improvement Industry Council
- Chicago area: The Professional Remodelers Association of Greater Chicago
- Cleveland area: Home Improvement Council of Greater Cleveland
- Denver area: Association of Remodeling Contractors
- Detroit area: Home Improvement Council of Metropolitan Detroit
- Erie, Pennsylvania, area: Home Improvement Council of Erie
- Houston area: Houston Home Improvement Council
- Kansas City, Missouri, area: Greater Kansas City Home Improvement Contractors Association
- Los Angeles area: Los Angeles NHIC-ABCA (National Home Improvement Council and American Building Contractors Association)
- Milwaukee area: Home Improvement Council of Greater Milwaukee
- Mobile, Alabama, area: Home Improvement Council of Mobile

- Orange County, California, area: Orange County Chapter, NHIC-ABCA
- Pittsburgh area: Approved Modernization Contractors Association
- Portland, Oregon, area: Oregon Remodelers Association, Inc.
- St. Louis area: The Remodeling Guild of Greater St. Louis
- San Diego area: San Diego Chapter, NHIC-ABCA
- San Fernando Valley, California, area: San Fernando Valley Chapter, NHIC-ABCA
- San Francisco area: Bay Area Home Improvement Council
- Seattle area: Washington Home Improvement Council
- Springfield, Massachusetts, area: Western Massachusetts Home Improvement Council, Springfield
- Washington, D.C., area: Metropolitan Washington Home Improvement Council

If informal mediation through a trade association isn't available or doesn't help, you may want to seek a more formal kind of arbitration. The contractor may refuse to go before a Better Business Bureau panel of arbitrators. But if he's willing, you may save a lot of time and money (in litigation costs) by taking this route. Your last resort, assuming that by now you've already filed complaints with your state consumer agency and any licensing agency your state has, is to go to court. The amount involved will probably exceed the limit of small claims court jurisdiction, so you'll need a lawyer. But his fee may be well spent if it helps you retrieve some money that otherwise would be gone with the wind.

We must also reckon with the possibility that the person who did, or at least was supposed to do, the work on your home has left town. One common ploy is for a home repair con artist to take a 33 per cent deposit, bring a few materials over to your garage, promise to show up next week, and then disappear. You're left with maybe $50 of materials for perhaps $1,000 of your hard-earned money. If this happens to you, notify your state consumer agency, your state Attorney General's office (if the two are distinct), and most of all—if you haven't already done so—the police!

Another variation on this endless theme is the roofer (or driveway paver, basement waterproofer, etc.) who offers what seems like a bargain price. It is, too. Perhaps the price was only $1,000 for a job that would normally cost $5,000. By the time you realize what a lousy job you got, this fellow has skipped town. Call the same three agencies.

One more variation is the contractor who lets you pay for his work on an installment basis (probably with a stiff interest rate). There's no hint in the price he charges that he's going to do anything but first-quality work. But in fact, the work he does is substandard. He then sells your installment contract to some finance company and leaves town. By the time the shingles start to fall off your roof, or it rains again and you find your basement still leaks, the contractor is long gone. Only the finance company is still around, demanding payment from you and claiming that it scarcely knew the gentleman from whom it bought the installment contract. For a summary of your rights in this situation, see the discussion of the holder-in-due-course doctrine in the entry under "Credit problems."

Hospitals. See Medical treatment.

Houses. If your brand-new house has been completed, but not quite to your satisfaction, there are several places you can turn. First, of course, try to thrash things out with the builder himself. If that fails, a local builders' association may be willing to mediate the dispute. Look in the telephone book under National Association of Home Builders (NAHB) to see if it has a local affiliate in your area. Also look under Builders Association of Greater (name of the nearest large city), or just Builders Association of (name of city or state). If you still can't find a local builders' association, call your city or town hall and ask the building inspector or buildings department for help.

The Better Business Bureau may also be able to help. In many places the BBB offers binding arbitration as a public service, when both parties agree to it. The American Arbitration Association might also be willing to arbitrate your complaint for a small fee (far less that it would cost you to go to court). Traditionally, the AAA has shied away from getting involved in arbitrating consumer disputes, but it is beginning to move in that direction. In Harrisburg, Tucson, Cleveland, Miami, and Pittsburgh, the AAA will definitely handle consumer complaints.

If none of these resources seems to hold the solution to your dispute with a builder, you can fall back on that reliable standby, your state consumer-protection agency (see Part II).

If your problem is with a house you've bought from the previous owner, you have far fewer recourses. Nothing requires the previous owner to tell you about the home's flaws. Even if you asked him whether the roof leaked, and he said no, and then you discovered it *does*, there's still not much you can charge him with except being an evil person. Your only protections are those written into your contract or other written agreements. That's why it's so important to have the assistance of a lawyer when buying a house. If you think a written agreement involved in your purchase has been breached, check with your lawyer. If you don't have a lawyer, get one. If you don't know how to get one, see the entry under "Lawyers."

Humidifiers. See Appliances and appliance repairs.

Inheritance. If you've inherited something, the executor of the will normally makes sure you get what's coming to you. Thus, you should be suspicious if you get a notice in the mail that someone sharing your surname is entitled to an inheritance, and it may be you. If the person sending the mail offers to check into the situation, *for a fee,* you should be doubly suspicious. In fact, you should probably drop a line to your state consumer-protection agency, and your state Attorney General's office (if they're distinct), as well as the Postal Inspector at the nearest major post office. If you've already paid the fee, it may be too late to get your money back. But you can try. Send your complaint to those same three agencies. By the way, thousands of people named Kelly fell for this scheme a couple of years ago.

If you have the opposite kind of inheritance problem—you really have strong reason to think you've inherited something, but it's being kept from you—your best bet is to hire a lawyer, probably on a contingency-fee basis. That means if he succeeds in getting something for you, he'll get an agreed-upon portion as a fee.

Insurance. You had one minor accident that wasn't even your fault, and you find your auto insurance rate has been raised. Or you had two accidents and suddenly found the company won't renew your policy. Or you bought a health insurance policy, but now that you've developed a heart condition the company wants to charge you extra. Or you were turned down for a life insurance policy, and you don't understand why. Or a tree fell on your house, and the homeowner's insurance company is being slow in paying for the damage. Or you have a dented fender, and the auto insurance company won't pay you as much to fix it as your body shop says it will actually cost. Or your spouse died seven weeks ago, and you need some of the life insurance money to pay bills, but your money hasn't come through yet.

With all of these, and the many other problems that can crop up in the realm of insurance, there is one basic governmental recourse for your problems: the state insurance department.

Some state insurance departments are fast to respond, competent, and eager to help. Others are slow, insensitive, and bureaucratic. I'm not going to give my opinion of which are which, because they can change fairly quickly. A new Governor usually appoints a new Insurance Commissioner. But here are their addresses. Thank heaven for the good ones, and pester the heck out of the bad ones.

- Department of Insurance, Administration Building, Montgomery, Ala. 36104
- Division of Insurance, Dept. of Commerce and Economic Development, Pouch D, Juneau, Alaska 99801
- Insurance Department, 1601 W. Jefferson St., Phoenix, Ariz. 85007
- Insurance Division, Department of Commerce, University Tower Building, Little Rock, Ark. 72204
- Department of Insurance, 600 S. Commonwealth Ave., Los Angeles, Calif. 90005
- Insurance Division, Dept. of Regulatory Affairs, 106 State Office Building, Denver, Colo. 80203

- Insurance Department, State Office Building, Hartford, Conn. 06115
- Insurance Department, 21 The Green, Dover, Del. 19901
- Department of Insurance, 614 H St., N.W., Washington, D.C. 20001
- Department of Insurance, The Capitol, Tallahassee, Fla. 32304
- Insurance Department, 238 State Capitol, Atlanta, Ga. 30334
- Insurance Division, Department of Regulatory Affairs, 1010 Richards St., Honolulu, Hawaii 96811
- Department of Insurance, 206 State House, Boise, Idaho 83720
- Department of Insurance, 215 E. Monroe, Springfield, Ill. 62706
- Insurance Department, State Office Building, Indianapolis, Ind. 46204
- Insurance Department, Lucas Building, Des Moines, Iowa 50319
- Insurance Department, Tenth and Topeka Avenue, Topeka, Kan. 66612
- Department of Insurance, Capitol Plaza Tower, Frankfort, Ky. 40601
- Insurance Commission, State Capitol, Baton Rouge, La. 70804
- Bureau of Insurance, Department of Business Regulation, - State House Annex, Augusta, Me. 04330
- Insurance Division, One S. Calvert St., Baltimore, Md. 21202
- Division of Insurance, Department of Banking and Insurance, State Office Building, Boston, Mass. 02202
- Insurance Bureau, Department of Commerce, 111 N. Hosmer St., Lansing, Mich. 48913
- Insurance Division, Department of Commerce, Metro Square Building, Saint Paul, Minn. 55101
- Insurance Department, 1804 Sillers Building, Jackson, Miss. 39205
- Division of Insurance, Department of Consumer Affairs, Regulation and Licensing, 515 E. High St., Jefferson City, Mo. 65101

- Commissioner of Insurance, Auditor's Office, 229 State Capitol, Helena, Mont. 59601
- Department of Insurance, Box 94699, Lincoln, Neb. 68509
- Insurance Division, Department of Commerce, Nye Building, Carson City, Nev. 89701
- Insurance Department, 169 Manchester St., Concord, N.H., 03301
- Department of Insurance, 201 E. State St., Trenton, N.J. 08625
- Insurance Department, Corporation Commission, PERA Building, Santa Fe, N.M. 87501
- Insurance Department, 324 State St., Albany, N.Y. 12210
- Department of Insurance, 316 Fayetteville St., Raleigh, N.C. 27601
- Insurance Department, State Capitol, Bismarck, N.D. 58505
- Department of Insurance, 447 E. Broad St., Columbus, Ohio 43215
- Insurance Department, 2401 Lincoln Boulevard, Oklahoma City, Okla. 73105
- Insurance Division, Department of Commerce, 158 Twelfth St., N.W., Salem, Ore. 97310
- Insurance Department, 108 Finance Building, Harrisburg, Pa. 17120
- Insurance Commissioner, Banking, Insurance and Securities Administration, Department of Business Regulation, 169 Weybosset St., Providence, R.I. 02903
- Department of Insurance, 2711 Middleburg Drive, Columbia, S.C. 29204
- Insurance Division, Department of Commerce and Consumer Affairs, Insurance Building, Pierre, S.D. 57501
- Department of Insurance, State Office Building, Nashville, Tenn. 37219
- Board of Insurance, 1110 San Jacinto, Austin, Tex. 78701
- Department of Insurance, 115 State Capitol, Salt Lake City, Utah 84114
- Deputy Commissioner of Insurance, Department of Banking and Insurance, 120 State St., Montpelier, Vt. 05602

- Bureau of Insurance, Corporation Commission, 1220 Bank St., Richmond, Va. 23219
- Office of Insurance Commissioner, Insurance Building, Olympia, Wash. 98504
- Department of Insurance, State Office Building #3, Charleston, W.Va. 25305
- Office of Commissioner of Insurance, 201 E. Washington Ave., Madison, Wis. 53703
- Insurance Commission, 500 Randall Avenue, Cheyenne, Wyo. 82001

Job-related Problems. (See also Discrimination.) If you are a member of a union, most job-related difficulties should be taken up first with your union. If you're not a union member or your union performs unsatisfactorily, the best recourse agencies for many problems are your state department of labor or the U.S. Department of Labor. Problems regarding job safety should be reported to the U.S. Occupational Safety and Health Administration (OSHA), which is listed in the phone book under the U.S. Labor Department in the government listings in the white pages. Environmental problems should be reported to your supervisors, the authorities mentioned in the entry under "Pollution," or both. Injuries that occur during working time should be reported immediately to your supervisor. If the company doesn't act immediately to provide you with medical care and rehabilitation for the injury, or if the injury was a serious one, report it promptly to your state workmen's compensation board.

Lakeside Lot Sites. See Real estate.

Land Sales. See Real estate.

Landlord-Tenant Problems. The tenants' rights movement is one whose time is finally coming—belatedly, but surely. The number of rights you have as a tenant varies greatly, however, from state to state and from city to city.

Two basic protections exist in most jurisdictions. One is a ban on retaliatory evictions—that is, evictions of a tenant in response to his joining a tenants' group or in response to his filing a complaint with a government agency. The other is a law putting some limits on how long a landlord may legally keep a tenant's security deposit after a lease has expired. Most security deposit laws also limit the size of the deposit (usually to one and a half or two months' rent), and a few require payment of interest on security deposits.

An increasing number of states now recognize the "implied warranty of habitability." This doctrine, parallel to the "implied warranty of merchantability" for consumer products, states that a landlord, by offering his premises for rent, is making an implicit promise that they're suitable for habitation. When a state recognizes this doctrine, either through legislation or through judicial decisions, tenants are much better off. They have a basic premise from which specific tenants' rights can be derived. The implied warranty of habitability where it exists, annuls the old common-law doctrine of "independent covenants." That doctrine held that the tenant's obligation to pay rent was completely separate from any obligation of the landlord to provide livable premises. In other words, you have to pay whether you're getting what you pay for or not. Most leases, if you read them carefully, still adhere to this outmoded philosophy. But many lease provisions will no longer hold up in court. The chief use of some parts of a lease nowadays is to terrorize uninformed tenants, to keep them from exercising their legal rights.

Once a state has recognized the implied warranty of habitability, it is only a small step to legalizing rent strikes, or rent withholding actions, under certain circumstances. And a fair number of states have done so, including almost all of the large, highly urban states. The form rent withholding may take varies, however. In some places, it's legal to make needed repairs yourself, if the landlord has failed to do so, and to take the cost out of the rent you pay. This remedy, called "repair-and-deduct," is useful, but it's almost always limited in terms of the dollar amount deductible. Often the limit is half of one month's rent, though in Massachusetts it's two months' rent, and there's no fixed limit in New Jersey.

The withholding of larger amounts either requires a court

action on your part or invites one from your landlord. Therefore, you should undertake such rent-withholding actions only in conjunction with a lawyer, a tenants' association, or both. Tenants' associations are much to be recommended, anyway, since tenants have much more power to deal with a landlord when they band together than when they work separately. A single person making complaints or withholding rent may be at most a nuisance for a landlord. A group of a third or more of his tenants doing the same thing poses an economic threat and a force that must be dealt with.

If there's no tenants' group in your building and you want to form one, try to do so in conjunction with a citywide or statewide tenants' group in your area. If you can't find a larger group to advise you or to affiliate with, write the National Housing and Economic Development Law Project, 2313 Warring St., Berkeley, Calif. 94704. They may be able to help you link up with a group, and they may also be able to provide you with useful information.

Your group, if it doesn't contain a lawyer, should consult with a lawyer for up-to-date information on applicable state laws. But your strategies needn't be limited solely to the remedies the law provides. Picketing or other forms of adverse publicity can be highly effective against some landlords. Voluntary consumer groups and the media have a fairly high level of interest in landlord-tenant disputes: You may be able to get additional help there. Research about your landlord, particularly his business ventures and his other real estate holdings, could give you an invaluable tactical edge. A book giving invaluable tips on how to conduct such research is *People Before Property,* published by Urban Planning Aid, Inc., 639 Massachusetts Ave., Cambridge, Mass. 02139.

A somewhat longer treatment of landlord-tenant problems and how to cope with them appeared in a series of three articles in *Consumer Reports* magazine (October and November 1974, and January 1975), collectively entitled "A Guide for Renters." A reprint of the three articles can be obtained for $1.00 from the Reprint and Book Department, Consumers Union, Orangeburg, N.Y. 10962.

Late Delivery. See Delivery of merchandise.

Lawyers. A good lawyer is an essential part of a consumer's arsenal. Several of the entries in this section ("Franchises," "Houses," and "Landlord-tenant problems," for example) allude to the need for legal advice. Lawyers, however, tend (as a lawyer might say) to charge fees commensurate with their training and ability. To use the vernacular, they don't come cheap.

If you need legal advice but fear you can't afford it, there are several ways of coping with the problem. If your income is at or near poverty level, you can use Legal Aid lawyers. Many of them are excellent, and most are highly dedicated. If you need only a limited amount of legal advice, your local Bar Association may be able to arrange a half hour's or an hour's consultation with a lawyer for a small fee. This may also be a good course to follow if you just want enough legal advice to find out if you have a good enough case to be worth hiring a lawyer! You can find a bar association in the phone book, under the [name of state, county, or large city] Bar Association.

In some kinds of cases, you can get a lawyer to take your case on a contingency-fee basis. That means that he or she gets paid only if you win. In that case, the fee will normally be some agreed-upon percentage of the amount the lawyer has helped to recover for you.

As a final way of getting relatively low-cost legal help, don't overlook the possibility of a plain old forthright discussion of the fees issue with a lawyer. You may find that he's willing to lower his normal fee because your case appeals to him . . . or even that he's just glad to have the business!

Lawyers, like other mortals, may have feet of clay. What's more, there are crooks in this profession as in any other. If you think you've encountered one, complain to your city, county, or state bar association. Send a copy of your complaint to your state consumer-protection agency and also (if they're distinct) to your state attorney general's office.

Licensed Occupations. The current philosophical swing, both in the consumer movement and in the federal administration, is antilicensing. Licensing boards, it is argued, often become the captives of the industries they are supposed to regulate. Indeed, very often it is the industries themselves that have pushed for licensing. One reason is that it allows them to use the licensing boards to keep out future competition, thus driving up prices and profits. Lewis Engman, chairman of the Federal Trade Commission, has said that an FTC study showed that licensing of television repairmen in Louisiana has not reduced fraud but has resulted in average repair prices higher than those that exist in unregulated jurisdictions. He has also mentioned, as an example of licensing boards that have turned into barriers to competition, the Florida Construction Industry Licensing Board. According to Engman, it has rejected every one of the 2,150 applicants that have come before it seeking a license. On top of everything else, the argument against licensing runs, the licensing boards impose red tape on industries, thus adding to overhead costs ultimately borne by the consumer.

The logic behind these attacks is compelling. But I, for one, do not believe the solution is necessarily to do away with as many licensing boards as possible. Where the boards are well run and include members chosen to represent consumers, they can provide a valuable check on unfair business practices. A board containing a good blend of consumer and industry representatives can combine close supervision and intimate knowledge of an industry with a concern for the public interest. The power to revoke licenses gives the boards a good regulatory club in the closet. And if the boards also have the power to temporarily suspend licenses and to levy fines, they have a good range of possible penalties to employ in discouraging wrongdoing. Such well-run licensing boards do exist. Some of the licensing and regulatory boards in California, for example, come close to fulfilling the model description given here. Even the study cited by Engman found that the number of incidents of fraud seemed to be lower in California, where television repairmen are regulated, than in unregulated jurisdictions. And California repair costs were no higher than those elsewhere, even though wages in California are generally above the national average.

So, licensing and regulation boards are at least a potential resource for you when you have a problem. The occupations that are licensed vary greatly from state to state. Some states seem to license everyone from acupuncturists to zoologists. Others license and regulate only a few professions or occupations. The states that currently license auto repair shops are mentioned here under "Automobile repairs." Those that currently license radio and television repairmen are mentioned in the entry on "Stereo, audio, and audio-visual equipment and repairs."

In most cases, any individual licensing boards are under the jurisdiction of a state agency for licensing and registration. Here are the names and addresses of such agencies, where they exist:

- Alaska Division of Occupational Licensing, Department of Commerce and Economic Development, Pouch D, Juneau, Alaska 99801
- California Department of Consumer Affairs, 1020 N St., Sacramento, Calif. 95814
- Colorado Department of Regulatory Agencies, 1845 Sherman St., Denver, Colo. 80203
- Delaware Division of Business and Occupational Registration, Department of Administrative Services, Old State House Annex, Dover, Del. 19901
- District of Columbia Office of Licenses and Permits, Department of Economic Development, Fourteenth and E Streets, N.W., Washington, D.C. 20004
- Florida Department of Professional and Occupational Registration, 315 S. Calhoun St., Tallahassee, Fla. 32302
- Georgia State Examining Board, Office of Secretary of State, 166 Pryor St., S.W., Atlanta, Ga. 30334
- Hawaii Department of Regulatory Agencies, 1010 Richards St., Honolulu, Hawaii 96813
- Idaho Bureau of Occupational Licensing, Department of Self-Governing Agencies, 2404 Bank Drive, Boise, Idaho 83705
- Illinois Department of Registration and Education, 628 E. Adams, Springfield, Ill. 62706
- Kentucky Division of Occupations and Professions, Execu-

tive Department for Finance and Administration, Box 456, Frankfort, Ky. 40601

- Louisiana Department of Occupational Standards, 721 Government St., Baton Rouge, La. 70801
- Maryland Department of Licensing and Registration, One S. Calvert St., Baltimore, Md. 21202
- Massachusetts Board of Registration, State Office Building, Boston, Mass. 02202
- Michigan Department of Licensing and Regulation, Executive Office, 1033 Washington Ave., Lansing, Mich. 48926
- Missouri Division of Professional Registration, Department of Consumer Affairs, Registration and Licensing, 112 N. Bemiston Ave., St. Louis, Mo. 63105
- Montana Department of Professional and Occupational Licensing, Lalonde Building, Helena, Mont. 59601
- New Jersey Division of Consumer Affairs, Department of Law and Public Safety, 224 E. Hanover, Trenton, N.J. 08608
- New York Division of Professional Licensing Services, Office of Higher and Professional Education, Education Department, 99 Washington Ave., Albany, N.Y. 12210
- North Dakota Licensing Department, Office of Attorney General, State Capitol, Bismarck, N.D. 58505
- Pennsylvania Bureau of Professional and Occupational Affairs, Department of State, 279 Boas St., Harrisburg, Pa. 17120
- Utah Registration Division, Department of Business Regulation, 330 E. Fourth South St., Salt Lake City, Utah 84111
- Vermont Licensing and Registration Division, Office of Secretary of State, Admas Building, Montpelier, Vt. 05602
- Virginia Department of Professional and Occupational Registration, Ninth and Main Streets, Richmond, Va. 23219
- Washington Administrator of Professional Licensing, Department of Motor Vehicles, Highways-Licenses Building, Olympia, Wash. 98504
- Wisconsin Department of Regulation and Licensing, 201 E. Washington Ave., Madison, Wis. 53703

Loan Companies.   See Credit problems; Debt collection.

Magazines. See Publications.

Mail. If a package you sent or expected to receive is lost, or if it appears, upon delivery, to have been handled by a gorilla, contact the Consumer Advocate, U.S. Postal Service, Room 5920, L'Enfant Plaza West, S.W., Washington, D.C. 20260. This is also the office to complain to for any other shortcomings of the U.S. Postal Service, such as excessive delivery time, rudeness of local post office personnel, or consistently long service lines at your local post office. Naturally, you should also complain to the local office.

If your complaint doesn't concern the Postal Service, but rather the sender, see the entry under "Mail-order houses."

Mail-Order Houses. Mail-order complaints are extremely common: They rank fourth in my GRIPE index, for example. But if you run into one, you have a number of strong recourses at your disposal.

A Federal Trade Commission regulation, which took effect on February 2, 1976, says that mail-order houses must deliver you the promised merchandise within the stated time, or within thirty days if no time is stated. If they fail to do this, they must furnish you with "an adequate cost-free means" of canceling the sale and getting a full refund. (A postage-paid card is an example.) If you choose to exercise this right, the house must send you your refund within seven days or credit it to your account on the next billing cycle, if you maintain a charge account with it. If you don't notify the seller that you want a refund, you're presumed to have consented to a thirty-day delay. But any further delay after that would require written consent from you.

The FTC said it issued the rule after holding hearings that produced "well over 10,000 pages of complaints regarding mail-order sales." If you encounter a violation of the rule, complain to the FTC, whose regional offices are listed on pages 34–35.

Let's suppose now that your complaint concerns something other than late delivery. Perhaps the item that came wasn't what you ordered, it was damaged, or it didn't live up to the claims in the catalog or the ad. In these cases, send your first complaint to the mail-order house itself. Wait a full thirty days for a reply.

If things aren't straightened out to your satisfaction in thirty days, send a copy of your original complaint letter, along with a short covering note, to the Mail Order Action Line, Direct Mail Marketing Association, Inc., 6 East Forty-third St., New York, N.Y. 10017. The association (DMMA) represents about 1,600 businesses that either advertise by mail or sell by mail. Naturally, its greatest success is in mediating complaints involving its own members. But it will also try to intercede on your behalf with other mail-order firms.

Send a second copy of your complaint letter to the consumer-protection agency in your own state and a third copy to the consumer-protection agency in the mail-order house's state. Send a fourth copy to the Postal Inspector in Charge at the nearest sizable post office. With these four lines in the water, you stand an excellent chance of getting some action—and of fishing your money back up into the sunlight.

You can, incidentally, lessen the chances that you'll have to file a mail-order complaint by noting extra facts on your order form. Instead of just putting down the order number, it's a good idea to include a description of the item (weight, size, color, and other specifications). Check the company's policy on returns. If it's unclear, you may want to write to the company to find out the policy on returns before you order anything. If you do receive defective merchandise, one thing you should not do is try to send a package back COD. This would only complicate things. Send a letter instead.

Medical Treatment. Doctors, dentists, hospitals, nursing homes, and clinics have all come under fire in recent years. Inadequate care, insensitivity to patients' needs, and ever escalating charges are among the most common complaints. But often these complaints are voiced only in the press or to third parties. Something in the atmosphere of the medical setting seems to discourage many patients from complaining directly to the institutions involved.

Some hospitals have appointed a patient advocate to hear patients' complaints and try to see that something is done about them. If that remedy fails or isn't available, you can direct a written complaint to the chairman of the hospital's board of directors. You can also write to the American Hospital Association, 840 North Lake Shore Drive, Chicago, Ill. 60611, and to your county or state medical society.

The American Hospital Association, incidentally, has promulgated a patient's bill of rights. Among the rights to which that document says you are entitled are:

- The right to be informed about your condition, treatment method, and chances for recovery
- The right *not* to have that same information bandied about to other people, without your consent.
- The right to a reasonable amount of personal attention from the hospital staff, delivered in a considerate manner
- The right to some continuity of care (In other words, you shouldn't be seeing a different doctor each time you see a doctor.)
- The right to have hospital bills explained to you

With nursing homes, you should take complaints to the director, if subordinate personnel haven't solved them. In clinics, you should speak to the physician in charge. After that, you can try the county or state medical society and also send a written complaint to your state consumer-protection agency. That agency may be able to refer your complaint to a specialized board that regulates medical treatment facilities in your state.

For complaints involving individual doctors or dentists, your county or state medical or dental society is the basic recourse agency. You may command more attention for your complaint if you send copies of it to your state health department, your state consumer-protection agency, and possibly the hospital with which your doctor is affiliated. But by no means rush into a formal complaint without trying to talk things over first. Patients who suffer silently under real or imagined wrongs do a disservice to both themselves and their physicians. This advice applies to the subject of fees as well as to purely medical matters. Some doctors and dentists are willing to adjust their fees. Others are not. If it becomes a question of "Pay my fee or go elsewhere," you may be better off going elsewhere. You may find a highly qualified practitioner who charges considerably less. And there are some good-quality health facilities operated on a low-cost basis by cities, counties, and universities.

If you think you have encountered real negligence or malpractice on the part of a doctor or dentist, you can hire a lawyer to file a malpractice suit. Doctors and dentists take these suits very seriously indeed, as the recent headlines about malpractice insurance costs around the country show. Your lawyer will probably take the case on a contingent-fee basis, so you won't have to pay him anything unless you win the suit. But such suits should be undertaken only if you feel your health has actually been impaired by a doctor's actions or inactions, and only if one or more professionals in the health field have told you they think you have a valid case.

Miscellaneous. With complaints that don't fall into one of the categories described in this chapter, a rereading of Chapters 2 and 3 of this book should give you constructive ideas on how to proceed.

Missing Heirs. See Inheritance.

Mobile Homes and Mobile-Home Parks. The days when mobile homes were really mobile have largely passed. Today, mobile home means cheap home. The mobile-home industry is, to a great extent, simply the low-cost end of the housing industry spectrum.

Low cost is not something to be ashamed of. It is, as a matter of fact, something to be proud of—for the seller as well as the buyer. However, some of the short cuts that some mobile-home manufacturers have taken in order to achieve this low cost are nothing to be proud of. That's one reason why mobile homes rank near the top of consumer complaint lists in so many states.

The other reason is that most mobile-home owners don't own the land on which their home rests. Instead, they rent it from a mobile-home park landlord. This means that mobile-home owners have most of the disadvantages of being a tenant. Indeed, in many states they have fewer rights than tenants in apartment buildings. A great many states still have no laws to prevent a mobile-home park landlord from evicting tenants whenever he pleases. Having that power, park landlords can engage in a variety of other abuses: frequent rent increases, added-on fees for the use of various park facilities, arbitrary enforcement of park rules and regulations, and kickback arrangements with local suppliers (of trailer skirting or trailer tie-down services, for example), to name but a few. Those tenants brave enough to risk eviction by complaining may be told, "Leave if you don't like it here." But moving is not a prospect the average mobile-home owner can cheerfully face. Most mobile-home owners have permanent jobs near where they live; space in other parks is limited; and moving a mobile home always entails at least a slight risk of structural damage.

If you have a problem involving either your mobile home itself or your park landlord, start by complaining to your state consumer-protection agency. Some complaints will have to be bounced to another government body. But your consumer-protection agency will probably be able to make connections with other agencies or bureaus faster than you could make them for yourself.

Some forty-six states have now established construction standards for new mobile homes. But only a handful of states have set standards for the warranties that come with the homes. The warranty is your best weapon when it comes to getting a home's defects fixed. A common problem, though, is that you'll be shuttled back and forth between the dealer and the manufacturer. If you find yourself in that position, try to put a stop to the shuttle by getting the dealer to agree to arbitration of the complaint by a Better Business Bureau. If that doesn't work, and the amount of money involved is below the small claims court limit in your state, file a suit in small claims court. On major problems, it may well be worth hiring a lawyer and going to a conventional court. Once they see that you mean business, your opponents may choose to settle.

Help for mobile-home warranty problems may be on the way, at long last. As this book was being written, the Federal Trade Commission was holding hearings regarding a proposed rule on mobile-home sales and services. The rule, if and when it becomes law, would require that manufacturers who delegate warranty responsibilities to dealers enter into service contracts that clearly delineate the responsibility of both the manufacturer and the dealer. When a consumer makes a complaint under the warranty, the necessary repairs would have to be done within thirty days. If the defect affected the safety of a mobile home or rendered it "substantially uninhabitable," the repairs would have to be started within three business days and completed "expeditiously." And manufacturers who delegated warranty-repair responsibilities to dealers would have to monitor the dealers' performance to make sure it was adequate. You can find out whether this proposed Trade Regulation Rule has taken effect by contacting the closest regional office of the Federal Trade Commission (listed on pages 34–35).

Moving.   Some of the most common complaints about movers are (1) they didn't show up on time, (2) they didn't deliver on time, (3) they broke things, (4) they didn't pay fair compensation for the things they broke, (5) their actual charge was far higher than their estimate, and (6) they charged extra for things we didn't know were going to cost extra.

You can avoid having a lot of these complaints come up in the first place by reading a seventeen-page booklet published by the Interstate Commerce Commission called *Summary of Information for Shippers of Household Goods*. The ICC also requires a mover to furnish consumers with "performance information" on themselves. This information, amounting to a sort of report card, includes the percentage of shipments that mover picked up and delivered on time last year; the percentage of shipments where the cost was within 10 per cent of the estimate; the percentage of shipments with goods lost or damaged; the percentage of shipments where consumers filed claims for damages; and the percentage of those claims that were paid. If you study the report cards of a few movers and get several estimates before picking a mover, you'll probably save yourself a lot of headaches.

I'm not going to list the addresses of headquarters of moving companies here, because the companies are legally obliged to give you these in case you want to file a claim. If you run into a problem you can't resolve by complaining to the company, the place to complain is the Interstate Commerce Commission. The

ICC has seventy-eight branch offices around the country. Its national address is simply Interstate Commerce Commission, Washington, D.C. 20423.

Nondelivery of Merchandise. See Delivery of merchandise.

Nursing Homes. See Medical treatment.

Ovens. See Appliances and appliance repairs.

Paving. See Home improvements and repairs.

Pensions. See Job-related problems.

Pharmacies. See Drugs.

Phonographs. See Stereo, audio, and audio-visual equipment and repairs.

Pollution. In most places there are three, or even four, levels of government concerned with pollution control. If you see an apparent violation that troubles you, report it to the appropriate agencies at the federal, state, and county levels—and at the city level, too, if the city in question has an antipollution agency. Local and state agencies often bear names like Department of Environmental Control or Environmental Protection Agency. If you're having trouble finding the appropriate agency, your local library's reference department or the switchboard operator at your county building can probably help you. On the federal level, report pollution complaints to the U.S. Environmental Protection Agency. Its nationwide headquarters are at 401 M St., S.W., Washington, D.C. 20460. Its ten regional offices are as follows:

- Region I (Connecticut, Massachusetts, New Hampshire, Vermont, Rhode Island, Maine) headquarters, John F. Kennedy Building, Room 2303, Boston, Mass. 02203
- Region II (New York, New Jersey, Puerto Rico, Virgin Islands) headquarters, 26 Federal Plaza, Room 908, New York, N.Y. 10007
- Region III (Pennsylvania, Delaware, Maryland, Virginia, West Virginia, and District of Columbia) headquarters, Cur-

tis Building, Sixth and Walnut Streets, Philadelphia, Pa. 19106

- Region IV (Georgia, Albama, Florida, Kentucky, Mississippi, North Carolina, South Carolina, Tennessee) headquarters, 1421 Peachtree St., N.E., Atlanta, Ga. 30309
- Region V (Illinois, Indiana, Michigan, Minnesota, Ohio, Wisconsin) headquarters, 1 N. Wacker Drive, Chicago, Ill. 60606
- Region VI (Texas, Arkansas, Louisiana, New Mexico, Oklahoma) headquarters, 1600 Patterson St., Suite 1100, Dallas, Tex. 75201
- Region VII (Iowa, Kansas, Missouri, Nebraska) headquarters, 1735 Baltimore Ave., Kansas City, Mo. 64108
- Region VIII (Colorado, Montana, North Dakota, South Dakota, Utah, Wyoming) headquarters, 1860 Lincoln St., Suite 900, Denver, Colo. 80203
- Region IX (California, Arizona, Hawaii, Nevada, American Samoa, Guam, Trust Territories of the Pacific, Wake Island) headquarters, 100 California St., San Francisco, Calif. 94111
- Region X (Washington, Idaho, Oregon, Alaska) headquarters, 1200 Sixth Ave., Seattle, Wash. 98101

Post Office. See Mail.

Precious Metals. The Federal Trade Commission has stated, "The purchase of an investment in gold is a potentially fertile area for unscrupulous promoters and fraudulent schemes, particularly in view of the inflationary state of the economy and the fascination that surrounds gold. Moreover, the price of gold is often dictated by speculative interests and is subject to significant and rapid fluctuations." Many of the same points can be made in relation to silver. In addition, no amateur can assess the purity of either metal; this has to be done by an expert, using specialized equipment. So, if you haven't already gotten involved in the purchase of precious metals, don't—at least until you've read up thoroughly on the subject.

Suppose, though, that you've already met up with one of those "unscrupulous promotors" or "fraudulent schemes." Complain in writing to the person or company that sold you the precious (or ostensibly precious) metal. Send a copy of your complaint letter to your state consumer-protection agency (see Part II), and to the Federal Trade Commission's closest regional office (see pages 34–35).

If the firm that sold you the metal is a dealer in securities, write to the Securities and Exchange Commission (see pages 39–40). If it was a bank or savings institution, call or write the appropriate banking authority (see under "Banks"). If the party that sold you the metal has skipped town, notify your state Attorney General's office (assuming you haven't already—this office *is* the consumer-protection agency in some states) and the police.

Publications. Most of the complaints about publications, I'm embarrassed as a former magazine editor to say, are about magazine subscriptions. You send your check in, and your subscription takes months to start—or perhaps it never starts. Sometimes it starts, but issues are skipped. Since you parted with your money in the first place because you're highly interested in the subjects the magazine covers, you're now highly annoyed. And well you should be. Editors and reporters I know at a number of magazines and newspapers are extremely embarrassed by their circulation problems.

Your first complaint, of course, should go to the manager of the subscription department or, in the case of newspapers, the circulation department. If the publication is local, follow up your letter with one or more telephone calls. If not, follow up your first letter with a second, two weeks later. If after a month you've had no response, send a letter to the publisher (his name is usually listed on the publication's masthead), enclosing copies of your earlier complaints. You might add a bit to the momentum by writing the Magazine Publishers Association, 575 Lexington Ave., New York, N.Y. 10022.

If a newspaper is involved, you may find it piquant (or even helpful) to write about your subscription problem in a letter to the editor or a letter to the paper's consumer action line.

A final resort, and one that should normally prove effective, is to complain to your state consumer-protection agency.

While complaints about subscriptions are the most common

gripes, you may have complaints about the content of the publication. If you find an advertisement to be deceptive or in bad taste, write the publication's advertising manager, or (for large publications) department of advertising acceptability. If your complaint concerns editorial content, try to find the chief editor's name on the masthead and write him. If you think fairness or accuracy demands a correction of an item previously printed, say so at the outset of your letter. This helps to crystallize the issues involved. It also improves the chances that your "letter-to-the-editor" will be published, since the chief editor may propose that route as a substitute for a correction.

If you encounter an item in a book that strikes you as misleading (or distasteful), you needn't assume that the damage has already been done. Many books go through more than one printing. So check the title page to see who the publishing house is, look up that publisher's address on the copyright page or at the library, and send a letter to the publisher.

One other subject of complaints in the publications realm is book clubs. See the entry under "Buying clubs" for suggestions on dealing with the problems that can arise here.

Pyramid Plans. See Unfair business practices.

Racial Discrimination. See Discrimination.

Radios. See stereo, audio, and audio-visual equipment and repairs.

Ranges. See Appliances and appliance repairs.

Real Estate. If you bought land in another state and are sorry you did, your problem may fall within the province of the Office of Interstate Land Sales Registration, Department of Housing and Urban Development, 451 Seventh St., S.W., Washington, D.C. 20410. Since 1973 HUD has had regulations requiring full disclosure of key facts involved in interstate land transactions. Among the things that must be disclosed—in a property report that must be furnished to prospective buyers—are these:

- Whether there is physical access to the property by car
- Whether there are legal encumbrances on the title to the property

- The availability of utilities
- The availability of sewage lines
- The availability of fire and flood insurance
- Whether decent drinking water is available (If this is not known, the report must say so.)
- Whether a building permit would be required to build on the land
- Information on the financial standing of the developer
- Special risk factors, such as restrictions on resale of the land
- Information on any lawsuits that have been filed against the developer, and about any actions by government agencies to prosecute or discipline the developer

If you can demonstrate that the information furnished in the property report you received was false or inadequate, HUD may be able to help you or direct you to someone who can. It might even launch its own investigation, which could indirectly help you in getting your money back.

Besides the federal agency, you should direct a copy of any real estate complaint you have to the appropriate state agency. Finding that agency isn't always easy, though. So send your complaint first to your state consumer-protection agency (see Part II). In your covering letter, ask whether there are any specialized agencies in the state, such as a real estate commission, to which your complaint should also be sent.

If the firm that sold you the land (or, in rarer cases, the building or buildings) was an out-of-state firm, file a complaint also with a consumer-protection agency in that firm's state.

Don't overlook the possibility of hiring a lawyer, possibly on a contingent-fee basis, to handle your complaint in the courts. The amount of money involved is probably sizable for you. If a lawyer can get it back, the money you spend on his fee would be worth spending.

Do not, in your anxiety to get rid of land you wish you hadn't bought, fall for the second half of a land swindler's one-two punch. Some firms specialize in offers to sell off land you don't want. They may take from you a fee or a deposit and then disappear, leaving you still stuck with the land, and out some additional money as well.

Record Clubs.   See Buying clubs.

Recreational Vehicles.   See Automobile repairs; Automobile sales.

Referral Selling.   See Unfair business practices.

Rentals.   The term "rental firms" actually refers to several quite distinct kinds of businesses. There are apartment rental referral agencies; rent-a-car firms; specialized equipment rental outfits; and general merchandise rental outlets. We'll say a word or two about each.

Apartment rental agencies, currently thriving mainly in big cities with housing shortages, don't rent anything to anyone themselves. Rather, they're referral agencies, matching up potential tenants with potential landlords, and theoretically saving trouble for each. In better times (times when housing was less scarce, anyway), the agencies' fees used to be paid by landlords. No more. Now it's the tenant who pays the agency's fee in exchange for its having helped him (or her) find a place to live. Such fees are sometimes a flat dollar sum. More often they're scaled to the rental of the apartment found, ranging from half a month's rent to as much as two months' rent. Such fees can well merit grumbling on your part. But they don't merit complaints, *if* the fees were openly stated and *if* the agency really was instrumental in your finding the apartment in question. Where that's not the case, or where an agency tries to charge you when it hasn't rendered you any services, complain to the Better Business Bureau, a local consumer-protection agency if there is one (in big cities there often is), and your state consumer-protection agency.

If you run into a problem with a rent-a-car firm, a good place to complain is the Federal Trade Commission (see pages 34–35 for a list of the FTC's regional offices). The FTC has been following activities in this industry with great interest; in 1975 it filed an antitrust action against the three largest rent-a-car firms. It also makes sense to send copies of your complaint to your state consumer agency or the state agency in the state where you rented the car and to any applicable local consumer agency. This should be done, of course, only after first complaining to the rent-a-car company's headquarters. Addresses for four of the largest companies are

- Hertz Corp., 660 Madison Ave., New York, N.Y. 10021 (Robert Stone, president)
- Avis Rent-a-Car System, Inc., 900 Old Country Road, Garden City, N.Y. 11530 (W. V. Morrow, Jr., president)
- National Car Rental System, Inc., 5501 Green Valley Drive, Minneapolis, Minn. 55437 (Joseph James, president)
- Budget Rent-a-Car Corp. of America, 35 E. Wacker Drive, Chicago, Ill. 60601 (Morris Belzberg, president)

The other two types of rental agencies—specialized equipment rental firms and general merchandise rental firms—are quite similar in the types of problems they pose and in the ways you can fight back. Indeed, which category a particular firm falls into can be a question of degree. Rental firms that are truly specialized (dealing only in, say, power tools or medical supplies) may be somewhat more dependent on repeat business. They might also be susceptible to intervention on your behalf from one of their large, steady customers. But, in general, your recourses here are likely to be small claims courts or local and state consumer-protection agencies. Better Business Bureau arbitration panels, where they exist, may also provide an excellent forum for settling a dispute with an equipment or merchandise rental firm.

Repairmen. See Licensed occupations; also see entry concerning item repaired.

Retail Stores. This is a bit of a catchall category: Most of the advice in Chapters 2 and 3 is applicable here. In complaining to retail stores, it's especially important to deal with people in authority. Don't talk to anybody who won't give you his or her name and title. Find out who can make the decision you need. "Do you have the power to authorize a refund?" "Do you have the authority to offer me a replacement?" Asking questions like these can save you a lot of time and irritation. They can also help speed your route to the person who can really cope with your complaint. Many times the store manager is the person who holds the keys to your refund. If he can't or won't help you, your next step is to find out whether the store is part of a chain or owned by another corporation. If so, write to the chain headquarters or to the chief executive of the parent company. This tactic often produces a startling change of attitude.

Only after you've exhausted the internal corporate remedies should you turn to an outside agency for help. You can and should, however, use the *threat* of bringing in outside agencies to help speed your complaint through a store's machinery. Which agency or agencies you ultimately choose is a question of tactics. Possibilities include small claims courts, the Better Business Bureau, a local consumer-protection agency, and a statewide consumer-protection agency. Copies of your previous complaint letters to the store should be sent to the agency in question or produced in small claims court. For this reason, you should always put your complaints in writing the minute you suspect a solution isn't going to be easy to reach. This should be done even if the store in question is just across the street from you. Not only will written complaints provide a valuable record, they will also demonstrate to the store that you mean business.

Retirement Benefits.   See Job-related problems.

Rugs.   See Carpeting.

Savings Institutions.   See Banks.

Securities.   In the broadest sense, a security is anything sold for its future investment value. However, the term is normally used to refer to stocks, bonds, and options to buy or sell stocks or bonds. If you feel your transaction has been handled improperly, your first complaint should go to your broker, and your second complaint should go to the president of your broker's firm. Put it in writing as well as orally. If this route fails to produce satisfaction, send copies of your complaint letter to the National Association of Securities Dealers, 1735 K St., N.W., Washington, D.C. 20006, and to the Securities and Exchange Commission (SEC).

The SEC is the federal agency with broad responsibilities and strong powers for regulating the entire securities industry. Its headquarters are at 500 North Capitol Street, Washington, D.C. 20549. It also maintains seventeen regional and branch offices in New York, Boston, Philadelphia, Arlington, Atlanta, Miami, Chicago, Detroit, Cleveland, Saint Louis, Houston, Fort Worth, Denver, Salt Lake City, Los Angeles, San Francisco, and Seattle. (Regional offices are listed on pages 39–40.)

If complaining to the SEC doesn't have any effect—or if its effect should be to get the brokerage firm disciplined but not to get you your money back—consider hiring a lawyer and going to court. In many states you may recover some or all your attorneys' fees if you win. If you believe many people may have been victimized in the same way you were, you and your lawyer may want to consider a class action suit. These are legal in some nineteen states. They're also legal, technically, in the federal courts, but there are substantial barriers to bringing them there.

Self-Improvement. See Vocational schools.

Sex Discrimination. See Discrimination.

Short Weight, Measure, or Count. What you do with this type of complaint depends in part on how mad you are. Personally, I get very mad.

If you are only mildly annoyed, the simplest thing to do would be to go straight back to the store and ask for a full or partial refund, or for an exchange. The store manager would probably give it to you. And you could drop things right there.

However, you may start to reflect on a few things. While a short weight (or measure or count) may affect you only slightly, it can result in a lot of ill-gotten gains for a merchant or manufacturer. Consider the case of the Dairylea Cooperative, which happened to be the oldest and largest dairy cooperative in New York State and one of the largest in the nation. For five and a half years, from 1967 to 1973, the cooperative adulterated fresh whole milk by adding powdered skim milk to it. It also altered the milk content of several of its other dairy products. And this cooperative was selling milk at the rate of about 1.75 billion quarts a year.

Foreign recipients of U.S. grain shipments have been receiving less grain than was called for in their agreements with this country. Reason: short-weighting as a virtual way of life at American export grain-loading docks.

The New York City Department of Consumer Affairs estimated, as Francis Cerra reported in the *New York Times,* "that New York City consumers bought $25 million worth of nothing in 1974."

And a Florida disk jockey made news when he started counting items packed by number and discovered that very often the count was short. Following his lead, the staff of the *Wall Street Journal* started counting the number of items found in containers packed by number—everything from paper clips and file cards to vitamin pills. Often they found short counts in as many as 40 per cent of the containers!

Reflecting on facts like these, you may get a little more riled up. If so, what should you do? Well, for a start, many cities and almost all counties have departments of weights and measures. Complain to them. You may want to hold onto the container in question or turn it over to the government agency. This may slow down your getting a refund, but it will preserve the evidence.

Especially if the goods were packaged in the store where you bought them, you may want to file a complaint with your state consumer-protection agency. If they were packaged elsewhere, you may want to file a complaint with the state agency in the home state of the manufacturer or shipper. See Part II of this book for the addresses of the appropriate agencies.

Silver.   See Precious metals.

Songwriting Companies.   See Unfair business practices.

Stereo, Audio, and Audio-visual Equipment and Repairs.   Complaints in this realm are fairly evenly divided between the defects of new products and the practices of the people who fix the products. Television sets, radios, and stereo equipment are the most frequent focuses of complaints, probably because they're the most widely used types of electronic equipment. But other items, from tape recorders to walkie-talkies, also fall into this category.

If you buy a new TV (or whatever) and it isn't working right, you'll naturally call the store for warranty service. If, after one or two service calls, the set still isn't working right, consider demanding a new set. Why should you be stuck for the next five or ten years with a lemon that's going to require frequent repairs? Demanding a new set may have two positive effects: (1) You may actually get a new set; (2) your demand may accelerate the store's attention to the necessary repairs. If these are done promptly and satisfactorily, you may decide you don't need a new set after all.

If the store's attempts to help you are unsuccessful, desultory, or unsatisfactory, I would take several simultaneous steps. Write the manufacturer. Send copies of your complaint letters to the store (I assume you've been following this book's advice and making at least some of your complaints in writing) to the Better Business Bureau, to a local consumer-protection agency if there is one (see Part II to find out), and to your statewide consumer-protection agency.

To save you time in writing the manufacturer, here are the addresses of some of the key firms in the stereo, audio, and audio-visual field:

- Admiral Corp., 3800 West Cortland, Chicago, Ill. 60647 (Ross D. Siragusa, Jr., president)
- General Electric Co., Appliance and Television Group, 570 Lexington Ave., New York, N.Y. 10022
- KLH Research and Development Corp., 30 Cross St., Cambridge, Mass. 02139
- The Magnavox Co. 345 Park Ave., New York, N.Y. 10022 (R. H. Platt, president)
- Motorola, Inc., 9401 West Grand Ave., Franklin Park, Ill. 60131 (William J. Weisz, president)
- North American Phillips Corp., 100 East Forty-second St., New York, N.Y. 10017 (Pieter C. Vink, president)
- RCA Corp., 30 Rockefeller Plaza, New York, N.Y. 10020 (Anthony L. Conrad, president)

- Sony Corp. of America, 9 W. Fifty-seventh St., New York, N.Y. 10019 (Harvey Schein, president)
- Zenith Radio Corp., 1900 N. Austin Ave., Chicago, Ill. 60639 (John J. Nevin, president)

If your complaint to the manufacturer bears no fruit, it's time to pick up the threads of your complaint against the retailer. If none of the agencies mentioned seems about to help bring the stituation to a head, your best bet may well be to file suit in small claims court. The amount of money involved in most cases will be below the maximum permitted in such courts.

Let's turn our attention now to complaints that involve the servicing of older sets. Your initial complaints, of course, will go to the firm that provides the servicing. Make these complaints both orally and in writing. The latter provides a written record of the facts, which could prove invaluable later; it also impresses the firm with your seriousness. If outside help should be necessary, there are several possible sources. In some states (at this writing, these include California, Connecticut, the District of Columbia, Florida, Indiana, Louisiana, Massachusetts, Oregon, Utah, and Vermont), television and radio repair dealers must be registered or licensed. The effectiveness of the licensing agencies in curbing fraud—or dealing with it—varies from state to state. And in some states (Louisiana, for example, according to an FTC study), the chief effect of licensing seems to have been to lessen competition and raise prices. So approach these agencies gingerly. But do approach them as one possible avenue to a solution. (For the addresses of state licensing bodies, see the entry under "Licensed occupations.")

Other sources of aid in disputes with repairmen include the Better Business Bureau, a local consumer-protection agency, your statewide consumer-protection agency, or filing suit in small claims court.

Stocks. See Securities.

Stoves. See Appliances and appliance repairs.

Subdivisions. See Real estate.

Swimming Pools. See Home improvements and repairs.

Tape Recorders. See Stereo, audio, and audio-visual equipment and repairs.

Telephone Company. See Utilities and utility bills.

Television Sets. See Stereo, audio, and audio-visual equipment and repairs.

Tenant Problems. See Landlord-tenant problems.

Termite Inspection. See Home improvements and repairs.

Toys. Complaints about toys have a special dimension because small children have such towering hopes. They are not yet cynical about advertising: If a rocket ship in an ad looks like they can climb inside, they'll expect to. They are not yet resigned to poor workmanship: If a new toy breaks, they'll be bitterly disappointed. They are not yet capable of using things with discretion: If an item is fragile, it will be broken. If an item has sharp edges, children will bump up against them. If an item has small, dangling parts, very young children will swallow them.

Thus, any complaint you have about a defective toy is fairly likely to wind up being a product safety complaint as well. If you feel a safety element is involved in your complaint, call the U.S. Consumer Product Safety Commission, Washington, D.C. 20207. The commission maintains a Safety Hot Line for complaints. The number is 800-638-2666. It won't cost you a dime, and it may save some child from being hurt. In Maryland, the number is 800-492-2937. In Alaska and Hawaii, the toll-free phone connection isn't available, so you'll have to write.

In addition to reporting any safety hazard, you'll want to get your money back. Here the remedies are similar to those for any unsatisfactory product purchased at a retail store. Complain to the retailer and the manufacturer. If that fails to produce results, get in touch with local and state consumer-protection agencies (see Part II), and the Better Business Bureau. If the toy was expensive or if you strongly believe in "the principle of the thing," you can also file suit in small claims court.

Trailers. See Mobile homes and mobile-home parks.

Travel. Chances are your travel complaint concerns either (1) a bus or train trip, (2) a travel agent, or (3) an airplane trip. We'll take up each of these areas in turn. (Car and rental-car complaints are discussed elsewhere. See the entries headed "Automobile repairs," "Automobile sales," and "Rentals.")

With bus or train problems, your first complaint should go to the station manager, your second to the president of the bus or train company. Three addresses may be useful at this juncture:

- National Railroad Passenger Corp. (AMTRAK), 955 L'Enfant Plaza North, S.W., Washington, D.C. 20260
- Greyhound Lines, Inc., Greyhound Tower, Phoenix, Ariz. 85013
- National Trailways Bus System, 1200 I St., N.W., Washington, D.C. 20005

If this course of action bears no fruit, you should complain to the Interstate Commerce Commission, and possibly to the agency that regulates bus and train passenger travel in the state where the problem took place. The state agency may be difficult to find, because each state assigns this thankless task to a different part of its administrative structure. In most states either the state transportation department or the state public utilities commission has this hot potato or can tell you who does. (See under "Utilities" for a list of public service commissions and public utility commissions.)

On the federal level, your recourse is always the Interstate Commerce Commission (ICC). It should be able to help you if a bus or train line loses or damages your luggage. It will also take complaints about other problems, including chronic lateness by some bus or train lines. What it does with these latter complaints, besides accept them, is a subject on which many people have wondered aloud. Anyway, the ICC's headquarters address is simply Washington, D.C. 20423. It also has seventy-eight regional offices scattered around the country.

If your complaint concerns a travel agent, it should go first to that agent and second to the president of the agency, if they are not one and the same. If you meet with indifference, send a copy of your complaint letter to the American Society of Travel

Agents (ASTA), 360 Lexington Ave., New York, N.Y. 10017. If this route doesn't produce results, your state consumer-protection agency is a logical next step.

With airline complaints, the stakes are often higher than with bus or train problems. The comedian Shelly Berman's main concern was that the plane might "come to a sudden stop—like against a mountain." Most airline problems are likely to be less dramatic than that, but still pretty annoying if and when they affect you. You may be (1) overcharged for your ticket, (2) bumped off a flight for which you held a confirmed reservation, (3) subjected to long delays or flight cancellations, (4) confounded by lost luggage, or (5) some combination of the above.

Your first recourse, in the case of any of these hassles, is the airline itself. We've noted that with any consumer complaint it's important to speak with someone in authority. This is even more applicable than usual when a problem arises at an airport. Unfortunately, in the rushed atmosphere of a terminal, it's sometimes hard to find the right person. Press underlings to let you talk with their superiors. Use the courtesy phones provided by some lines. Or go to a pay phone, if necessary, in an attempt to reach the person who can help you.

If this hectic effort fails, you're going to be trying to straighten things out by letter. Here are the home office addresses of some of the major airlines:

- American Airlines, Inc., 633 Third Ave., New York, N.Y. 10017 (Albert V. Casey, president)
- Braniff International, Braniff Tower, Exchange Park, Dallas, Tex. 75235 (C. Edward Acker, president)
- Continental Air Lines, Inc., Los Angeles International Airport, Los Angeles, Calif. 90009 (Robert Six, president)
- Delta Air Lines, Atlanta Airport, Atlanta, Ga. 30320 (Daniel Garrett, Jr., president)
- Eastern Air Lines, Inc., 10 Rockefeller Plaza, New York, N.Y. 10020 (S. C. Higginbottom, president)
- National Airlines, Inc., International Airport, Miami, Fla. 33159 (L. B. Maytag, president)
- Northwest Orient Airlines, Minneapolis-Saint Paul Inter-

national Airport, Saint Paul, Minn. 55111 (Donald Nyrop, president)
- Pan American World Airways, Pan Am Building, New York, N.Y. 10017 (William Seawell, president)
- Trans World Airlines, Inc., 605 Third Ave., New York, N.Y. 10016 (F. C. Wiser, Jr., president)

Both at the airport and when you're writing a protest letter, you should be armed with a pretty good idea of what your rights are. If you discover that you were overcharged for a ticket (a not uncommon occurrence, thanks to the immense complications of the airlines' fare structures), you're entitled to the difference between what you paid and what you should have paid. If you're bumped from a flight because the airline overbooked that flight, you're entitled to what's called "denied boarding compensation." This consists of the price of your ticket (up to $200), *plus* your original ticket back. Thus, if your total fare was less than $200, you get what amounts to a free (though late) ride. If you no longer care to go wherever you were going, you can cash in your ticket and get what amounts to double your money back (or your money back plus $200—whichever is less).

If you're delayed for four hours or more (because of weather, equipment troubles, or whatever), ask to see the airline's tariff book. (By law, they must show it to you.) Look under "delayed flights." You'll probably find the airline is obliged to pay for your meals while you're waiting. If the delay occurs at night, they may well be obliged to pay for your overnight lodgings. Sometimes the personnel at the airport will volunteer these amenities. Often they'll provide them if you ask for them. But if not, you should be able to win reimbursement by writing the airline.

If your luggage should be bruised, banged, broken, shredded, or just plain lost, you again have rights to compensation. But the law limits the airline's liability to $500 for *all* of your bags. If you carry valuable things in your luggage, you should probably purchase extra insurance from the airline. Its cost was recently about 10 cents for each extra $100 of insurance. If the airline damages your goods you're entitled to the actual amount of the damage, up to $500, or a higher ceiling if you've bought the insurance.

If your reasonable, factual letter to the airline fails to bring you prompt redress, complain to the Office of Consumer Affairs, Civil Aeronautics Board, 1825 Connecticut Ave., N.W., Washington, D.C. 20428. The CAB has the final say on all complaints regarding the airlines. If it can't help you, your only further recourses are lawsuits and publicity. You may also want to write the Aviation Consumer Action Project (ACAP) a nonprofit public-action group that Ralph Nader helped form. ACAP probably can't help you with your individual complaint, but it can use the information you provide as it fights for various reforms in the airline industry. ACAP's address is 1346 Connecticut Ave., N.W., Washington, D.C. 20036.

Truck-Driving Schools. See Vocational schools.

Unfair Business Practices. The number of possible unfair or deceptive business practices is as limitless as the fertility of the greed-inspired mind. We'll discuss thirteen such practices very briefly here, with a view to helping you recognize them quickly, so you can take appropriate action as soon as possible. The full arsenal of complaint methods described in Chapter 3 is applicable to most of these situations. But your basic recourse, when you encounter unfair business practices, is your state consumer-protection agency. These agencies are set up, after all, to enforce a state's unfair and deceptive trade practices act.

Bait and Switch Tactics. A department store had a sale on "personal size" nine-inch black-and-white television sets—only $68, according to the ad in the paper. So the young man walked in to buy one. Well, said the salesman, those TVs have to be specially ordered. It would take a few weeks to get one. "But they're on sale!" exclaimed the young man. "The ad's in the paper today." Sorry, said the salesman, but each store only has one of those sets on hand, for demonstration purposes. If the young man wanted a set right now, he could select a twelve-inch model that also happened to be on sale. It would cost only $79.88.

That scenario (a true one, by the way, involving a major department store in mid-1975) is a classic example of bait and switch tactics. Something is advertised at an attractively low price. When you come into the store, the salesman either starts disparaging the advertised item or tells you it's not available right away. He tries to "trade you up" to a more expensive item, whose good qualities and immediate availability seem to know no limits.

Bait and switch tactics are illegal in almost every state, either through an explicit statutory prohibition or through the state's unfair and deceptive trade practices act. Some cities also have ordinances banning the tactic. And the Federal Trade Commission has had guidelines against what it calls "bait advertising" since 1959. (The FTC rules can be used against any merchant big enough to "affect" interstate commerce.) So if you encounter bait and switch tactics, complain to your state and local agencies (see Part II) and to the FTC regional office nearest you.

The young man who was looking for a television set didn't know where to complain, but he knew bait and switch tactics were illegal, so he called the police. Much commotion followed, but when the dust had settled, the young man left the store with a television that normally cost $89.99, having paid for it the sum of $66.39. One more complaining consumer taken care of. "The television," he reports, "works beautifully. I just love it."

Business Opportunities. "Do you write songs? We'll market them for you. Pay us a modest fee of $50 and we'll arrange for your songs to be looked at by major musical and publishing houses." That (fictitious) ad capsulizes in brief form what's wrong with all too many business opportunities. They may be opportunities for the person getting your money, but not necessarily for you. All too often you pay money to get started in a business and receive token or desultory help—or perhaps none at all. In getting involved in any business venture, you should know exactly whom you're getting in with, what their past record is, and exactly what they're committed—on paper, in a signed contract—to do for you. If you've been caught in a phony business opportunity (and if so, you'd be lucky if $50 is all you've lost), your state consumer-protection agency is a logical first recourse. See the passages below for further details on two kinds of business opportunities fraught with their own particular hazards, distributorships and franchises.

Contests. The letter always seems to be written in bold type. "Good news for the [your name filled in by typewriter] family," it may begin. "You have won a valuable prize!" In the long run, what you've won is often a chance to pay your good money to buy something from the company whose "contest" you have just "won." Sometimes you actually have to do something to win such a contest—something hard, like telling how many states there are in the United States. Much of the time such ploys are merely annoying. Personally, I throw all such "good news" into the garbage. However, if you're told you've won something, and when you try to collect there turn out to be strings attached, you should smell fraud. Report it to your state consumer-protection agency and also (if they're distinct) your state Attorney General's office.

Distributorships. Being a distributor for a product is fine, but there are certain danger signs that will help you distinguish a legitimate distributorship from a pyramid scheme. If a legitimate firm tries to recruit you as a distributor, it won't promise you instant riches. It will probably offer to buy back from you any goods that you can't sell, at something like 90 per cent of what you paid for them. It will not charge you a large initial investment fee. And, most of all, it will emphasize selling its product, *not* recruiting subdistributors.

The hallmark of a pyramid scheme is that you're supposed to make money by recruiting subdistributors into the scheme. In this regard, it resembles nothing so much as an old-fashioned chain letter. Chain letters are widely illegal, and so are pyramid schemes, for the same reason: There aren't enough potential recruits in the world to make either kind of scheme profitable for anyone except those who get in early in the game. Those who come in later are bound to lose; their money winds up in the pockets of the earlybirds who win. That "win," however, could end in a jail sentence, as more and more states outlaw pyramid plans. If you encounter one, report it to your state consumer-protection agency and, if they're distinct, also to your state Attorney General's office.

False Advertising. See separate entry under "Advertising."

Franchises. The best time to get advice regarding a franchise is before you commit any money to it. You should do complete research on both the individual company for whom you may become a franchisee and on the industry it's in. One helpful source of information about the mechanics of the franchise game is the International Franchise Association, 7315 Wisconsin Ave., Bethesda, Md. 20014.

Let's say, though, that you're already committed. Now, the franchisor is not giving you the guidance and financial help he promised. Or he's failing to give your branch of the franchise as much advertising support as you thought you had coming. Or he's charging you large fees for equipment. What do you do?

Take your problem, and your contract, to a good lawyer. You may want to try to cancel your whole contract and sue for the return of some or all of your franchise fee. Or you may be able to pressure the franchisor into giving you more support, especially if he's not living up to the written terms of your contract. Hold off writing to government agencies at first. The threat of doing so may be needed as a bargaining tool. If you do need government help, some agencies to turn to would be your state consumer-protection agency, your state Attorney General's office (if they're distinct), and the federal Small Business Administration. The national headquarters of the Small Business Administration are at 1030 Fifteenth St., N.W., Washington, D.C. 20417, but there may be a branch office near you. Let your lawyer advise you on when, and whether, to launch any of these complaints.

It should be emphasized that many franchise operations are entirely legitimate and potentially very profitable. But getting stuck with the other kind is the financial equivalent of being caught in a bear trap.

Fraud. The dictionary defines fraud as "A deception deliberately practiced in order to secure unfair or unlawful gain." In that sense, much of this book is about fraud and how to fight it. But note that word "deliberately." If someone sells you shoddy goods, you can and should fight to get your money back or a replacement or repairs. But that's not fraud, *unless* the seller led you to believe you were getting one thing while knowing all along you were going to get something else. If someone does a lousy roofing job on your house, that's a pain in the neck and cause for complaint. If someone puts on lightweight shingles after telling you he would use heavyweight ones, that's fraud.

Fraud should always be reported to your state consumer-protection agency and to your state Attorney General's office, if they're different. It may also be reported to a large variety of other agencies, depending on the type of abuse involved.

Future Services Contracts. Dating services, health spas, book clubs, country clubs—all of these enterprises are normally marketed in the form of a future services contract. That is, you pay now for what you anticipate will be a series of times in the future when you will use the organization's facilities. Suppose, however, that you don't like the people at the country club. Suppose the dating service introduces you only to sex maniacs (or, depending on what you expected, fails to introduce you to any sex maniacs). Suppose, in short, that once you start using the service you don't like it, or for some other reason want to back out. Can you get most or all of your money back? With many future services contracts the answer is no.

For the most part, your rights here are limited by the contract you signed. In the case of health spas, though, a proposed Federal Trade Commission regulation would require the issuing of pro rata refunds. (See separate entry on "Health spas.") If the service has in some way misrepresented its terms, you should then be able to force cancellation of your contract and gain at least a partial refund. Your state consumer agency would be a logical recourse here. So would a local consumer-protection agency and the Better Business Bureau, if a local company is involved. If it's a long-distance contract, write the consumer-protection agency in the seller's home state.

Late Delivery and Nondelivery of Merchandise. See the separate entries under "Delivery of merchandise" and "Mail-order houses."

Referral Selling. This one can be made to sound like a real golden opportunity. The seller will sell you something—say a roofing job on your house—for a certain fee. But for every additional customer you dig up for the seller, you'll get a rebate. By the time you've found a few customers, you wind up paying little or nothing for the job or whatever the goods in question are. This deal can sound so good that you fail at first to ask some key questions that later seem startlingly obvious. Was the initial price a good price? Probably not. What are my chances of scaring up some additional customers for this seller? Probably poor. If it were easy to find buyers for his particular wares, why would he resort to a referral scheme in the first place?

Another question worth asking is, "Was his offer legal?" The answer varies from state to state. But in quite a few states the answer is no. Call your state consumer-protection agency to find out.

Shoddy Workmanship. This complaint arises most often in connection with home improvements and repairs. (See the separate entry on that subject.) It helps if you have a clause in your contract saying, "All work shall be done in a workmanlike manner." But such a clause isn't legally necessary in most cases. Under the "implied warranty of merchantibility" recognized in most states, any goods or services sold must be reasonably free of defects. Withholding payment, suing in small claims court or larger courts for a full or partial refund, and complaining to local and state consumer-protection agencies are some of the tactics to pursue here. Better Business Bureaus and trade associations may also be of help. As they are rarely suspected of proconsumer bias, their opinion that a particular piece of work is shoddy should carry considerable weight.

Showcase Merchandise. This is a variant on referral selling. But here you're told that your home siding (or your refrigerator, or whatever) will be a model. All you need do is let others come and look at it from time to time. In return, you'll get a substantial discount on the price. There's really only one crucial question here. A discount from what? If it's a discount from that merchant's standard astronomically inflated price, then it falls considerably short of being a bargain. Once you've fallen for this ploy, it's often difficult to get your money back, since it's quite hard to prove that a skillful operator used fraud or misleading tactics. The deceptive promises are usually made orally. Nonetheless, complain to your state consumer-protection agency and your Better Business Bureau. At best, you may gain some or all of your money back. At worst, your complaint will serve to help warn other potential victims.

Unsolicited Merchandise. The people who peddle unsolicited merchandise must all have gotten master's degrees in guilt inducement from the psychology department of some warped university. If you keep the merchandise and don't order from their company or give to their charity, they do their best to make you feel like a crook, a thief, or at least an ingrate. Sometimes they even dun you to pay for the item they sent you completely unprovoked. But the law here is clear. If you receive unsolicited merchandise in the mail, U.S. Postal regulations say you may keep it as a gift. Period, end of controversy. If the merchandise is delivered to you some other way (dropped on your doorstep, for example), state laws in forty-five states still say it's yours to do with as you please. According to the federal Office of Consumer Affairs, the five states without such specific laws are Alabama, Colorado, New Mexico, North Dakota, and Utah. If you live in one of those five states, you may want to play it safe and offer to return the merchandise to the sender. Make your offer in writing (keeping a copy), and make it clear that the sender, not you, should bear any shipping costs involved.

Used Cars.   See Automobile repairs; Automobile sales.

Utilities and Utility Bills.   In common usage, the term "utilities" includes the services of the heating company, the water company, the electric company, and the telephone company. One or more of these services (most often water) may be supplied by your municipality. Where that's the case, complaints go to city hall.

With telephone complaints, one resource (after it becomes clear that the phone company can't or won't help you with your problem) is the Federal Communications Commission, 1919 M St., N.W., Washington, D.C. 20554. But telephone complaints should also go to the state agency that handles utility complaints in general.

With most other utility complaints, the state utility agency is the best—often the only—place to go. Copies of your complaint can also be sent to your state consumer-protection agency. In most cases your complaint will simply be bounced back to the utility agency. But occasionally you'll find a consumer-protection agency that can't resist going to bat for you, even if it means stepping on a sister agency's toes.

The state utility agencies are as follows:

- Alabama Public Service Commision, P.O. Box 991, Montgomery, Ala. 36102
- Alaska Public Utilities Commission, 338 Denali St., Anchorage, Alaska 99501
- Arizona Corporation Commission, Room 216, 1688 West Adams, Phoenix, Ariz. 85007
- Arkansas Public Service Commission, Justice Building, Little Rock, Ark. 72201
- California Public Utilities Commission, 350 McAllister St., San Francisco, Calif. 94102
- Colorado Public Utilities Commission, 1845 Sherman St., Denver, Colo. 80203
- Connecticut Public Utilities Commission, 165 Capitol Ave., Hartford, Conn. 06115
- Delaware Public Service Commission, Old State House Annex, Dover, Del. 19901
- District of Columbia Public Service Commission, 1625 I St., N.W., Washington, D.C. 20006
- Florida Public Service Commission, 700 S. Adams St., Tallahassee, Fla. 32304
- Georgia Public Service Commission, 244 Washington St., S.W., Atlanta, Ga. 30334
- Hawaii Public Utilities Commission, P.O. Box 541, Honolulu, Hawaii 96809
- Idaho Public Utilities Commission, Statehouse, Boise, Idaho 83720
- Illinois Commerce Commission, 527 E. Capitol Ave., Springfield, Ill. 62706
- Indiana Public Service Commission, 901 State Office Building, Indianapolis, Ind. 46204
- Iowa State Commerce Commission, State Capitol, Des Moines, Iowa 50319
- Kansas State Corporation Commission, State Office Building, Topeka, Kan. 66612

- Kentucky Public Service Commission, P.O. Box 496, Frankfort, Ky. 40601
- Louisiana Public Service Commission, P.O. Box 44035, Capitol Station, Baton Rouge, La. 70804
- Maine Public Utilities Commission, State House Annex, Capitol Shopping Center, Augusta, Me. 04330
- Maryland Public Service Commission, 904 State Office Building, 301 West Preston St., Baltimore, Md. 21201
- Massachusetts Department of Public Utilities, 100 Cambridge St., Boston, Mass. 02202
- Michigan Public Service Commission, 525 West Ottawa St., Lansing, Mich. 48913
- Minnesota Public Service Commission, Kellogg and Robert Sts., St. Paul, Minn. 55101
- Mississippi Public Service Commission, Box 1174, Jackson, Miss. 39205
- Missouri Public Service Commission, Jefferson Building, Jefferson City, Mo. 65101
- Montana Public Service Commission, 1227 Eleventh Ave., Helena, Mont. 59601
- Nebraska Public Service Commission, 3d floor, 1342 M St., Lincoln, Neb. 68508
- Nevada Public Service Commission, 225 E. Washington St., Carson City, Nev. 89701
- New Hampshire Public Utilities Commission, 26 Pleasant St., Concord, N.H. 03301
- New Jersey Board of Public Utility Commissioners, 101 Commerce St., Newark, N.J. 07102
- New Mexico Public Service Commission, State Capitol Building, Santa Fe, N.M. 87501
- New York Public Service Commission, 44 Holland Ave., Albany, N.Y. 12208
- North Carolina Utilities Commission, P.O. Box 991, Raleigh, N.C. 27602
- North Dakota Public Service Commission, State Capitol Building, Bismarck, N.D. 58501
- Ohio Public Utilities Commission, 111 N. High St., Columbus, Ohio 43215

- Oklahoma Corporation Commission, Jim Thorpe Office Building, Oklahoma City, Okla. 73105
- Oregon Public Utility Commissioner, Labor and Industries Building, Salem, Ore. 97310
- Pennsylvania Public Utility Commission, P.O. Box 3265, Harrisburg, Pa. 17120
- Rhode Island Public Utility Commission, 169 Weybossett St., Providence, R.I. 02903
- South Carolina Public Service Commission, P.O. Box 11649, Columbia, S.C. 29211
- South Dakota Public Utilities Commission, Capitol Building, Pierre, S.D. 57501
- Tennessee Public Service Commission, C1-102 Cordell Hull Building, Nashville, Tenn. 37219
- Texas Railroad Commission, Utilities Division, Drawer 12967, Capitol Station, Austin, Tex. 78711
- Utah Public Service Commission, 330 E. Fourth South St., Salt Lake City, Utah 84111
- Vermont Public Service Board, 7 School St., Montpelier, Vt. 05602
- Virginia State Corporation Commission, P.O. Box 1197, Richmond, Va. 23209
- Washington Utilities and Transportation Commission, Highways-Licenses Building, Olympia, Wash. 98504
- West Virginia Public Service Commission, Room E-217, Capitol Building, Charleston, W.Va. 25305
- Wisconsin Public Service Commission, 432 Hill Farms State Office Building, Madison, Wis. 53702
- Wyoming Public Service Commission, Supreme Court Building, Cheyenne, Wyo. 82001

Vacation Giveaways. See discussion of contests in entry on Unfair business practices.

Vacations. See Travel.

Vocational Schools. Countless men and women who want to be models, truck drivers, beauticians, airline stewardesses, or members of a wide variety of other professions have thought to realize their hopes by going to a vocational school. Such schools are also called trade schools, training schools, self-improvement schools, or—when the course is given by mail—correspondence schools. The best such schools perform an extremely valuable service, helping people upgrade their lot in life. The worst trade meanly and greedily on people's hopes.

The first thing to realize about vocational schools is that none of them offer a quick route of entry into certain professions. No short course can make you a doctor, lawyer, or registered nurse, though a good vocational school course can prepare you to *assist* one of these people. Schools that offer to prepare you to be a long-distance truck driver are often misleading in their advertising. Those high-paying long-haul jobs are usually something you have to work your way up to, one step at a time. In fact, many truck drivers don't even start out driving trucks; they have to start out loading them. Similarly, courses that claim to prepare you to be a stewardess are usually misleading. In fact, all the major airlines train their own stewardesses.

The first thing you should do if you're thinking of attending a vocational school is to check with employers in your intended occupation to see how highly they regard that school's graduates. Employers are often quite glad to help you with such inquiries. The next thing you should do is check with your state department of education to see whether the school is accredited, and *by whom.* Certain accrediting bodies exist primarily to provide rubber-stamp accreditation for their members. They would accredit a school run by a colony of gophers if the price were right. Among the groups whose seal of approval does mean something are the National Home Study Council (for correspondence schools), the National Association of Trade and Technical Schools (for technical training), and the Association of Independent Colleges and Schools (for business training).

You should pay special attention to what happens if you sign up for a course and discover early in the game that you don't like it. Responsible schools will provide for pro rata refunds, but others will hang onto your money for dear life. Don't accept oral promises in this area. Be guided only by the school's written contract, which you should study carefully before signing.

If you already have a complaint about a vocational school, possibly because you didn't know about certain of the problems and precautions described here, complain in writing to the director of the school. If your problem isn't cleared up in a reasonably short time, send copies of your complaint to your state department of education, the school's accrediting body (if any) and your state consumer-protection agency (see Part II for addresses). One or more of these agencies may be able to help you. If not, they can probably advise you on whether you have a strong enough case to make it worth your while to hire a lawyer to sue the school.

Wages.   See Job-related problems.

Warranties.   See Chapter 2.

Washing Machines.   See Appliances and appliance repairs.

Water Heaters.   See Appliances and appliance repairs.

Waterproofing.   See Home improvements and repairs.

Working Conditions.   See Job-related problems.

Workmanship, shoddy.   See Unfair business practices.